THE RULE OF REASON IN ANTITRUST LAW

American, German and Common Market Laws in Comparative Perspective

COLLECTION SCIENTIFIQUE
DE LA FACULTÉ DE DROIT DE L'UNIVERSITÉ DE LIÈGE
26

THE RULE OF REASON IN ANTITRUST LAW

American, German and Common Market Laws in Comparative Perspective

by

RENÉ JOLIET
Assistant à l'Université de Liège
LL.M.

with a foreword
by

JAMES A. RAHL
Professor of Law, Northwestern University

SPRINGER-SCIENCE+BUSINESS MEDIA, B.V. 1967

ISBN 978-94-017-5640-2 ISBN 978-94-017-5900-7 (eBook)
DOI 10.1007/978-94-017-5900-7
Softcover reprint of the hardcover 1st edition 1967

FOREWORD

Two great problems of legal theory underlie most questions of antitrust and anticartel law: (1) how are prohibitions of restrictive agreements and practices to be tempered, if at all, by tests of reasonableness, or of public interest? and (2) with what tests and qualifications shall problems of monopoly, dominant power and business size be approached? This book examines the first of these problems in terms of American, German and European Common Market law, subjecting each to searching comparative analysis. The book is the work of a highly-qualified comparative legal scholar, René Joliet, who at this writing is an Associate of the Faculty of Law of the University of Liège, on leave for the years 1965-1967, as Senior Research Fellow at Northwestern University School of Law.

In the United States, problems with the Rule of Reason and its per se rule counterparts are as old as the Sherman Act of 1890. Perhaps no American antitrust doctrine has been more perplexing and controversial, doubtless in part because most of the law's hardest problems of policy take shape within the ambit of the question of how the Rule should be applied in given cases.

From the moment that Section 1 of the German Anticartel Law and Article 85 of the Rome Treaty were adopted, both in 1957, these legal systems became subject to the same kind of difficulty, and early signs are that this experience will be as intense and persistent as it has been in the United States. Naturally, approaches to this common problem have developed subjectively in Europe and America, in view of different origins, philosophies, conditions and institutions. The American rule quickly grew away from its only contemporaneous European analogy, the English common law. History is now repeating itself; early suggestions that Article 85(1) should be interpreted like the

Sherman Act Section 1 model (whic'; it almost copies in language) have been rejected by many commentators because of seemingly decisive differences in conditions. Indeed, Mr. Joliet finds that the EEC Commission interpretation of Article 85 has tended to follow the approach of the German Law, which the Rome Treaty provision does not really resemble nearly so closely as it does the American provision.

Given the big differences of opinion within and among these systems, a comparative approach to them is an enormous undertaking. At the same time, the wide perspective and sharp focus which comparative study at its best can provide has much to offer. To our knowlegde, Mr. Joliet is the first scholar on either side of the ocean to approach the Rule of Reason on this broad scale. The thoroughness with which he has done this will be sufficient reward for any reader who seeks basic understanding of the development of reasonableness tests in any or all of the systems concerned.

But beyond the expository, what contribution is here made to the more satisfactory development of the law? For American law, it is certain that Mr. Joliet's statement is an important one which, if heeded, promises to remove some very serious and deep misconceptions and to narrow greatly the area of doubt and controversy that will remain. To express pleasant surprise that this could be achieved by a non-American, a Belgian, might be an appropriate way to show admiration, but it might seem to overlook the tradition of outstanding work on American antitrust law by non-Americans already established by such scholars as Hans Thorelli of Sweden and A.D. Neale of England. Better it would be to say that Mr. Joliet's work is in this tradition and that it leads us to hope for more of the same kind of discerning scholarship at a time when American antitrust law is at another one of its famous crossroads!

As for European law, we are confident that both German and Common Market approaches to the reasonableness question will be much better understood as a result of Mr. Joliet's writing. It is, of course, possible that his conclusions on European law will encounter somewhat more disagreement than will his observations on American law. It would indeed be surprising if it should be otherwise, for Mr. Joliet has walked boldly into the middle of a substantial difference of opinion on basic approach which currently divides the EEC Commission and the Court of Justice. Further, he has taken sides in the controversy by advocating the use of a limited reasonableness test for the prohibitions of Article 85(1), independently of the exculpatory provisions of Article 85(3). This position was fully developed in his completed thesis before the Court of Justice decisions in 1966 in the cases of Grundig-Consten, Maschinenbau, *and the* Italian Government*—decisions which rather substantially confirmed his analysis. Since those decisions, he has revised the work to take account of them, and also to reaffirm his argument the more confidently because of them.*

We forecast that opponents of his view will find the cogency of his comparative analysis hard to counter, and that there will be many who will be persuaded by it. We may further hazard that in the long run he will be proved substantially right in his belief that a general prohibition of restrictive agreements cannot be administered intelligently without some kind of flexible test to separate the significant from the inconsequential, and thereby to maximize both efficiency of prohibition and freedom of enterprise.

It is understandable, therefore, that we await with great interest the completion of the work in which Mr. Joliet is presently engaged at Northwestern—a comparative study of the theories of monopoly and dominant power in antitrust law, the other of the two fundamental problems of antitrust policy mentioned above.

Northwestern University, Chicago.
December 1966. James A. Rahl.

PREFACE

« Oui, j'ai une patrie : la langue française ». When I read these words of Albert Camus some years ago, my immediate reaction was the nostalgic thought that even if they were not meant in that sense, they could serve as a wonderful rallying cry for all the French-speaking minorities, to one of which I belong. At that time, I was, of course, completely unaware that one day, through the fortuity of academic life, I would be writing a study of a controversial issue of antitrust law in a language which is not my own. My purpose in recalling this quotation is not only to reaffirm an allegiance, but also to point out the difficulties of my venture, and perhaps to ask the reader for his indulgence insofar as this study was also a philological exercise.

This study was originally written as a dissertation which was submitted in partial fulfillment of the requirements for the degree of master of laws at Northwestern University in June 1966. It was revised and completed during the fall of 1966 to accommodate the latest developments of the EEC antitrust law which had occurred during the summer.

The idea of a comparative study of the Rule of Reason was suggested by Professor James A. Rahl of Northwestern University and I am very pleased to record here my great debt to him. It was he who brought me to Northwestern and thoughout my stay here he has, despite heavy commitments, been a constant source of advice, inspiration and encouragement without which this study would never have been completed. To work under his guidance has been an enriching and unforgettable experience. Various aspects of my work have also been discussed, always to my profit, with Professor Dawn C. Netsch who was a member of my examining committee.

I am grateful to the General Electric Foundation, which, through a grant to Northwestern University for research in the field of comparative and international antitrust law, provided the generous financial support which made this study possible. I must also express my gratitude to the United States Educational Foundation in Belgium which recommended me for a Fulbright travel grant.

At various stages of the drafting of the text, I received from my friends Timothy Razzall, Philip M. Kayman, Nicholas Wilson and Andrew Walker invaluable assistance in revising the language and style.

Finally I wish to thank Professor L. Dabin of the University of Liège who encouraged me to gain the experience of American antitrust law and granted me leave of absence. I am grateful to the Law Faculty of the University of Liège which accepted this volume for publication in its series.

To all these many friends my thanks are due. They are of course in no way responsible for the shortcomings of this study.

Northwestern University, Chicago.

December 1966. René JOLIET.

TABLE OF CONTENTS

INTRODUCTION

1. - American and European Misconceptions about the Rule of Reason . . 3

2. - What is Reasonable? Two views 5

3. - Scope of this Study 7

4. - Trends in EEC Antitrust Policy prior to the *Grundig-Consten*, *Technique Minière* and the *Italian Government* Cases 8

5. - Consequent Need for a Comparative Study of the Rule of Reason . . 11

6. - German Law as an Influence upon the Development of the EEC Anti-cartel Law 12

CHAPTER I

RULE OF REASON AND PER SE VIOLATIONS UNDER SECTION 1 OF THE SHERMAN ACT

1. - The Standard of Reasonableness, *Appalachian Coals* and the Four Tests of Article 85(3) of the Rome Treaty 17

2. - The Origins of the Rule of Reason 20

3. - The Rule of Reason as a Synthesis 23

4. - *Transmissouri Freight Association* and the so-called Literalist Approach of Justice Peckham 25

5. - Taft's Review of the Common Law and his Concept of Ancillary Restraints 26

6. - The Foundations of the Modern Rule of Reason: *Standard Oil* and *American Tobacco* 29
   - A. - A Policy Against "Undue Limitations on Competitive Conditions" 29
   - B. - Loose-Knit Confederations and Close-Knit Combinations . . . 30
   - C. - No Distinction between Good and Bad Cartels 32

7. - Justice Brandeis' Version of the Rule of Reason 35
   - A. - Regulation and Promotion, as Opposed to Destruction, of Competition 35
   - B. - No Adverse Effect upon Market Conditions 36
   - C. - Limited License to Cartelize? 37
   - D. - *Chicago Board of Trade*: No Deviation from the Main Tradition of the Rule of Reason 39

8. - The Rule of Reason as Applied in *Appalachian Coals* 40
A. - The "Concentric Circle" Approach 40
B. - Competition no longer the Supreme Good? 41
C. - *Appalachian Coals* Superseded as a Rule for Price-Fixing . . . 41
D. - Unsuccessful Attempt to Apply the Same Standard to Mergers and Cartels 42

9. - The Development of *Per Se* Rules 43
A. - The Price-Fixing Rule 43
a) *Trenton Potteries* and the Element of Market Control . . . 43
b) *Socony Vacuum*: the First Use of the *Per Se* Formula . . . 45
I. - Rejection of the "Reasonable Prices" Justification . . 46
II. - Expansion of the *Trenton Potteries* Rule: Market Control not Necessary 46
III. - Actual Effect on Market Prices not a Prerequisite of the Price-fixing Offense 48
B. - The Boycott Rule 49
a) *Fashion Originator's Guild of America* 50
b) The *Klor's* case 51
c) Neither Purpose nor Effect of Agreement Relevant. - A Critical Appraisal 53
C. - Tying Arrangements: the Inadequacies of the *Per Se* Formula . . 54
D. - Market Sharing Agreements: False Analogy with Price-Fixing . . 56

10. - Conclusions 59
A. - Free Competition: Undoubted Policy Behind the Sherman Act . . 59
B. - European Anticartel Law Represents a Different Philosophy . . 60
C. - The Sherman Act does not Discriminate between Good and Bad Restraints 60
D. - Restraints on the Freedom of Action of the Individual Business Man not Necessarily an Excessive Impediment to Market Competition. - *White Motor* as a Possible Example 61
E. - Difficulties in Administering the Reasonableness Test Lead to the Development of *Per Se* Rules 63
F. - Approach to the Legal Definition of "Restraint of Trade": Object of this Comparative Study 66

CHAPTER II

THE NOTION OF RESTRAINT OF TRADE UNDER SECTION 1 OF THE GERMAN ANTICARTEL LAW

1. - General Characteristics of the German Statute Against Restraints of Competition 69

2. - Difficulties and Dangers Involved in a Comparative Study 70

3. - Object of this Study: What is a Restraint of Competition Under Section 1 of the German Statute Against Restraints of Competition? . 70

4. - Comparison with the British Restrictive Trade Practices Act: the Use of the Word "Competition" 71

5. - Section 1 of the German Anticartel Law: a *Per Se* Rule? 73

6. - Relationship Between Substantive Law and Procedural Rules . . . 74

7. - Two Possible Approaches to the Definition of Restraint of Competition . 76

8. - Competition and Restraint of Competition under Section 1 of the German Anticartel Law 77

A. - Legislative History 77

B. - Definitions of Competition Proposed by the German Legal Literature 78

C. - Restraint of Competition Defined as Contractual Limitation on the Individual Firm's Freedom to Compete 80

D. - Whether Competition is Restrained Can be Decided Abstractly . . 81

E. - No Limitation on the Cartel Prohibition Beyond the Scope of the Exemption of Sections 2-8 of the Statute 83

F. - The "*Gegenstandstheorie*": the Restriction as an Express Part of the Content of a Binding Agreement 84

9. - The Likelihood of Influencing Market Conditions: a Limited Rule of Reason for Section 1? 87

10. - "Probable Market Effect" Test and Analysis of the Case Law . . . 91

A. - *Gasglükörper* 91

B. - *Kohlenhandel* 93

C. - The *Spar* case 94

D. - Critical Appraisal of the *Spar* case 96

E. - The *Bockhorner Klinker* case 98

11. - Conclusions 99

A. - A Very Formalistic Approach to the Definition of Restraint of Trade under Section 1 99

B. - Other Uses of the Word "Competition". - Section 18 as an Example of a Different Competitive Test 103

CHAPTER III

A RULE OF REASON FOR ARTICLE 85(1) OF THE ROME TREATY

1. - Recent Developments of the EEC Antitrust Law: the *Grundig-Consten, Technique Minière* and the *Italian Government* Cases 109

2. - Substantive Test of Restraint of Competition and Jurisdictional Requirement under Article 85(1) of the Rome Treaty 110

3. - The American Rule of Reason as Viewed in Europe 112

4. - The Sherman Act Does not Permit a Consideration of the Economic Advantages Resulting from Restrictive Agreements 113

5. - The Need for a Rule of Reason under Article 85(1) of the Rome Treaty 115

6. - The EEC Commission's Doctrine: Regurgitation of the German Theories 116

7. - The Construction of Article 85(1) Proposed by German Writers: Restraint of Competition Equated with "*Wettbewerbsbeschränkung*" under Section 1 of the German Statute 119

8. - Arguments Against the Application of the German Theory to Article 85 of the Rome Treaty 124

A. - Linguistic Discrepancies Between Article 85(1) and Section 1 of the German Statute: Test of Anticompetitive "Object" or "Effect" 121

B. - Inadequacies of the *Gegenstandstheorie* in Interpreting Article 85. - The Ban on Concerted Practices 124

C. - Unlike the German Act, the Rome Treaty Does not Discriminate between Horizontal and Vertical Restraints of Trade 126

D. - The Prevention of Dominant Positions by Article 85(3) . . . 126

E. - Market Competition Is the Policy Behind Article 85(1); *e.g.*, Price Information Agreements, Joint Ventures and the *Grundig-Consten* Understanding on the Trade-Mark Gint 129

9. - The Test of "Purpose" or "Effect" in Article 85(1). - Its Use in the American Cases 133

10. - Review of the EEC Commission Decisions: Approach to the Problem of Restraint of Competition 136

A. - The Convention *Faïence*: a Collective Exclusive Dealing Agreement 138

B. - *Groxfillex*: a Case of Prohibition on Reexport to the Common Market and the Notion of Perceptible Restraint of Competition . 140

C. - *Vitapro*: An Example of An Ancillary Covenant not to Compete . 141

D. - *Grundig-Consten*: a Vertical Division of Territory Between Grundig Dealers 143

E. - *Blondel, Hummel* and *Jallate*: a Literal and Mechanical Approach to the Definition of Restraint of Trade. - Exclusive Dealing Promises and Exclusive Franchises Inherently Violate Article 85(1). - The Prospect of a Group Exemption Regulation 146

11. - The *Voma Exquisit* Case 152

A. - Another Illustration of the Literal Approach 152

B. - Criticism of the View that Every Technical Restraint Is Necessarily a Limitation on Market Competition 154

12. - The Doctrine Developed by the European Court of Justice 155

A. - The Rule of Reason under Article 85(1): Not a Mere Academic Discussion 155

B. - *Grundig-Consten v. EEC Commission* 156

I. - Arguments Expounded by Grundig and Consten 156

II. - The Commission's Theory 158

III. - The Doctrine Suggested by Advocate General Roemer . . 161

IV. - The Ruling of the Court 162

C. - *Société Technique Minière v. Maschinenbau Ulm GmbH* . . . 166

I. - The Questions Posed by the Court of Appeal of Paris . . 166

II. - The Thesis Defended by the EEC Commission 168

III. - The Theory Proposed by Advocate General Roemer . . . 168

IV. - The Ruling of the Court 170

D. - *Italy v. EEC Council and EEC Commission* 173
I. - Prior Developments in the Policy of the European Authorities Towards Vertical Agreements 173
II. - Regulation no. 19/65 Sustained by the Court 176
III. - Evaluation of the Court's decision 178
IV. - The Commission's Draft Regulation Exempting Exclusive Franchises and Exclusive Dealing Provisions 179
V. - Conclusions 182

13. - Conclusions 183
A. - Necessity for a Case-by-case Approach and Need for Economic Analysis 183
B. - Rule of Reason Approach Partly Endorsed by the European Court of Justice 185
C. - The Debate on the Application of a Rule of Reason to Article 85(1) Still Unresolved 187
D. - We Must Have a More Vigorous Antitrust Policy. - The EEC Commission as a Prosecuting Body 188
E. - More Flexibility Essential for Greater Effectiveness 188
F. - Risk that the Adoption of a Rule of Reason will Lead to Divergent Decisions Within the Six 190
G. - The Value of Comparative Anticartel Law 191

LIST OF ABREVIATIONS

ABA	American Bar Association
AktG	Die Aktiengesellschaft - Zeitschrift
AM. ECON. REV.	American Economic Review
ANTITRUST BULL.	Antitrust Bulletin
AWD BB	Aussenwirtschaftsdienst des Betriebsberaters
BB	Der Betriebsberater
BGBl	Bundesgesetzblatt
BGH	Bundesgerichtshof
BkartA	Bundeskartellamt
BUS. LAW.	Business Lawyer
CALIF. L. REV.	California Law Review
CCH	Commerce Clearing House
CCH TRADE REG. REP.	Commerce Clearing House Trade Regulation Reporter
CECA	Communauté Européenne du Charbon et de l'Acier
CEE	Communauté Economique Européenne
Cir.	Circuit Court of Appeals
COLUM. L. REV.	Columbia Law Review
D.	District Court
DB	Der Betrieb
ECSC	European Coal and Steel Community
EEC	European Economic Community
EGKS	Europäische Gemeinschaft für Kohle und Stahl
EWG	Europäische Wirtschaftsgemeinschaft
Fed.	Federal Reporter
F.2d.	Federal Reporter, Second Series
F. Supp.	Federal Supplement
FTC	Federal Trade Commission
GRUR	Gewerblicher Rechtsschutz und Urheberrecht - Zeitschrift
GWB	Gesetz gegen Wettbewerbsbeschränkungen
HARV. BUS. REV.	Harvard Business Review
HARV. L. REV.	Harvard Law Review
ILL. L. REV.	Illinois Law Review
JT	Journal des Tribunaux
JZ	Juristenzeitung

KG	Kammergericht
LG	Landgericht
MA	Der Markenartikel
MICH. L. REV.	Michigan Law Review
MINN. L. REV.	Minnesota Law Review
NJW	Neue Juristische Wochenschrift
NW. U. L. REV.	Northwestern University Law Review
OLG	Oberlandesgericht
RECORD OF N.Y.C.B.A.	Record of the Association of the Bar of the City of New York
RGZ	Reichsgericht in Zivilsachen - Amtliche Sammlung
TNEC	Temporary National Economic Committee
TRADEMARK REP.	Trademark Reporter
U.C.L.A.L. REV.	University of California Los Angeles Law Review
U. CHI. L. REV.	University of Chicago Law Review
U.S.	United States
U.S.	United States Supreme Court Reports
VA. L. REV.	Virginia Law Review
WRP	Wettbewerb in Recht und Praxis
WuW	Wirtschaft und Wettbewerb
WuW/E	Wirtschaft und Wettbewerb - Entscheidungssammlung
WuW/E BGH	Wirtschaft und Wettbewerb - Entscheidungen des Bundesgerichtshofes
WuW/E BKartA	Wirtschaft und Wettbewerb - Entscheidungen des Bundeskartellamtes
WuW/E EV	Wirtschaft und Wettbewerb - Entscheidungen der Europäischen Verwaltungsbehörden
WuW/E LG/AG	Wirtschaft und Wettbewerb - Entscheidungen des Land- oder Amtsgerichts
WuW/E OLG	Wirtschaft und Wettbewerb - Entscheidungen des Oberlandesgerichts
YALE L. J.	Yale Law Journal

INTRODUCTION

1. - American and European Misconceptions about the Rule of Reason

The Rule of Reason has been the subject of so many controversies in American legal literature that one must really wonder whether it is still possible to shed new light on this ancient debate. Several of the most learned American experts in the antitrust field have in turn devoted some of their reflections to this fundamental question (1) . Throughout more than seventy years of the Sherman Act's existence the United States Supreme Court has made numerous pronouncements and some of its most celebrated opinions are entirely concerned with this basic issue. However, to view the problem in a comparative perspective may now, perhaps, be the sole remaining way to dissipate the misunderstandings and the misconceptions which have so

(1) See *e.g.* W. Adams, *Rule of Reason: Workable Competition of Workable Monopoly*, 63 YALE L.J. 348 (1954); R.H. Bork, *The Rule of Reason and the Per se Concept: Price Fixing and Market Division*, 74 YALE L. J. 775 (1965) and 75 YALE L. J. 375 (1965); *id. Ancillary Restraints and the Sherman Act*, 15 ABA ANTITRUST SECTION 211 (1959); John T. Chadwell, *Competition and Section I of the Sherman Act - Instant Antitrust or Long-run Policy?*, 27 ABA ANTITRUST SECTION, 60 (1965); HANDLER, *A Study of the Construction and Enforcement of the Federal Antitrust Laws*, TNEC Monograph n° 38, 3-9 (1941); *id., The Judicial Architects of the Rule of Reason* in ANTITRUST IN PERSPECTIVE (1957); L. Loevinger, *The Rule of Reason in Antitrust Law*, 50 VA L. REV. 23 (1964), Montague, *Per Se Illegality and the Rule of Reason*, 12 ABA ANTITRUST SECTION 69 (1958); Oppenheim, *Federal Antitrust Policy: Guideposts to a Revised National Antitrust Policy*, 50 MICH. L. REV. 1139 (1951-1952); *id. Selected Antitrust Developments in the Courts and Federal Trade Commission during Past Year*, 15 ABA ANTITRUST SECTION, 37-42 (1959); *id., Antitrust Booms and Boomerang*, 9 ANTITRUST BULL. 641 (1964); Peppin, *Price-Fixing Agreement under the Sherman Antitrust Law*, 28 CALIF. L. REV. 297, 677 (1940); James A. Rahl, *Symposium on "Price Competition and Antitrust Policy"*, 57 NW. U. L. REV. 137 (1962); *id., Per Se Rules and Boycotts under the Sherman Act: Some Reflections on the Klor's Case*, 45 VA. L. REV. 1165 (1959); L. Schwartz, *The Schwartz Dissent*, 1 ANTITRUST BULL. 37 (1955-56); Smith, Berge and Burns, *Proposals for Extended Application of the Rule of Reason*, U. of Mich. Law School Summer Institute, Federal Antitrust Law, 231-262 (1953); Stocking, *Rule of Reason, Workable Competition and Monopoly*, 64 YALE L. J. 1107 (1955); *id., The Rule of Reason, Workable Competition and the Legality of Trade Associations Activities*, 21 U. CHI. L. REV. 527 (1954); TAFT, THE ANTITRUST ACT AND THE SUPREME COURT (1914); J. Van Cise, *The Future of Per se in Antitrust Law*, 50 VA. L. REV. 1165 (1964); Wiley, *The Per Se Illegality of Price-Fixing: Sans Power, Purpose or Effect*, 19 U. CHI. L. REV. 837 (1952).

often obscured (and which continue to obscure) the proper scope of the rule of reason.

Undoubtedly misunderstandings exist on both sides of the Atlantic. To some European writers who have dealt with this problem, the rule of reason appears as a device permitting the validation of almost any restrictive scheme when it is demonstrated that the beneficial effect of the agreement outweighs its pernicious effect ([1]). The view of these European observers is that it is within the discretion of the American Courts to draw the line between good and bad. Without questioning the accuracy of this premise, these authors have ruled *ex cathedra* that no room for such a vague and discretionary principle is available under the continental system of statutory law ([2]). This was the case, it was thought, of the anticartel provisions contained in the Rome Treaty. Agreements which have as their object or effect the restriction, prevention or distortion of competition within the Common Market and which are likely to affect interstate commerce, are banned by Article 85 (1). However, even when embraced by this broad prohibition, the agreements in question may be exempted if they fulfill the requirements of Article 85(3): they must improve production or distribution, or promote technical or economic progress and at the same time allow consumers a fair share of the resulting profit without imposing restrictions not essential for achieving these aims or giving the contracting parties the power to eliminate

---

(1) See 1961 *B Kart A Report* 62 [The German Federal Cartel Office publishes yearly reports entitled BERICHT DES BUNDESKARTELLAMTES ÜBER SEINE TÄTIGKEIT IM JAHRE ... SOWIE UBER DIE LAGE UND ENTWICKLUNG AUF SEINEM AUFGABENGEBIET. They will be hereinafter cited as *B Kart A* Report preceded by the applicable year]; Deringer, WuW/EWG - Wettbewersrecht, in WIRTSCHAFT UND WETTBEWERB (hereinafter cited as WuW) 866 (1962). Kurt Market, Book Review, WuW 343 (1963), speaking of some American decisions which held lawful the statistical activity of certain trade associations (price information agreements), wrote that they could only be instructive in a comparative perspective if one would know whether these agreements were sustained because no restraint of competition was found or because the Rule of Reason was applied. In his mind, it seems that the Rule of Reason opens the door to an economic justification of restrictive agreements. *Contra*, Wolf, *Zum Kartellrecht der EWG*, WuW 645 (1962): this author advocates the existence of a Rule of Reason under Article 85(1) of the Rome Treaty, but his conception of the American principle is no more accurate than that of the other writers.

(2) See OBERDORFER, GLEISS AND HIRSCH, COMMON MARKET CARTEL LAW, 25-26 (1963).

competition for a substantial proportion of the goods concerned. A majority of the European students of Article 85 have considered, without extensive inquiry, that this exempting provision, which enables the EEC Commission to give its blessing to certain " progressive " cartels, was nothing other than the codification of the American rule of reason(1).

But the same misconception is fairly common on the other side of the Atlantic too. Some American experts have thought that the purpose behind Article 85(3) was to write the American rule of reason into the prohibitions of Article 85 (2). To say the least, such statements reveal a great deal of confusion as to the actual function of the rule in American law itself.

2. - What is Reasonable ? Two Views

What is included within the concept of reasonableness? There are two conflicting views. According to one theory, the Rule of Reason would admit an inquiry into whether restrictive practices are likely, under certain circumstances, to better serve the public good than unfettered competition. In that context reasonableness would refer to the rationality of the agreement and the judicial discretion would extend to the determination of the economic and social expediency of

(1) Kurt Markert, *Alleinvertriebsverträge und Antitrustrecht* WuW 307 (1963) considers the exculpatory provision of Art. 85 of the Rome Treaty as a kind of codified Rule of Reason. See also, GÜNTHER, *Europäische und nationale Wettbewerbspolitik* in WIRTSCHAFTSORDNUNG UND RECHTSORDNUNG, FESTSCHRIFT FÜR FRANZ BÖHM (1965) at 294 and footnote (53).

(2) See the statement of LOEVINGER in ANTITRUST DEVELOPMENTS IN THE EUROPEAN COMMON MARKET,*Hearing Before the Sucommittee on Antitrust and Monopoly of the Committee on the Judiciary*, 88th Cong., 1st Session, pursuant to S. Res. 56, Part 1, 66 (1963). In the view of Fulda [*The First Antitrust Decisions of the Commission of the EEC*, 65 COLUM. L. REV. 643, 644 (1965)], " Article 85(3) seems to avoid splitting the field of the law into the two categories of per se violations and activities subject to a 'rule of reason'. It subjects all restrictive transactions to a single codified 'rule of reason' which may prescribe more precise standards than are available in American law for accepting 'business purposes' as a justification, or for weighing the advantages and disadvantages of competition versus restriction. "

cartels [1]. The public interest would still be the ultimate criterion but the Sherman Act would not be predicated on the premise that competition is always the best way to preserve the public. The Rule of Reason would be a principle opening the door to the justification of all restraints on competition. Although this conception is certainly not predominant, some judicial pronouncements bear its imprint, thereby causing much confusion. Such a view of the Rule of Reason would be very similar to the standards embodied by the EEC antitrust law in article 85(3) and by the British Restrictive Trade Practices Act in its series of gateways. However, while these statutes have strictly codified the tests which are to be followed by the Courts or the enforcement agency in balancing good and bad restraints, this view of the American law would leave the determination of what is in the public interest in a given case entirely to the discretion of the Courts.

In contrast, the currently prevailing view of the Rule of Reason is as a rule of construction of the Sherman Act, a rule which holds competition to be at the basis of Congressional policy. The inquiry under this conception of the Rule is limited to whether a certain practice has produced an anticompetitive effect or was intended to impair competition. All considerations which the Rule permits to be taken into account pertain exclusively to the purpose and the effect of the challenged agreement. The question of reasonableness is a question of degree. Reductions of competition which, because of their insignificance, do not offend the policy of the statute, can escape the ban of the Sherman Act. The judicial discretion only relates to the significance of the restraint. Not every agreement by which a trader limits his freedom and ability to compete is automatically deemed an excessive restriction of market competition. When

(1) HANDLER [*A Study of the Construction and Enforcement of the Federal Antitrust Laws*, TNEC Monograph n° 38, 8 (1941)] noted "a tendency to regard the rule of reason as opening the door to the validation of any scheme or device for the curtailment of competition which may be justified on grounds of business expediency. Reasonable in this context means rational, and if an arrangement is not irrational, having regard for the circumstances of its formation and operation, it should be free from censure". But Handler added that "though occasional official utterances and isolated passages in judicial opinions may point in that direction, the decisions of the Supreme Court in the past 30 years, viewed in their entirety, clearly reject this construction of the rule of reason".

the agreement under attack falls short of an anticompetitive result, business considerations and good motives can be adduced to show that no wrongful purpose has inspired the conduct of the traders.

Obviously, the meaning of the *per se* rules, which are qualifications of the principle, is determined by the conception of the Rule of Reason that one advocates. If reasonable means expedient or rational, *per se* unlawful will imply that all justifications are precluded in certain cases; defined types of behavior would be presumed detrimental to the public good. But if unreasonable means excessively inimical to competition, the *per se* formula would then obviate the inquiry into the effect of the practices on competition: certain types of behavior or certain kinds of agreements which, by their terms, relate to the competitive activity of traders will be considered inherently anticompetitive and injurious to the public without any need to determine if they have actually injured market competition.

As I will adopt the second definition of reasonableness, I will also adhere to the second meaning of *per se*. And whenever I use the terms " rule of reason " or " *per se* rule ", I will do so in that sense.

3. - Scope of this Study

Even reduced to these narrower limits, the American rule of reason offers a valuable field of comparison. Of course, some differences in economic policy appear if one contrasts the Sherman Act as presently construed with the European anticartel statutes. The latter generally provide for a long series of exemptions [1]. The premise on which the Sherman Act is based has been questioned in European law: competition is not always the summum bonum. The American philosophy

(1) See for instance the British Restrictive Trade Practices Act of 1956; the art. 59*bis* and 59*ter* of the French Price Ordinance n° 45-1483 of June 30, 1945; art. 65 of the ECSC Treaty. These laws are reproduced in ORGANISATION FOR EUROPEAN ECONOMIC COOPERATION (OEEC), GUIDE TO LEGISLATION ON RESTRICTIVE BUSINESS PRACTICES (1960).

has received several qualifications. Because of these differences, I will confine my study to the comparison of the American and the European (especially the EEC and the German) approaches to the problem of restraint of trade. What are the tests to which the American Courts resort for identifying the presence of an injury to competition under Section 1 of the Sherman Act? Can the same tests be employed under Article 85(1) of the Rome Treaty? It is necessary to indicate that when the term *per se* is used in a European context, this does not preclude a possibility of exemption. It is taken merely to refer to the method followed to find a restraint of competition. In most of the cases, this is only the preliminary step; it remains to be seen whether the group participating in the agreement can claim the benefit of one of the gateways set out in the German "Gesetz gegen Wettbewerbsbeschränkungen" (1) or meet the four tests formulated by Article 85(3) of the Rome Treaty.

In a long dissertation on a revised antitrust policy, Professor Oppenheim wrote a few years ago that "antitrust reflects the never-ending conflict between the desire for certainty and the desire for flexibility that is as old as the process of law itself" (2). This conflict is certainly not absent from the developing Common Market antitrust laws.

4. - Trends in EEC Antitrust Policy prior to the *Grundig-Consten, Technique Minière* and the *Italian Government* Cases

The first draft of this study was written prior to the pronouncements of the European Court of Justice in the *Grundig-Consten, Technique Minière* and the *Italian Government* cases (3).

(1) Literally translated, Act against restraints of competition, enacted July 27, 1957, hereinafter referred to as the German anticartel law.

(2) See Oppenheim, *Federal Antitrust Legislation: Guideposts to a Revised National Antitrust Policy*, 50 Mich. L. Rev. 1149 (1951-1952).

(3) Grundig-Consten v. EEC Commission, case no. 56/65, June 30, 1966, 2 CCH Common Market Reporter par. 8046; Société Technique Minière v. Maschinenbau Ulm GmbH, case no. 56/65, June 30, 1966, 2 CCH Common Market Reporter par. 8047; Italy v. EEC Council and EEC Commission, case no. 32/65, July 13, 1966, 2 CCH Common Market Reporter par. 8048. See my discussion of these cases, *infra* chapter III at 155-183.

At that time, a plea in favor of a Rule of Reason for Article 85(1) of the Rome Treaty could appear in several respects to be a vain crusade. The then current tendencies of the policy followed by the EEC Commission had revealed a very literal approach toward the concept of restraint of trade. Article 85(1), it was implied, does not give the enforcement agency any discretion to determine whether an agreement, although regulating the market behavior of competitors, is likely to improve rather than to impair the competitive process. Every restraint that businessmen and firms impose upon themselves should be filed with the Commission in order to be able later to claim the benefit of the exempting provision of Article 85(3) of the Rome Treaty. Engaging in market analysis in some cases (1), the Commission had in the large majority of them rejected any kind of rule of reason, dening the necessity of economic investigation to ascertain the anticompetitive purpose and effect of an agreement (2). Instead of proceeding on a case-by-case basis, the European agency had devoted much of its effort to formulate general and abstract rules which were reminiscent of a *per se* approach. This was especially the case in the field of vertical arrangements. In the early stage of the Common Market anticartel law, the Commission had, for instance, decided *in abstracto* that exclusive franchises and exclusive dealing terms were, by their very nature, restraints of competition under Article 85(1) (3). As a result, thousands of agreements of that kind were registered and the EEC Commission faced the overwhelming

(1) The best example is the *Grosfillex* case where the Commission granted a negative clearance. See decision of the EEC Commission of March 11, 1964, *Official Journal of the European Communities*, 915 (1964). Unofficial English translation in 3 COMMON MARKET LAW REPORTS 237 (1964). See my discussion of this case, *infra* chapter III at 140-141.

(2) In *Blondel*, *Hummel-Isbecque* and *Jallate*, the Commission exempted three exclusive franchise agreements pursuant to Article 85(3). However, its approach in regard to Article 85(1) and to the question of restraint of trade is a very mechanical one. For references and discussion of these cases, see *infra* chapter III at 146-152.

(3) See Official Notice on Contracts for Exclusive Representation Concluded with Commercial Agents, *Official Journal of the European Communities*, 2921 (1962) and 1 CCH COMMON MARKET REPORTER par. 2697; Regulation no. 153 Supplementing and Modifying Regulation no. 27 of May, 1962, issued by the EEC Commission December 21, 1962, *Official Journal of the European Communities*,, 2918 (1962) and 1 CCH COMMON MARKET REPORTER par. 2694.

task of examining specifically each case to decide whether the four tests of Article 85(3) were satisfied. This led the Commission to ask the Council for the power to exempt, by way of regulation, certain defined classes of restrictive agreements and to try thus to solve by a procedural device the administrative problem it had itself at least partly created (1). These tendencies might be explained, if not defended, by several factors: a trend toward abstraction and categorization which is inherent in the continental legal tradition; a desire to give business men clear-cut rules of thumb as to what they are allowed or forbidden to do and thus to assure a maximum of legal predictability; and, finally, a laudable concern with a uniform development of the law in the different countries despite a system which had not achieved a completely federal character. Nevertheless, this policy could also be assailed on several grounds. The search for certainty might well be justified—a lesson can be learnt from the American example—but conversely the lack of flexibility seemed to be the major defect of the emerging European antitrust law. The concept of competition had been narrowed arbitrarily by the Commission. One might wonder whether a certain amount of uncertainty was not inherent in the nature of an antitrust policy. If antitrust law so often appears unpredictable in America, the reason may be that " what is and what is not consistent with the maintenance of competition is not easy of determination " (2). Also the administrative control which consisted of submitting every restrictive agreement to the advance approval of the Commission, had prevented that body from playing more fully the role of a prosecuting agency.

---

(1) Regulation no. 19/65, Application of article 85(3) of the Treaty to Groups of Agreements and Concerted Practices, issued by the Council, March 2, 1965, *Official Journal of the European Communities*, 533 (1965) and 1 CCH COMMON MARKET REPORTER par. 2725; the constitutionality of this regulation was upheld by the European Court of Justice in the case no. 32/65, Italy v. EEC Council and EEC Commission, July 13, 1966, 2 CCH COMMON MARKET REPORTER par. 8048. See also the Proposed Regulation on the Application of article 85(3) of the Treaty to Certain Groups of Bilateral Exclusive Dealing Agreements and Concerted Practices, *Official Journal of the European Communities*, 2863 (1966) and 2 CCH COMMON MARKET REPORTER par. 9125. For a discussion of these regulations and of the *Italian* case, see *infra* chapter III at 173-182.

(2) HANDLER, *op. cit.*, at 9.

5. - Consequent Need for a Comparative Study of the Rule of Reason

These were the terms of the debate over the Rule of Reason before the three landmark decisions recently rendered by the Court of Jusice. When this dissertation was first written, I knew that these cases were pending. I also knew that Advocate General Roemer had pleaded for a theory of restraint of trade very close to the one applied in American Law under the Rule of Reason. But it was very risky to try to forecast the final outcome of the cases. The Court could have ratified entirely the approach taken by the Commission or, even worse, the Court could have avoided facing the problem. In that event, this dissertation would have been little more than a futile battle against windmills. Fortunately, the three cases decided by the Court make even more necessary and topical a comparative study of the Rule of Reason. Unexpectedly the Court did not close the door to any kind of rule of reason in the interpretation of article 85(1). The three cases—*Consten and Grundig v. EEC Commission, Société Technique Minière v. Maschinenbau Ulm GmbH* and *Italy v. EEC Council and EEC Commission*—have all raised this issue either directly or indirectly.

Two different interpretations of article 85(1) were advanced in these cases. On one side, Advocate General Roemer supported the view that a restraint of competition could not be ascertained in the abstract, but only on a case-by-case analysis after a thorough economic investigation, while the EEC Commission held to its theory that Article 85(1) formulates a mechanical standard prohibiting nearly every restraint of trade, within the technical meaning of that phrase, and thus does not require evaluation of the market situation in a specific case. The American Rule of Reason was explicitly mentioned: it was invoked by those who advocated more flexibility for Article 85(1), but it was denied any precedential value by the EEC Commission. The European Court faced a decisive choice of policy. Forced to decide which of these conflicting views should prevail, the Court developed a doctrine which is not entirely unequivocal. The *Grundig* case seems to be a *per se* condemnation of any territorial confinement system coinciding with the geographical boundaries of the member nations and involving distributors of the same brand, while, on the contrary, the construction given by the Court in *Société Technique Minière* leaves some room for the application of a Rule of Reason to exclusive franchises [1]. These seemingly contradictory decisions can be best understood in the light of a comparison with the American law which originated this opposition between the reasonableness test and the *per se* violations.

6. - German Law as an Influence upon the Development of the EEC Anticartel Law

This comparative study will use the German law as a conduit between the Sherman Act and the Rome Treaty. The reasons are multiple. Cartelization has long flourished in Germany, a development which reached its climax during the Hitler era when the cartels officially became instrumentalities of a regulated economy [2]. After World War II, when Germany was placed under strong American influence, a most stringent

(1) See my analysis of these three cases *infra* chapter III at 156-173.

(2) For an excellent historical survey of the German law in the field of cartels, see KAUFMANN, RAUTMANN ET AL. KOMMENTAR ZUM GESETZ GEGEN WETTBEWERBSBESCHRÄNKUNGEN, hereinafter referred to as FRANKFURTER KOMMENTAR, Introduction, Part B. See also *e.g.* Ivo Schwartz, *Antitrust Legislation and Policy in Germany - A Comparative Study*, 105 U. PA. L. REV. 617 (1957).

The judicial history of cartels in Germany may be traced to the decision of the REICHSGERICHT in 1897 in the *B. v. den Sachsischen Holzstaff-Fabrikranten-Verband* case (vi. Zivilsenat, Febr. 4, 1897, 38 RGZ 155). Facing a choice between freedom of trade and freedom of contract, the Reichsgericht gave priority to the latter.

In 1923 an Ordinance against Abuse of Economic Power was enacted which provided for a mere control of cartels (as opposed to a prohibition) and empowered a special Kartellgericht to step in against abuses. The best textbooks on the German cartel law of that period are: CALLMAN, DAS DEUTSCHE KARTELLRECHT (1934) and YSAY-TSCHIERSCHKY, KARTELLVERORDNUNG, VERORDNUNG GEGEN MISSBRAUCH WIRSCHAFTLICHER MACHTSTELLUNGEN (1930).

Under the Nazis, cartels "became a vehicle of an administration - planned economy". Schwartz, *op. cit.* at 641. This found its expression in the Law on Establishment of Compulsory Cartels.

anticartel law was imposed [1]. At that time, an American concept like the Rule of Reason, deeply rooted in a common law tradition, was surprisingly embraced several times by the German Courts to soften the ban against cartels and concentration [2]. Thus, long before the Common Market came into existence, the Rule of Reason was imported into a continental system, although under very exceptional circumstances. Later, when the Germans had adopted a statute of their own, the Rule of Reason continued to be the subject of many discussions.

On the other hand, the German anticartel law, rightly or wrongly, has the reputation of being the most vigorous of all antitrust statutes in effect among the EEC member nations. Germans have exerted a real and deep influence on the development of the European anticartel law [3]. The administrative system of enforcement with the extensive use of " notifications " was undoubtedly inspired by the German law. But also the decisions of the EEC Commission indicate the influence of the German definition of restraint of trade (" Wettbewerbsbeschränkung "). The German statute against restraints of competition is, however, drafted in quite different language from that of Article 85(1). The American tradition, and the policy followed in the enforcement of the Sherman Act, should, in my view, have been given more consideration by the European authorities. It must be questioned whether, by sticking so closely to the formalistic German approach, the enforcement agency has not defeated the purposes embodied in Article 85. Through an analysis of the Rule of Reason in American Law, in comparison with Section 1 of the German anticartel law and Article 85 of the Rome Treaty, this study represents an endeavor to answer this crucial question.

---

(1) § 12 of the Potsdam Agreement contained a provision relating to the decartelization and deconcentration of the German Economy. The three Western powers separately enacted military government decartelization laws in their respective zones of occupation. At that time, only America had a strong antitrust tradition.

(2) See the cases decided by the German Federal Supreme Court (*Bundesgerichtshof* hereinafter cited as BGH) referred to in BAUMBACH-HEFERMEHL, WETTBEWERS- UND WARENZEICHENRECHT, 1212 (1960).

(3) The adoption by the EEC Council of the Regulation no. 17 implementing Art. 85 and 86 of the Rome Treaty was described as the triumph of the German theories. See Françon, *Les Ententes et les Monopoles selon le Traité de Rome, Premier Règlement d'Application des Art. 85 et 86* in, 89 JOURNAL DU DROIT INTERNATIONAL (CLUNET) 400 (1962).

CHAPTER I

RULE OF REASON AND PER SE VIOLATIONS UNDER SECTION I OF THE SHERMAN ACT

1. - The Standard of Reasonableness, *Appalachian Coals* and the Four Tests of Article 85(3) of the Rome Treaty

The European lawyer who would confine his study of the Rule of Reason to *Appalachian Coals, Inc. v. United States* [1] would certainly have some support for equating the Sherman Act, as construed in the light of reason, with the cartel prohibition of the Rome Treaty, as qualified by its exempting clause. The facts of this case are now so famous that one can dispense with a detailed analysis. It will be remembered however that, confronted with a severe crisis, the producers in the Appalachian territory—combining 74.4 per cent of the production of bituminous coal in this area but possessing only a share of 11.96 of the relevant selling market—created a common and exclusive selling agency with the overt purpose of achieving greater efficiency. Their plan, examined in advance of its operation, was upheld as justifiable under the Rule of Reason.

There would have been no different result, it is submitted, if the United States Supreme Court had had to apply statutory provisions phrased in the same terms as Article 85 instead of Section 1 of the Sherman Act. The reasoning followed by the Court reflects a policy susbstantially similar to that embodied in the EEC law. Agreements in restraint of competition are declared prohibted by Article 85(1), but even if they do come within the prohibition, these agreements can be sustained and exempted if they meet the four tests set up in Article 85(3): (1) That the agreement contributes to improvement of production, distribution or to technological or economic progress; (2) that the public will share in the benefits of this improvement; (3) that the restriction is indispensable to the improvement; and (4) that the restriction does not afford the enterprises concerned the

(1) 288 U.S.344 (1933).

possibility to eliminate competition in a substantial part of the commodity.

In regard to Article 85(1), the plan of the Appalachian producers would have been viewed as in restraint of competition. Competition was eliminated between the defendants as the necessary consequence of a common selling agency with power to establish the prices at which it would make sales for its principals [1]. Indeed it was not denied that the plan might effect a change in market conditions [2]. Thus, Article 85(1) of the Rome Treaty would have caught the plan within the scope of its prohibition.

The United States Supreme Court decided, however, that the facts of the case were not sufficient to condemn the scheme. Under the EEC law, the exculpatory provision of Article 85(3) would have come into play. Comparing the Sherman Act and the Rome Treaty in regard to this particular set of facts, one cannot help being struck by the analogy of certain of the tests applied.

Improvement of production or distribution. As Chief Justice Hughes said, " the industry was in distress. It suffered from overexpansion and from a serious relative decline through the growing use of substitute fuels. It was afflicted by injurious practices within itself... " [3]. The evidence left no doubt that " defendants were engaged in a fair and open endeavor to aid the industry in a measurable recovery from its plight " [4]. Restraining competition *inter se*, the partners could claim that it was with the primary purpose of increasing their sales and thus the production of Appalachian Coals through better methods of distribution [5].

Consumers sharing in the benefits of the improvement. Consumers could certainly have been regarded as enjoying a fair share of the profit resulting from the plan. Chief Justice

(1) *Ibid.*, at 367.
(2) *Ibid.*, at 358-359 and 373-374.
(3) *Ibid.*, at 373.
(4) *Ibid.*, at 372.
(5) *Ibid.*, at 359.

Hughes noted: " The interests of producers and consumers are interlinked. When industry is grievously hurt, when producing concerns fail, when unemployment mounts and communities dependent upon profitable production are prostrated, the wells of commerce go dry [1]. "

Restriction no greater than required. The record did not reveal that the mitigation of the recognized evils could have been achieved otherwise. The agreement was not more restrictive than required to accomplish the alleged purposes. For instance, no attempt had been made to limit production [2].

Absence of monopoly power. Even though the agency was determining common prices for its shareholders, it was held that it had no power to fix market prices, and to eliminate outside competition. " [T]he group must still meet effective competition in a fair market and neither seeks nor was able to effect a domination of prices [3]. " The final test of Article 85 would have been met [4].

The rationale of the case, as viewed by Chief Justice Hughes, was that it should not be unlawful " to aid in relieving a depressed industry and in reviving commerce by placing competition upon a sounder basis [5]. " The plan was, in his judgment, fostering rather than impairing fair competitive opportunities. It put an end to injurious practices and consequently improved the *competitive* position of a group of producers which lacked any power to dominate the market [6]. Thus, albeit through different paths, the United States Supreme Court was able to come to the same conclusion as that which would have been reached under Article 85(1) as qualified by Article 85(3). The crucial issue remaining was whether *Appalachian Coals* could be construed as a license for minority groups to cartelize [7].

(1) *Ibid.*, at 372.
(2) *Ibid.*, at 367.
(3) *Ibid.*, at 374.
(4) *Cf. infra*, chapter III, at 126-129.
(5) Appalachian Coals, Inc. v. United States, 288 U.S. 344, 374 (1933).
(6) *Ibid.*, at 374.
(7) *Cf.* the discussion of Appalachian Coals in Robert H. Bork, *The Rule of Reason and the per se concept: Price-fixing and Market Division*, 74 YALE L.J. 822-826 (1964-1965).

Such an analogy is however misleading. Even assuming that *Appalachian Coals* is still good law, it remains nevertheless a rather isolated case, decided under exceptional circumstances [1]. I used it to show a possible application of the system embodied in Article 85. But it is certainly not conclusive as to what the proper scope of the Rule of Reason is today, nor as to the reasons why a statute, on its face absolute and all-encompassing, (" *Every* contract, combination in the form of trust or otherwise, or conspiracy in restraint of trade ... ") has been, and had to be, qualified by way of judicial construction.

2. - The Origins of the Rule of Reason

To explore in any depth the origin, the evolution and the present role of the Rule of Reason would require nothing less than an attempt to retrace the entire history of the Sherman Act and its enforcement. Such an undertaking would surpass the necessarily limited purpose of this chapter which is to show which of the two conflicting views of the Rule of Reason stated previously [2] prevails today, and to demonstrate that, despite some possible overlapping, Article 85(3) of the Rome Treaty is not a codification of the Rule of Reason but the by-product of a different philosophy. I believe that, so limited, the question can be answered by a review of the leading cases.

Essentially it may now be agreed that the decisive contribution of the Rule of Reason was to enable the courts to transform a statute, drafted in the language of the old common law, into a statute with a more modern orientation designed primarily to maintain market competition, and to make of the Sherman Act a workable and major " instrument of economic policy [3]. "

It is a long way from the early *United States v. Transmissouri Freight Association* [4] to the contemporaneous restatements of

---

(1) See NEALE, THE ANTITRUST LAW OF THE UNITED STATES OF AMERICA, 41 (1962); *contra,* J.A. Rahl, *Price Competition and the Price-fixing Rules,* 57 NW. U. L. REV. 144-145 and note 43 (1962).

(2) See *supra,* the introduction, at 5-7.

(3) See NEALE, *op. cit.,* at 29.

(4) United States v. Transmissouri Freight Association, 166 U.S. 290 (1897).

the Rule of Reason and of the *per se* rule contained in the *Northern Pacific Railway* [1] and *Klor's* [2] cases. To a civil lawyer, that such an evolution was possible without basic amendment of the Sherman Act provides a basis for admiration of the flexibility permitted by a common law system. True antitrust law is statutory. But the relationships between the common law and the Sherman Act are multiple. Common law is case law. And to ascertain on a case-by-case analysis, as is done under the Sherman Act, whether there is or is not a significant and unreasonable impairment of competition may be viewed as a device closely related to a common law tradition. On the other hand, if the search for certainty and predictability, for definitions and abstract categorization, is generally said to be more characteristic of a civil law system, this too is quite clearly visible in this area of American law. Whether or not they are reconcilable with the Rule of Reason, the *per se* rules developed by the American courts are a manifestation of this striving toward certainty. This may be one of the reasons why *per se* rules appear closer to the techniques used by the European anticartel statutes to ascertain an injury to competition [3].

It is well known that Senator Sherman did not write " his " Act in the same form as it was finally enacted. The initial bill setting in motion the congressional machinery which was to produce the first antitrust statute was directed against " all arrangements, contracts, agreements, trusts or combinations between persons or corporations, *made with a view*, or which *tend* to prevent free and full *competition* [4]. " Protection of competition was the senator's main concern and the now well-settled distinction between intent and effect was already present in this formulation, as in Article 85(1) of the Rome Treaty.

The adherence of Congress to the traditional common law language has been regarded as the source of most of the problems

---

(1) Northern Pacific Railway Co. v. United States, 356 U.S. 1 (1958).

(2) Klor's, Inc. v. Broadway-Hale Stores, Inc., 359 U.S. 207 (1959).

(3) See my evaluation of the German law, *infra*, chapter II, at 99-103 and the position of the EEC Commission, *infra*, chapter III, at 116-118.

(4) See THORELLI, THE FEDERAL ANTITRUST POLICY, 166 (1954) (Emphasis supplied).

which finally found their solution in the policy announced by Chief Justice White in *Standard Oil* (1) (2).

The origin of the Rule of Reason is to be explained mainly by the fact that Congress left undefined the central concept of restraint of trade. " The phrase was the creature of the English courts in private suits for the enforcement of an agreement by the defendant to refrain from competing with the plaintiff, the obligation usually being ancillary to the execution of a property or employment transaction between the parties... The 'trade' restrained... was the vocation of the obligor " (3). Restraint of trade conveyed the idea that the covenantor had agreed to eliminate *his competition* entirely or not to compete within a certain area or time (4). Thus it implied that a trader had imposed on himself some restriction of his freedom and ability to compete (5).

" The doctrine took on additional duties in the nineteenth century American cases where the courts began to use it as the vehicle for expression of the growing public policy of free competition and it was applied in the price-fixing, profit-pooling and market-sharing confederacy cases of the day (6). " Restraint of trade could be taken to refer to an agreement of which the sole purpose was to eliminate competition between the participants or to designate an arrangement by which a group of businessmen sought to impair a third person's ability to trade, as in boycott cases. But whether the restraint was purely internal or external, it still consisted of a self-imposed limitation upon tradesmen pursuant to an agreement. In the case of price-fixing, conspirators restrict their freedom to establish prices according to their own judgment. In the case of boycott, they restrict their freedom to deal with third parties. The element of restraint

(1) Standard Oil Co. of New Jersey v. United States, 221 U.S. 1 (1911).

(2) See John T. Chadwell, *Competition and Section 1 of the Sherman Act—Instant Antitrust or Long-run Policy?*, 27 ABA AANTITRUST SECTION, 60 (1965).

(3) J.A. Rahl, *Conspiracy and the Anti-Trust Laws*, 44 ILL. R. REV. 745 (1950).

(4) See OPPENHEIM, FEDERAL ANTITRUST LAWS, 1 (1958).

(5) *Cf.* United States v. Addyston Pipe and Steel Co., 85 Fed. 271, 279 (6th Cir. 1898), aff'd, 175 U.S. 211 (1899).

(6) See Rahl, *op. cit.*, at 745.

put on the competitive freedom of the members of the group is present in both situations, even though in the latter, the emphasis is placed more upon the coercion exerted upon outsiders.

The concern of the law changed in the latter part of the nineteenth century. Originally preoccupied with preserving the ability of individuals to earn a livelihood, and avoiding the risk of their becoming a public charge, the law came to be more concerned with arrangements which threaten " the desired automatic play of competitive forces in a free market place (1) ".

As the terms of the Sherman Act were capable of embracing a large variety of restrictive covenants and agreements, it was inevitable that the issue would sooner or later arise as to whether the statute should be read literally or whether it should be injected with some flexibility by an interpretation which would take into account the later developments of the common law. Did the Sherman Act have the effect of rendering unlawful any kind of contractual limitation on the freedom of economic activity accepted by individual traders? Was the statute designed to cover the separate covenants which are subordinate to the main lawful purpose of a larger transaction such as ancillary restraints? Was it even meant to make unlawful transactions in which the primary purpose is to eliminate or restrict competition as such, regardless of the significance of the effect actually produced in the market place? An answer to these questions required a return to the basic policy of the statute.

3. - The Rule of Reason as a Synthesis

The conflict which led to the Rule of Reason is generally viewed as one between literalists and those who wanted to save the Sherman Act from its vagueness by imparting to it the gloss of history (2).

(1) See Rahl, *op. cit.*, at 746.

(2) As to the latter formula, I am referring to the words of Justice Frankfurther in his dissent in Federal Trade Commission v. Motion Picture Advertising Service Co., 344 U.S. 392, 405 (1953).

However this view seems to be oversimplified. Recent students of the Rule of Reason have shown convincingly that the debate was not as to " whether the Act should be flexible or rigid but by what criteria it flexibility was controlled [1] ".

The dissent of Justice White in *United States v. Transmissouri Freight Association* [2] throws much light on the motives which led Justice Peckham to read the Sherman Act literally and to put emphasis on the word " every " in Section 1. Defendants were claiming that the agreement was a perfectly proper, legitimate and salutary one, and that it was necessary to the prosperity of the companies [3]. In this case Justice White advocated a conception of the Rule of Reason very different from that which he finally formulated in *Standard Oil.* The standard of reasonableness which he supported at that time was based mainly on the reasonableness of the prices fixed by a combination, or, more broadly, on its social expediency [4].

In opposition to this conception—which would have greatly weakened the Sherman Act—was a strict construction. But, contrary to what has long been thought, the reaction of the literalists, which found its expression in the majority opinion of Justice Peckham, was not " the result of a single-minded application of the statutory language [5] "; it was dialectical in character.

In *Standard Oil* and in *American Tobacco,* Chief Justice White was able to persuade a majority of the Court to adopt the Rule of Reason, because he had considerably changed his own theory. The policy announced in 1911 by Chief Justice White appears in thoses cases to be a compromise between his early views and those of his opponents. Thus, from this synthesis of opposing views arose the basis for the modern Rule of Reason.

---

(1) Bork, *op. cit.*, at 785.

(2) United States v. Transmissouri Freight Association, 166 U.S. 290 (1897).

(3) *Ibid.*, at 308.

(4) Bork, *op. cit.*, at 786.

(5) Bork, *op. cit.*, at 786-787 and 790.

4. - *Transmissouri Freight Association* and the so-called Literalist Approach of Justice Peckham

United States v. Transmissouri Freight Association involved eighteen railroads, banded together in an association of freight carriers which had agreed upon rates and other terms of service. The main claim of the defendants was that the agreement had been entered into for the purpose of maintaining reasonable rates. Pointing to the language of the statute, Peckham stressed that " every " could not mean anything other than " every ". " So far as the very terms of the statute go, they apply to any contract of the nature described (1). " The Justice saw no escape from the conclusion that if any agreement restrains trade, it is condemned by the Act. Consequently, he rejected the view that the Act should cover only agreements which are in unreasonable restraint of trade, because, he said, such a construction would alter the plain meaning of the statute (2). Furthermore, he felt that a standard of reasonableness, as he understood it, would be unworkable, and would emasculate the Act. He said:—

> If only that kind of contract which is in unreasonable restraint of trade be within the meaning of the statute, and declared therein to be illegal, it is at once apparent that the subject of what is a reasonable rate is attended with great uncertainty. What is a proper standard by which to judge the fact of reasonable rates? [...] To say, therefore, that the act excludes agreements which are not in unreasonable restraint of trade, and which tend simply to keep up reasonable rates for transportation, is substantially to leave the question of reasonableness to the companies themselves (3).

If Justice Peckham refused to read into the statute, by way of judicial legislation, an exception that was not placed there by the law-making branch of the Government (4), it was because of the vagueness of the claimed qualification. " Reasonable " related to the reasonableness of rates, and all his argument

(1) United States v. Transmissouri Freight Association, 166 U.S. 290, 312 (1897).

(2) *Ibid.*, at 329.

(3) *Ibid.*, 331-312.

(4) *Ibid.*, at 340.

rested solely on the uncertainty of such a test. He read the Act literally and mechanically, not in order to oppose flexibility as such, but rather in order to counteract the loose and fuzzy conceptions expressed by Justice White in his dissent (1).

This may explain why Peckham was more concerned with refuting misconception than with giving the Act a comprehensible content.

Was Peckham " redefining " " restraint of trade " to refer to the elimination of competition in the general market (2)? Was he, as one recent analyst asserts, the first initiator of a Rule of Reason in the modern sense (3)? I would not go so far as this. But one can at least acknowkledge the importance of his role. It seems fair to say that by rejecting the " reasonable-price standard of legality (4) " " he helped to prevent the statute from becoming a licence to cartelize (5) ".

5. - Taft's Review of the Common Law and his Concept of Ancillary Restraints

The masterful review of the common law by Taft in *Addyston Pipe and Steel Co.* (6) was the first, if hesitant, step away from Peckham's strict approach. Described as "one of the imperishable landmarks of our law " (7), the opinion of Taft has not had an influence proportionate to the clarity of its argument.

The case had to do with a division of territory coupled with a collusive bidding scheme and price-fixing agreement. Assuming, without necessarily deciding, that the Sherman Act codified the common law, Taft rejected the contention of defendants that their agreement would have been upheld at common law as reasonable. For him, " no conventional restraint

(1) See Bork, *op. cit.*, at 790.
(2) *Id.*, at 794.
(3) *Id.*, at 785.
(4) *Id.*, at 796.
(5) *Id.*, at 796.
(6) United States v. Addyston Pipe and Steel Co., 85 Fed. 271 (6th Cir. 1898), aff'd, 175 U.S. 211 (1899).
(7) HANDLER, *The Judicial Architects of the Rule of Reason*, in ANTITRUST IN PERSPECTIVE, 9 (1957).

of trade can be enforced unless the covenant embodying it is merely ancillary to the main purpose of a lawful contract, and necessary to protect the covenantee in the enjoyment of the legitimate fruits of the contract, or to protect him from the dangers of an unjust use of those fruits by the other party (1)." But "where the sole object of both parties in making the contract as expressed therein is merely to restrain competition and enhance or maintain prices, it would seem that there is nothing to justify or excuse the restraint, that it would necessarily have a tendency to monopoly, and therefore would be void (2)."

Courts which had relaxed the rules for determining the unreasonableness of restraints were accused of having "set sail on a sea of doubt" (3). In Taft's view, these courts had assumed the power to say how much restraint of competition is in the public interest and how much is not (4). "The manifest danger in the administration of justice according to so shifting, vague and indeterminate standards would seem to be a strong reason against adopting it. (5)"

The opinion of Taft had two merits. First, as had been done in *United States v. Transmissouri Freight Association*, it rejected any possibility of justifying or excusing, on the basis of its social expediency or of its utility to the participants, an agreement which was merely restrictive of competition. Reasonableness of prices fixed or business reasons for the combination were held to be wholly irrelevant in deciding the lawfulness of such an agreement (6). Second, unlike Justice Peckham, Taft attempted to find a foundation in logic for excepting from invalidity at common law covenants in restraint of trade which are ancillary to a main lawful transaction and which do not exceed the "measure of protection needed (7)."

But the shortcomings of Taft's doctrine are nevertheless apparent. Its central test was defined in terms of *purpose* of

---

(1) United States v. Addyston Pipe and Steel Co., 85 Fed. 271, 282 (6th Cir. 1898).
(2) *Ibid.*, at 282-283.
(3) *Ibid.*, at 283-284.
(4) *Ibid.*, at 284.
(5) *Id.*
(6) *Ibid.*, at 291.
(7) *Ibid.*, at 282.

restraining competition. It seems that in Taft's view, competition meant the freedom of traders to compete rather than being descriptive of general market conditions. All agreements whose naked purpose is to impede businessmen's freedom to compete would thus be deemed unlawful regardless of whether their *effect* on competition at large was *de minimis*. Taft did not leave any room for appraising, as a factual matter, the competitive significance of restrictive practices (1). On the other hand, his theory was completely inadequate in regard to mergers, holding companies, trusts and consolidation (2). A merger for instance has, at least as one purpose, the removal of any competition between the merging companies. Should it be therefore considered illegal?

It is even doubtful whether Taft's distinction between ancillary and non-ancillary restraints may be accepted without reservation under the modern Sherman Act. However helpful, his theory has to be re-evaluated under the later law and especially under the Rule of Reason as expressed by White. While Taft did not directly state the ancillary restraints are *ipso facto* valid under the Sherman Act, his opinion has been frequently invoked for supporting the proposition that any restraint is valid, if ancillary. But even though ancillary, a restraint can be upheld under present law only if its *effect* on market competition is quite insubstantial (3). A transaction, lawful in itself, may mask a cartel. Taft's doctrine has been the refuge of such subtly presented agreements (4).

(1) See Chadwell, *op. cit.*, at 60.

(2) It should be noted, however, that Taft might have been speaking of a process of integration when he wrote: "But, in recent years, even the fact that the contract is one for the making of a partnership or a corporation, has not saved it from invalidity if it could be shown that it was only part of a plan to acquire all the property used in a business by one management with a view to establishing a monopoly." United States v. Addyston Pipe and Steel Co., 85 Fed. 271, 291 (6th Cir. 1898).

(3) *Cf.*, Denisson Mattress Factory v. Spring Air Co., 308 F. 2d 1642, 1647 (5th Cir. 1962). This is not to suggest that only ancillary restraints may be lawful under Section 1 of the Sherman Act. The test is one of competitive effect. Therefore even non-ancillary restraints which have only a minimum effect on competition may be upheld.

(4) See *e.g.* in the field of international cartels, Timken Roller Bearing Co. v. United States, 341 U.S. 593 (1950); United States v. National Lead Co., 63 F. Supp. 513 (S.D.N.Y. 1945), aff'd 312 U.S. 319 (1947); United States v. General Electric Co., 82 F. Supp. 753 (D.N.J. 1949). However in these cases, the courts rejected defendants' arguments that the restraints were merely ancillary.

Thus, apart from being a work of art in legal literature, *United States v. Addyston Pipe and Steel Co.* has little influence for the contemporary observer.

6. - The Foundations of the Modern Rule of Reason : *Standard Oil* and *American Tobacco*

A. - A Policy Against " Undue Limitations on Competitive Conditions "

The dicta of Chief Justice White in *Standard Oil* (1) and *American Tobacco* (2) set up the foundations for the development of the modern Rule of Reason. They accomplished the synthesis between White's early views as expressed in his dissent in *United States Transmissouri Freight Association* and Peckham's literal construction of the statute and established the Sherman Act as making unlawful only undue limitations on competitive conditions.

Although White's opinion in *Standard Oil* is the starting point of the modern interpretation of the Sherman Act, it lacks all the qualities which make the language of Taft's doctrine so admirable. Drafted in long, complicated and confusing sentences, *Standard Oil* was—not suprisingly—the source of many misunderstandings. One explanation may be that the Rule of Reason that he finally announced was susbtantially different from the version he had advocated a few years earlier.

Fortunately, White himself later elucidated his doctrine in *American Tobacco*. He restated that since the statute had not defined the phrase " restraints of trade ", it became necessary to construe those words—a duty which could only be discharged by a resort to reason (3).

> It was held in the *Standard Oil* case that as the words " restraints of trade " at common law and in the law of this country at the time

---

(1) Standard Oil of New Jersey v. United States, 221 U.S. 1 (1911).
(2) United States v. American Tobacco Company, 221 U.S. 106 (1911).
(3) *Ibid.*, at 179.

of the adoption of the antitrust act only embraced acts or contracts or agreements or combinations which operated to the prejudice of the public interest by unduly restricting competition, or unduly obstructing the due course of trade, or which either because of the inherent nature or effect or because of the evident purpose of the acts, etc., injuriously restrained trade, that the words as used in the statute were designed to have and did have but a like significance (1).

White's construction of the statute was certainly the only feasible way to transform the Sherman Act into a workable instrument of economic policy. As Section 1 was designed to cover cartel agreements as well as the combination of companies by trust, holding company, merger or consolidation, some guidance had to be sought. Did Section 1 " mean that every agreement between two or more competitors constituting a technical restraint was prohibited? Was the purchase of a competing business, no matter how extenuating the circumstances, forbidden? (2) "

Competition was declared to be the policy of the statute, and became the regulating factor of the economic system. The test of injury to the public clearly implied that only such contractual limitations on individual freedom of action which placed an excessive burden on the competitive process were to be considered unreasonable.

B. - Loose-Knit Confederations and Close-Knit Combinations

Although White did not discriminate between them, the standards he set up were certainly of greater importance in regard to close-knit combinations than to loose-knit confederations. It is elementary that a merger between two competitors removes any competition between them. But is it *ipso facto* to be considered as having an anticompetitive effect on the general market? The merging firms may be small companies and only their combination may enable them to compete with larger units (3) White himself

(1) *Id.*

(2) HANDLER, A STUDY OF THE CONSTRUCTION AND ENFORCEMENT OF THE FEDERAL ANTITRUST LAWS, TNEC Monograph no. 38, 2 (1941).

(3) *Cf.* Brown Shoe Co. v. United States, 370 U.S. 294, 319 (1962).

seemed aware of the efficiency which flows from mergers and stock transfer (1). " If some integration was permissible, at what point did the combinations of companies become unlawful? (2) " A greater discretion is needed for determining when the acquisition of the corporate stock or physical assets of a competitor becomes anticompetitive. Without the test of anticompetitive effect or purpose formulated by White, the Sherman Act might have led to the prohibition of any merger or consolidation. But, as a matter of fact, White's Rule of Reason accounts perhaps for the relaxation of the antitrust policy on mergers (3) and for the later cases interpreting the Sherman Act as virtually requiring proof of illegal monopolization to invalidate a merger or a consolidation. (4) It has been stressed that " one of the very few important antitrust cases which the Government has lost in the Supreme Court since World War II was the *Columbia Steel* merger case. (5) " As early as 1941, Professor Handler noted that " the adoption of the Rule of Reason effected more of a change in theory than in actual doctrine, insofar as loose-knit combinations were concerned. Greater effect is to be discerned in the field of close-knit combinations... (6) "

(1) See Bork, *op. cit.*, at 804-805.

(2) HANDLER, *op. cit.*, at 2.

(3) This is, for instance, the opinion expressed by Blake and Jones, *The Goals of Antitrust: A Dialogue on Policy — In Defense of Antitrust*, 65 COLUM. L. REV. 376, 381 and footnote (35) (1965).

(4) J.A. Rahl, *Antimerger Law in Search of a Policy*, Proceedings of the Fourth Annual Corporate Counsel Institute, 74 (1965). Professor Rahl refers to United States v. United States Steel Corp., 251 U.S. 417 (1920) (Consolidation of 50 % of industry upheld); United States v. International Harvester Co., 274 U.S. 630 (1927) (64 % allowed to stand).

(5) J.A. Rahl, *op. cit.*, at 74.

(6) HANDLER, *op. cit.*, at 8. HANDLER (*Id.*, at 74) summarized his review of the Supreme Court cases as follows: " The course of decision in the field of mergers and consolidations has been erratic and unpredictable ... There is today virtually as much doubt and uncertainty regarding the permissive limits of capital combinations as there was in 1890. " Furthermore, he wrote (*Id.*, at 83): " The standard of reason has permitted the Court to sit as censor on corporate integrations and undoubtelly has resulted in a more tolerant attitude toward such combines than would have been the case had the rule of reason been rejected. Once it was decided that the statute does not, on the one hand, prohibit every business consolidation, nor permit, on the other, integrations just short of complete domination, the Court, with or without a rule of reason, was compelled to draw the line somewhere in the scale from 1 to 100 %. The rule of reason has not altered the nature of the problem with which the courts have been confronted and except for its doubtful psychological value, has not assisted the courts in the formulation of any clear and predictable tests by which the legality of corporate integrations might be measured. "

Naked restrictive agreements between competitors are less likely to promote efficiency. A common selling agency is the best example of an agreement which may improve the competitive position of a group without affecting competition on the market itself. But this is in reality a case where the firms are *merging* one of the functions of the enterprise. Sound reasons exist for treating mergers and cartels differently ([1]). At best, cartels will be constituted to remedy certain evils; but generally the main result will be to keep the least efficient business unit in existence ([2]). They will hamper rather than foster the economic progress. Thus, cartels could be thought to be caught by the test of inherently anticompetitive effect, and at any rate a lesser degree of discretion is involved in measuring their purpose or effect of hampering competition than in the case of concentration. In the field of loose-knit confederations, the standard formulated by Chief Justice White provided the basis for *per se* rules in the modern sense. As shown later by the *Klor's* case ([3]), the courts could avoid extensive inquiry into the effect or the purpose of a practice by considering it as *inherently* anticompetitive ([4]).

C. - No Distinction between Good and Bad Cartels

As competition was the general standard, no room was left to determine the expediency or inexpediency of cartel agreements: social or economic justifications unrelated to competition were not permitted. White himself took the precaution to stress that acts which the statute prohibited could not be removed from the control of its prohibitions by a finding that they are reasonable. As stated in *Standard Oil* ([5]), once it

(1) J.A. Rahl, *op. cit.*, at 74.

(2) But certain European anticartel statutes (see *e.g.* Section 5(2) of the German Law against Restraints of Competition and Art. 59*bis* and *ter* of the French Ordinance No. 45-1483 of June 30, 1945) favor, for instance, market-sharing arrangements as to types of products (so-called "specialization" cartels). In that respect, these cartels may be considered as furthering economic progress. But it is to be stressed that cartels then become instrumentalities of the government's economic policy. This illustrates that European legislatures do not have full confidence in the free play of market forces.

(3) Klor's Inc. v. Broadway-Hale Stores, 359 U.S. 207 (1959).

(4) See *infra*, this chapter, at 52.

(5) Standard Oil of New Jersey v. United States, 221 U.S. 1, 65 (1911).

was established that contracts or agreements "were clearly restraints of trade, they could not be taken out of that category by indulging in general reasoning as to the expediency or non-expediency of having made the contracts, or the wisdom or want of wisdom of the statute which prohibited their being made." (1)

This passage shows that Chief Justice White had modified the conception of the Rule of Reason which he had espoused earlier in *United States v. Transmissouri Freight Association.* In this manner, he was able to hold that the *Freight Association* and the *Joint Traffic* decisions (2) were an application of the Rule of Reason. The Sherman Act applied only to unreasonable restraints, but on their facts these combinations were unreasonable in the sense in which he now defined the policy of the Act (3).

If discretion was involved in the Rule of Reason, it did not extend to a balance of the advantages of restraint versus competition. As Professor Handler put it in 1941:—

> The standard of reason though related to the statutory objectives is still vague and indefinite. This is, however, inherent in the very nature of the standard. What is and what is not consistent with the maintenance of competition is not easy of determination. Integrating the rule of reason into the purposes of the legislation does not eliminate the element of discretion. It does, however, establish the metes and bounds of such discretion and precludes the voyage upon the chartless sea of doubt which was so greatly feared by Judge Taft (4).

The same interpretation has been adopted by the Attorney General's Committee:—

> While *Standard Oil* gave the courts discretion in interpreting the word "every" in Section 1, such discretion is confined to consideration of whether in each case the conduct being reviewed under the Act constitutes an undue restraint of competitive conditions, or a monopolization, or an attempt to monopolize. This standard permits the courts to decide whether conduct is significantly

(1) *Id., cf.* United States v. American Tobacco Co., 221 U.S. 106, 179-180 (1911).
(2) United States v. Joint Traffic Association, 171 U.S. 505 (1898).
(3) Standard Oil of New Jersey v. United States, 221 U.S. 1, 64-68 (1911).
(4) HANDLER, *op. cit.,* at 9. A similar view of the Rule of Reason has been proposed by Eugen V. Rostow, *Monopoly Under the Sherman Act: Power or Purpose?*, 43 ILL. L. REV. 754, 751, 752 (1948-1949).

and unreasonably anticompetitive in character or effect; it makes obsolete once prevalent arguments, such as, whether monopoly arrangements would be socially preferable to competition in a particular industry, because, for example, of high fixed cost, or the risks of "cutthroat" competition or other similar unusual conditions. (1)

Neither *Standard Oil* nor *American Tobacco* could be the basis for a distinction between bad and good cartels. The courts did not have the burden, as they now have under the British Restrictive Trade Practices Act, of choosing between or balancing conflicting economic and social interests (2). The standard of competition provided an answer. Judicial discretion existed only as to the issue of whether the restraint was undue: this was a question of degree.

Thus, Chief Justice White did not deserve the criticism he received (3). However, some observers felt that the Rule of Reason had weakened the Act, and this feeling led to the enactment of the Clayton Act. As the Senate Interstate Commerce Committee declared in a 1913 Report :—

> The Committee has full confidence in the integrity, intelligence and patriotism of the Supreme Court of the United States, but it is unwilling to repose in that Court, or any other Court, the vast and undefined power which it must exercise in the administration of the statute under the rule which it has promulgated. It substitutes the Court in the place of Congress, for whenever the rule is invoked, the Court does not administer the law, but makes the law. (4)

Paradoxically, the Clayton Act, which was passed presumably to remedy these evils, was interpreted fifty years later as codifying the standard of reason announced by Chief Justice White. Aside from the question that the Clayton Act requires a lower standard of proof (5), the test of effect on competition is nothing else than a built-in Rule of Reason (6).

---

(1) Report of the Attorney General's National Committee to Study the Antitrust Laws, 11 (1955).

(2) *Cf.*, Turner, *Conglomerate Mergers and Section 7 of the Clayton Act.*, 78 Harv. L. Rev. 1313, 1395 (1965).

(3) J.T. Chadwell, *op. cit.*, at 61.

(4) See Rep. No. 1326, 62d Cong., 3d Sess., 1913.

(5) See Adelman, *Acquire the Whole or Part of the Stock or Assets of Another Corporation,* Aba Antitrust Section 111, 118 (1953). *Accord* J.A. Rahl, *op. cit.*, at 77.

(6) Neale, *op. cit.*, at 23.

7. - Justice Brandeis' Version of the Rule of Reason

A. - Regulation and Promotion, as Opposed to Destruction, of Competition

In *Chicago Board of Trade* (1), a few years after the real birth of the Sherman Act, Justice Brandeis gave another version of the Rule of Reason.

The regulation adopted by the Board and challenged by the Government prohibited members " who bought after the close of business from making such purchases at any price other than the closing bid at the Exchange's 'call' session (2). "

No attempt was made by the Government to show that the rule had the purpose or the effect of limiting the amount of grain shipped to Chicago; or of retarding or accelerating shipment; or of raising or depressing prices; or of discriminating against any part of the public; or that it resulted in hardship to anyone (3). *Absolutely no evidence had been advanced by the Government to show an adverse effect on market conditions.* The Government had rested its case entirely on the mere proposition that " a rule or agreement by which men, occupying positions of strength in any branch of trade, fixed prices at which they would buy or sell during an important part of the business day is an illegal restraint of trade under the Antitrust Law (4). "

The Government's contention was rejected in the following passage which is often quoted as the most perfect formulation of the Rule of Reason:—

> But the legality of an agreement or regulation cannot be determined by so simple a test, as whether it restrains competition. Every agreement concerning trade, every regulation of trade, restrains. To bind, to restrain is of their very essence. The true test of

(1) Board of Trade of City of Chicago v. United States, 246 U.S. 231 (1918).

(2) I am quoting the analysis of the REPORT OF THE ATTORNEY GENERAL'S NATIONAL COMMITTEE TO STUDY THE ANTITRUST LAWNS, 23 (1955).

(3) Board of Trade of City of Chicago v. United States, 246 U.S. 231, 238 (1918).

(4) *Ibid.*, at 238.

legality is whether the restraint imposed is such as merely regulates and perhaps thereby promotes competition or whether it is such as may suppress or even destroy competition. To determine that question the Court must ordinarily consider the facts peculiar to the business to which the restraint is applied; its condition before and after the restraint was imposed; the nature of the restraint and its effect, actual or probable. The history of the restraint, the evil believed to exist, the reason for adopting the particular remedy, the purpose and end sought to be attained, are all relevant factors. This is not because a good intention will save an otherwise objectionable regulation or the reverse; but because knowledge of intent may help the Court to interpret facts and to predict consequences. (1)

B. - No Adverse Effect upon Market Conditions

Obviously, the restraint which was upheld by the Court had no significant effect on the market. It was even likely to improve market conditions. Brandeis, by analyzing the nature, the scope and the effect of the rule, endeavored to demonstrate this. Stressing the narrow limits of the " call " rule, he listed several reasons why within its narrow limits the rule helped to improve market conditions. It was, of course, decisive that the restriction, although it pertained clearly to price formation, was essentially upon the " period of price-making " (2). The price itself was still determined by free competition in the open market. This enabled the Court to regard the restriction as being one related to " the hours in which business may be done " (3), rather than as a price-fixing agreement. The analysis of the Attorney General's Committee has become classic:—

After a full review of the available facts, the Court concluded that the rule had no appreciable effect on general market prices, nor on the volume of grain coming to Chicago. On the contrary, the Court found that the rule served legitimate regulatory purposes of the exchange, other than price-fixing objectives. The Court treated the rule, therefore, not as a species of price-fixing, but as a regulation of the hours of trading, whose effect would be to bring more of the class of transactions affected into the regular and fully competitive sessions of the Exchange. (4)

(1) *Id.*
(2) *Ibid.*, at 239.
(3) *Ibid.*, at 241.
(4) *Op. cit.*, at 23.

Although the tendency of the Court was to limit the case to its facts ([1]), it could at least stand for the proposition that *not every* restraint upon the conduct of businessmen is likely to suppress competition.

C. - Limited License to Cartelize?

The language of the opinion has been said to invite a further step. In 1941, Professor Handler already looked at the case as leaning " toward the view that arrangements which have a partial and not a controlling effect on market prices may be permissible " ([2]). Later, the same author engaged in an even broader generalization. He inferred from *Chicago Board of Trade* that Brandeis seemingly identified reasonable restraint of trade with the absence of monopoly. ([3]) " The fact that a combination eliminates competition *inter se* is not controlling, if the quality of competition in the market as a whole remains unimpaired. ([4]) " The issue is then whether Brandeis intended to give minority groups a limited license to cartelize. To another observer, Brandeis' language " sounds as though regulation of competition—which seems difficult to differentiate from mitigation of competition—might be lawful as an end in itself " ([5]).

But the distinction set up by Brandeis between a restraint which regulates competition or a restraint which suppresses competition may be dangerous when applied to other factual situations. I think that these authors are reinterpreting *Chicago Board of Trade* in the light of *Appalachian Coals* ([6]) in which Chief Justice Hughes relied heavily on Brandeis' language. This approach is fallacious. Nothing in the facts of *Chicago Board of Trade* indicates that Brandeis intended to go as far as these commentators have claimed. A narrower interpretation seems to me preferable. *Chicago Board of Trade* is still good law. In my view, it can be invoked to support the proposition that not every restriction put on the conduct of business men

(1) HANDLER, *op. cit., supra*, note (2), p. 30, at 31.
(2) *Id.*
(3) HANDLER, *op. cit., supra*, note (7), p. 26, at 19.
(4) *Id.*
(5) Bork, *op. cit.*, at 817.
(6) Appalachian Coals Inc. v. United States, 288 U.S. 344 (1933).

is likely to affect market competition. *White Motor* [1] shows for instance that Brandeis' doctrine could serve to justify a restraint on *intraband* competition, which promotes rather than destroys *interbrand* competition.

It is submitted that knowledge of Brandeis' own philosophy should not prejudice the interpreters of *Chicago Board of Trade.* Some of Brandeis' philosophy has been articulated in his dissent in *American Column and Lumber Co. v. United States* [2]. There he would have sustained " a voluntary system for collecting from these independent concerns detailed information concerning the business operations of each and its opinions as to trade conditions, prospects, policy; and of collating, interpreting and distributing the data so received among the members of the Association and others. " [3] He eloquently advocated the lawfulness of the open price system involved, saying that the Sherman Act did not command that competition should be pursued blindly, and that the aim of the plan in this case was to make competition more rational. [4] The decisive passage is where he declared:—

> The refusal to permit a multitude of small rivals to cooperate ... in order to protect themselves and the public from the chaos and havoc wrought in their trade by ignorance, may result in suppressing competition in the hardwood industry.

Referring to the *U.S. Steel* and *United Shoe Machinery* cases where vast aggregations of capital in a single corporation had been upheld by the Court, Brandeis went on to say:—

> May not these hardwood lumber concerns, frustrated in their efforts to rationalize competition, be led to enter the inviting field of sonsolidation? And if they do, may not another huge trust with highly centralized control over vast resources, natural, manufacturing, and financial, become so powerful as to dominate competitors, wholesalers, retailers, consumers, employees, and in large measure, the community? [5]

---

(1) White Motor Co. v. United States, 372 U.S. 253 (1963).

(2) American Column and Lumber Co. v. United States, 257 U.S. 377 (1921).

(3) *Ibid.*, at 415.

(4) *Id.*

(5) *Id.*, at 418-419.

This passage suggests that in Brandeis' view mergers and cartels should not be treated differently, since a strict position against loose-knit arrangements, accompanied by a more favorable treatment of mergers, could only produce an increased trend toward concentration. " The essential key to his thinking " may be " in his attitude toward bigness on the one hand and small business on the other. "[1] But I do not agree with the inferences drawn by Bork from *Chicago Board of Trade.* According to that author, " Brandeis believed that private regulation of competition might legitimately have other than economic aims; it might go beyond regulating, and thereby promoting competition, to the achievement of non-economic goals. To that extent, a Sherman Act court would be required to balance economic goals against more broadly social or humanitarian goals. " [2]

D. - Chicago Board of Trade: *No Deviation from the Main Tradition of the Rule of Reason*

Brandeis' Rule of Reason, as it is expressed in *Chicago Board of Trade,* does not permit taking restraints out of the prohibitions of the Sherman Act by indulging in reasoning as to their social or economic justification, once they have been found to be destructive of market competition. *Chicago Board of Trade* is not the equivalent of Article 85(3) of the Rome Treaty which involves such a process of justifying restraints on competition. It is not a deviation from the main tradition of the Rule of Reason. [3] It differs from White's theory only to the extent that it could not be a springboard for the development of *per se* rules. [4] As I have already stated, a *per se* rule is not incompatible with *Standard Oil* and *American Tobacco,* but it is more difficult to reconcile with *Chicago Board of Trade.*

---

(1) HANDLER, *op. cit.,* at 17. To support his proposition, Professor Handler refers mainly to BRANDEIS, THE CURSE OF BIGNESS, Pt. 3 and to Brandeis' defense of resale price maintenance (see HANDLER, *op. cit.,* and note 138, at 95).

(2) Bork, *op. cit.,* at 819.

(3) *Id.,* at 811.

(4) Cf. HANDLER, *op. cit.,* at 18.

8. - The Rule of Reason as Applied in *Appalachian Coals*

A. - The " Concentric Circle " Approach

As I have pointed out at the beginning of this chapter, the rule of reason applied by Chief Justice Hughes in *Appalachian Coals Inc. v. United States* (1) presents some overlapping with the third clause of Article 85 of the Rome Treaty. *Appalachian Coals*—not *Chicago Board of Trade*—is the best example of what has been denominated the " concentric circle " approach. " Treating the boundaries of the market as the outside and the combine as the inside circle, there is no violation if the smaller circle remains at a respectable distance from the outer periphery. " (2)

Similarly, Article 85 of the Rome Treaty, as qualified by the exculpatory clause, permits the sustaining of an agreement which suppresses competition within one group, provided that the agreement brings about certain specified benefits, and that the group making it is in no position to dominate the market.

The joint selling agreement involved in *Appalachian Coals* was considered to promote efficiency, and, although suppressing competition between the parties, it was upheld by the Court. It should not be unlawful, the Court said, to prevent certain " distress practices " in the production and marketing of coal, when defendants are found to have neither intent nor power to reduce price competition in the market. (3) Under Article 85(3), it would have been claimed that the combination improved *production and distribution.* The United States Supreme Court was able to sustain the plan of the coal producers by deciding that it contributed to improving their *competitive position* without conferring market power on them. Through a different analysis the United States Supreme Court reached in fact a result very similar to that permitted by Article 85(3) of the Rome Treaty.

---

(1) 288 U.S. 344 (1933).

(2) HANDLER, *op. cit.*, at 20.

(3) See J.A. Rahl, *Price Competition and the Pricefixing Rule*, 57 NW. U. L. REV. 141 (1962).

B. - Competition no longer the Supreme Good?

One may perhaps agree, without tracing Hughes' thought back to *Chicago Board of Trade*, that Chief Justice Hughes exhibited a willingness " to judge how much regulation and elimination of competition, as an end in itself, was an allowable or even praiseworthy goal. " ([1]) This trend would come very close to the philosophy underlying Article 85 of the Rome Treaty. Competition is no longer the supreme good. It is a means of achieving certain aims of economic policy: improvement of production or distribution; promotion of technology; a higher standard of living for consumers. Where these aims are better accomplished by elimination of competition, cartels may be justified.

Did Chief Justice Hughes take an unreasonable restraint out of the prohibitions of the Sherman Act by indulging in analysis of its economic expediency, or did he simply redefine what a significant impairment of competition was in the sense of White's Rule of Reason? This question has not yet been answered.

C. - Appalachian Coals *Superseded as a Rule for Price-Fixing*

It is difficult not to admit that *Appalachian Coals* is a rather isolated case. In 1941, Professor Handler reported that " prior to the *Appalachian Coals* case it was held consistently that the suppression of competition by agreement was unlawful regardless of the market position of the parties to the agreement. "([2]) After that, the Supreme Court in *Socony Vacuum*([3])

([1]) Bork, *op. cit.*, at 823.

([2]) HANDLER, *op. cit.*, *supra*, note (2), p. 30, at 85. To support his proposition, this author referrend *e.g.* to *Chesapeake and Ohio Fuel Co., v. United States* [115 Fed. 610 (6th Cir. 1902)] where " the court held illegal an exclusive sales agency which had been formed to market about 30 % of the coal and about 45 % of the coke which was produced in the Kanawha district of West Virginia. The coal of the combine was less than 1 % of that sold in the same markets in which it competed and the coke sold met 'severe' competition in all markets. The sales agency was given the power to fix the prices and to control the production of the members of the group. Although the combination was subject to effective competition in all markets, it was held illegal since it deprived the public of the benefits of competition within the group. " (HANDLER, *id.*, at 30). " The law reaches combinations which may fall short of complete control of a trade or business, and does not await the consolidation of many small combinations into the huge 'trust' which shall control the production and sale of a commodity. " [115 Fed. 610, 624 (6th Cir. 1902)].

([3]) United States v. Socony Vacuum Oil Co., 310 U.S. 150 (1940).

condemned price-fixing even by groups which lack market power. Without being overruled, *Appalachian Coals* has at least been superseded.

D. - Unsucccessful Attempt to Apply the Same Standard to Mergers as to Cartels

Appalachian Coals is also significant in that it retained the ideas expressed by Brandeis in his dissent in the *American Column and Lumber* case. (1) The decision recognized the necessity of applying the same tests to both mergers and cartels. Relying on certain cases which had found close-knit integrations lawful, defendants insisted that no valid objection could have been raised if they had followed the road to complete integration of their mining properties in a single ownership. The argument was accepted by Chief Justice Hughes when he stated:—

> The Antitrust Act aims at substance. Nothing in theory or experience indicates that the selection of a common selling agency to represent a number of producers should be deemed to be more abnormal than the formation of a huge corporation bringing various independent units into one ownership. (2)

But, in that respect also, *Appalachian Coals* represents an isolated decision. Prior to that, the doctrine, as summarized by Professor Handler, was that:—

> Where competition is restrained by agreement or understanding between ostensibly independent competitors, the courts have perceived that the public sustains injury notwithstanding that the conspirators may lack monopoly power. Where, however, competing businesses are fused by merger or consolidation, the courts have not regarded the consequent disappearance of competition as serious where the new unit lacked at least a semblance of monopoly power. Hence for many years a sharp distinction in fact obtained between the doctrines laid down in the loose-knit and merger cases. (3)

This attempt to apply the same rule to cartels as to concentration by way of merger has failed as far as Section 1

(1) American Column and Lumber Co. v. United States, 257 U.S. 377 (1921).

(2) Appalachian Coals Inc. v. United States, 288 U.S. 344, 377 (1933).

(3) HANDLER, *op. cit.*, at 85.

of the Sherman Act is concerned. [1] Later developments of the law have shown an undeniable discriminatory treatment in favor of integration. [2]

9. - The Development of *Per Se* Rules

First adduced to short-circuit all the traditional defences based on the social or economic expediency of cartels, the per se rules have been progressively developed to the point of permitting the courts to dispense with lengthy economic investigations into the challenged practices.

An identical trend is to be observed in the field of price-fixing agreements and boycotts which are now, it is submitted, the true examples of per se rules. The same evolution goes from *Trenton Potteries* [3] to *Socony Vacuum* [4] as from *Fashion Originator's Guild* [5] to the *Klor's* case. [6]

A. - The Price-Fixing Rule

a) Trenton Potteries *and the Element of Market Control.*

As a matter of fact, *Trenton Potteries*, which is considered to have originated the per se rule in the area of price-fixing, was a straight application of Chief Justice White's doctrine. [7] The trial judge had charged the jury that the combinations

---

(1) See J.A. Rahl, *op. cit., supra*, note (4), p. 31, at 73-74; HANDLER, *op. cit., supra*, note (2), p. 30, at 85, had raised the question as to whether the coalescence of both rules "should be effected by the adoption of the more liberal rule applicable to mergers, as suggested in the Appalachian case, or of the more stringent rule applicable to restraint of trade."

(2) Professor Rahl noted in regard to amended Section 7 of the Clayton Act that "antitrust evolution has finally ironed out its old ambivalence, and has brought anti-merger policy alongside the policy of loose arrangements." (*Op. cit.*, at 86.)

(3) United States v. Trenton Potteries Co., 273 U.S. 392 (1927).

(4) United States v. Socony Vacuum Oil Co., 310 U.S. 150 (1940).

(5) Fashion Originator's Guild of America, Inc. v. Federal Trade Commission, 312 U.S. 417 (1941).

(6) Klor's Inc. v. Broadway-Hale Stores, Inc., 359 U.S. 207 (1959).

(7) See J.T. Chadwell, *op. cit.*, at 62.

alleged in the indictments, if found in fact to exist, were violations of the statute as a matter of law, saying:—

> ... the law is clear that an agreement on the part of the members of a combination controlling a substantial part of an industry, upon the prices which the members are to charge for their commodity, is in itself an undue and unreasonable restraint of trade and commerce. (1)

The Supreme Court affirmed that this was the correct legal standard, and rejected any further inquiry into the reasonableness of the combination, because to do so would have led it to enter into non-economic considerations which were found irrelevant. To determine the social utility of the combination was not within the province of the Court.

The rationale of *Trenton Potteries* was that what is required under the Sherman Act is only a determination of the effect on competition. This test is inherent in the Rule of Reason approach laid down in *Standard Oil.* Although often said to be the beginning of a per se rule, it was not really that, because the Supreme Court did not decide that price-fixing was inherently anticompetitive regardless of the degree of market control of the members. What was once more repudiated was the old " reasonable price legality standard ". This stands out clearly in the following passage:—

> Our view of what is a reasonable restraint of commerce is controlled by the recognized purpose of the Sherman Act itself. Whether this type of restraint is reasonable or not must be judged in part at least, in light of its effect on competition, for whatever differences of opinion there may be among economists as to the social and economic desirability of an unrestrained competitive system, it cannot be doubted that the Sherman Act and the judicial decisions interpreting it are based upon the assumption that the public interest is best protected from the evils of monopoly and price control by the maintenance of competition. (2)

It was thus repeated that the policy of the Act is to maintain competition, that the public interest lies in the preservation of the competitive system, and that every agreement or combination placing an undue burden on competition must be presumed to be

---

(1) United States v. Trenton Potteries Co., 273 U.S. 392, 396 (1927).

(2) *Ibid.*, at 397.

injurious to the public. By reinterpreting *Standard Oil* and *American Tobacco, Trenton Potteries* showed, if that was still necessary, that Chief Justice White had not, by declaring competition to be the policy of the Sherman Act, committed such a usurpation of power as was charged by those who thought that the rule of reason authorized general use of dicretion to lift the Act's prohibitions. If judicial discretion was involved, it was only to ascertain the anticompetitive effect of the challenged practices. In *Trenton Potteries,* the adverse impact on competition could be easily inferred from the power of the combination over the market. Because *Trenton Potteries* once more put to rest the old conception of the Rule of Reason, it has been thought that it set up a *per se* rule, but this view is clearly inaccurate.

Whether or not *Trenton Potteries* is incompatible with *Chicago Board of Trade* is a more delicate question. Justice Stone of course distinguished the cases carefully, but his distinction does not go to the heart of the matter. Indeed, although Brandeis believed that some " regulation " of competition would be beneficial, he had certainly never advocated the legitimacy of cartels with as clear a monopolistic tendency as was present in *Trenton Potteries.*

b) Socony Vacuum: *the First Use of the* Per Se *Formula.*

The per se illegality of price-fixing stems from *Socony-Vacuum* where the latin formula was used for the first time. (1) It is sufficient to recall that to prevent " distress " gasoline from having a depressing effect on retail prices, major oil companies had engaged in two concerted buying programs to remove from the market the surpluses of small independent producers. Justice Douglas, in reviewing previous cases decided by the Court, inferred that it " has consistently and without deviation adhered to the principle that price-fixing agreements are unlawful per se and that no showing of so-called competitive abuses or evils which those agreements were designed to eliminate or alleviate may be interposed as a defense. " (2)

(1) United States v. Socony-Vacuum Oil Co., Inc., 310 U.S. 150 (1940).

(2) *Ibid.*, at 218.

I. - Rejection of the "Reasonable Price" Justification

The justification sought in the reasonableness of prices was unequivocally put aside by the Court:—

> The elimination of so-called competitive evils is no legal justification for such buying programs [...]. Fairer competitive prices, it is claimed, resulted when distress gasoline was removed from the market. But such defense is typical of the protestations usually made in price-fixing cases. Ruinous competition, financial disaster, evils of price cutting and the like appear throughout our history as ostensible justifications for price-fixing. If the so-called competitive abuses were to be appraised here, the reasonableness of prices would necessarily become an issue in every price-fixing case. In that event the Sherman Act would be supplanted by one which is wholly alien to a system of free competition; it would not be the charter of freedom which its framers intended. (1)

On this point nothing new was said by the Court. Justice Douglas could be thought to be repudiating once more the old conception of the Rule of Reason advocated by Chief Justice White in the early days of *United States v. Transmissouri Freight Association.* Chief Justice White in *Standard Oil* and *American Tobacco* had himself already barred any analysis of the expediency of agreements which place an undue burden on the competitive system. *Socony-Vacuum* merely repeated solemnly that competition was the unqualified policy of the Sherman Act. No excuse would be accepted for interfering with the free play of market forces. This was still a rule of reason approach.

II. - Expansion of the *Trenton Potteries* Rule: Market Control not Necessary

True, Justice Douglas clearly expanded the rule of *Trenton Potteries.* This latter case was the condemnation of a direct price-fixing combination which evidently exerted its control over a whole industry. Defendants tried to distinguish *Trenton Potteries* from their case in asserting that there "the parties had substituted an agreed-on price for one determined by competition." (2) They contended that they had neither the

---

(1) *Ibid*, at 220-221.

(2) *Ibid*, at 218.

purpose nor the intent to do anything more than to free competition from the effect of distress gasoline.(1) They then claimed the benefit of *Appalachian Coals.* The reply of Justice Douglas was twofold. First, he stressed that " the thrust of the rule is deeper and reaches more than monopoly power. " (2) Therein lies the expansion of *Trenton Potteries*: " Any combination which tampers with price structure is engaged in an unlawful activity. Even though the members of the price-fixing group were in no position to control the market, to the extent that they raised, lowered or stabilized prices they would be directly interfering with the free play of market forces. " (3) Moreover, Justice Douglas stated that it was not important " that the prices paid by the combination were not fixed in the sense that they were uniform and inflexible. " (4) Agreements to raise or lower prices are unlawful " whatever machinery for price-fixing was used. " (5) Second, Justice Douglas distinguished the instant case from *Appalachian Coals.* The only essential similarity between the two situations, he said, was " the presence in each of so-called demoralizing or injurious practices. " (6) But he pointed out the differences in dealing with them. " Unlike the plan in the instant case, the plan in Appalachian Coals was not *designed* to operate vis-a-vis the general consuming market and to fix the prices on that market. Furthermore, the *effect*, if any, of that plan on prices was not only wholly incidental but also highly conjectural. " (7) Thus, the fact that in *Appalachian Coals* market competition remained unimpaired was deemed decisive. A similar distinction was made in regard to *Chicago Board of Trade.* The restriction involved there " was not aimed at price manipulation or the control of market prices. " (8) The prices were determined competitively and openly. (9)

However, even up to that point, *Socony-Vacuum* could still be considered consistent with previous cases. The test was

---

(1) *Ibid.*, at 219.
(2) *Ibid.*, at 221.
(3) *Id.*
(4) *Ibid.*, at 222.
(5) *Id.*
(6) *Ibid.*, at 216.
(7) *Id.*
(8) *Ibid.*, at 217.
(9) *Id.*

one of purpose *and* effect to influence market prices. [1] And to meet the test, the members of the group should at least be *able* to influence the prices. In *Socony-Vacuum,* ample evidence supported the charge that the conspiracy was intended to, and actually did alter market prices. If Douglas' interpretation had been so restricted, the term *per se* would have had no new significance. This is, however, not the actual teaching of *Socony-Vacuum.*

III. - Actual Effect on Market Prices not a Prerequisite of the Price-Fixing Offense

The crux of the case is in what Professor Rahl has called " one of the most important footnotes in Supreme Court annals " [2]: footnote 59 in which Justice Douglas has really laid down the doctrine of the court regarding price-fixing. This is where Justice Douglas explained the reasons why he treated the case " as one where exertion of the power to fix prices (*i.e.* the actual fixing of prices) was an ingredient of the offense. " [3] " Under this indictment proof that prices in the Mid-Western area were raised as a result of the activities of the combination was essential, since sales of gasoline by respondents at the increased prices in that area were necessary in order to establish jurisdiction in the Western district of Wisconsin. " [4] The Justice then proceeded to emphasize that his treatment of the case did not imply that both a purpose and a power to fix prices were necessary for the establishment of a conspiracy under Section 1 of the Sherman Act. [5] The concerted activity struck down by Section 1 may be " wholly nascent or abortive on the one hand or successful on the other. " [6]

> ... a conspiracy to fix prices violates § 1 of the Act though no overt act is shown, though it is not established that the conspirators

---

(1) *Ibid.*, at 223 and at 219.

(2) J.A. Rahl, *Price-competition and the Price-Fixing Rule* — Preface and Perspective, 57 NW U. L. Rev. 141 (1962).

(3) United States v. Socony Vacuum Oil Co. Inc., 310 U.S. 150, 224, 225 (1940).

(4) *Id.*

(5) *Id.*

(6) *Id.*

had not the means available for acccomplishment of their objective, and though the conspiracy embraced but a part of the commerce in the commodity. (1)

" Intent to alter the operation of price competition in the market is the illegal distillate of *Socony Vacuum...* " (2) In this way, the first per se rule was formulated: price-fixing is inherently anticompetitive, so that one can dispense with any inquiry into its actual effect on competition. If effect had still been required, the per se rule would not have differed from the Rule of Reason: the latin formula would not have served to express a specific principle of law. Where it is demonstrated that competition is adversely affected, there is no place for the term *per se.* For, in itself, this demonstration is the indication that a full " rule of reason " inquiry has been made. (3) *Appalachian Coals* might still be reconcilable with *Socony Vacuum* on the ground that the Appalachian Coal producers had no intent to alter market prices. (4)

B. - The Boycott Rule

Similar developments are to be studied in the area of boycotts. Concerted refusals to deal have not been held inherently anticompetitive until very recently. Although often cited in support of *per se* illegality for boycotts, *Fashion Originator's Guild of America* (5) is actually a good example of a rule of reason approach. There, as in *Trenton Potteries,* which is also often erroneously thought to be the origin of a per se rule for price-fixing, ample evidence sustained a finding of anticompetitive effect.

---

(1) *Id.*

(2) J.A. Rahl, *op. cit.,* at 145.

(3) *Cf.* J.A. Rahl, *op. cit.,* at 146.

(4) See J.A. Rahl, *id.,* at 145. We must ask however whether in *Appalachian Coals* there was not a sufficient effect on market prices. Granting that the parties had no intent to affect general market conditions, it should be stressed that it was not disclaimed that their plan was likely to affect market prices in some discernible way. For this reason, I insist that *Appalachiam Coals* is rather an isolated case. Douglas' opinion would be intellectually more satisfactory if *Appalachian Coals* had been frankly overruled instead of being merely distinguished.

(5) Fashion Originators' Guild of America Inc. v. Federal Trade Commission, 312 U.S. 457 (1941).

a) Fashion Originators' Guild of America.

Manufacturers of women's garments and manufacturers of textiles used in their making, claiming the authorship of original creations, had combined to combat the competition of outsiders who were copying their designs and fabrics. The members of the Federation of Textiles, affiliated with the Guild, had agreed to sell their products only to those garment manufacturers who undertook not to use or deal in textiles which were copied from the designs of textile manufacturing Guild members. In turn, the garment manufacturers were committed to sell only to such retailers as would not use or deal in copied designs.

Justice Black, delivering the opinion of the Court, emphasized the magnitude of the conspiracy, the power of the combining groups, and the fact that the Guild amounted to an " extra-governmental agency " (1), and expressly pointed to the adverse effects on competition produced by the conspiracy. The Guild's plan ran contrary to the competition policy of the Sherman Act in several respects. The necessary tendency, as well as the purpose and effect of the combination, was the direct suppression of competition in the sale of unregistered textiles and copied designs. The petitioners might not yet have achieved a complete monopoly, he said, but they were well under way. (2) The Commission had found " that the combination exercised sufficient control and power in the women's garments and textiles businesses to exclude from the industry those manufacturers and distributors who do not conform to the rules of said respondents, and thus tend to create in themselves a monopoly in the said industries. " (3)

No other factual finding would have been necessary to condemn the whole plan as an undue restraint. Justice Black considered this evidence sufficient and then went on to reject the contention that the practices of FOGA were reasonable because necessary to protect the industry against the evils of piracy. He said:—

> ... the reasonableness of the methods pursued by the combination to accomplish its unlawful object is no more material

---

(1) *Ibid.*, at 465.
(2) *Ibid.*, at 466.
(3) *Ibid.*, at 466-467.

than would be the reasonableness of the prices fixed by unlawful combination. (1)

The parallel with *Trenton Potteries* appears obvious. What Justice Black was rejecting here was again a conception of the Rule of Reason which would have opened the door to a judgment regarding the social expediency of a restraint. But *Standard Oil* and *American Tobacco* had already precluded such a conception. (2)

Certainly no support could be found in *Fashion Originators' Guild of America* for an abstract proposition of law that a boycott having only minimal effect, such as a boycott of one person, is per se illegal, regardless of its effect on competition at large. (3) This step was made, however, in the *Klor's* case. Just as Douglas in *Socony Vacuum* had destroyed " the last vestige of a market power test " (4) in regard to price fixing, so Justice Black in *Klor's* put to rest the necessity of showing an anticompetitive effect in boycott cases. (5)

b) *The* Klor's *case.*

The plaintiff, operator of a small retail store in San Francisco, was claiming that a chain of departement stores, competing with it in the sale of household appliances, had conspired with ten national manufacturers not to sell to it. The allegations of conspiracy were not disputed, but defendants contended that the boycott had not produced any anticompetitive effect, since there were hundreds of other household appliance retailers, many within a few blocks of Klor's, who sold many competing brands of appliances. The opportunities for customers to buy in a competitive market had thus not been reduced, it was argued. The Court of Appeals had " attempted to state antitrust policy purely along the lines of the public's interest in economic markets, providing good and adequate alternatives and in

(1) *Ibid.*, at 468.

(2) See this chapter *supra*, at 46-49.

(3) *Cf.* Interborough News Co. v. Curtis Pub. Co., 127 F. Supp. 286, 300 (S.D.N.Y. 1954), *aff'd* 225 F. 2d 289 (2d cir. 1955).

(4) See J.A. Rahl, *op. cit., supra*, note 135, at 145.

(5) Klor's Inc. v. Broadway-Hale Stores, Inc., 359 U.S. 207 (1959).

protection of competition in prices, quality and service." [1] It had found "no significant change in the structure, nor in the state of economic performance." [2]

The Supreme Court, however, reversed the decision. The opinion by Justice Black traces to *Standard Oil* the distinction between a rule of reason approach and per se illegality (although it did not use the term). [3] The Court restated that there were some agreements whose validity could not be determined without study of the surrounding circumstances. [4] Quoting *Standard Oil,* it emphasized however, "that there were classes of restraints which from their 'nature or character' were unduly restrictive, and hence forbidden by both the common law and the statute." [5]

In this passage, which I think is completely warranted by Chief Justice White's doctrine, Justice Black sharpened the traditional dichotomy. Professor Oppenheim expressed the view that "reaffirmation of these two categories of Sherman Act restraints constitutes a gain in semantic clarification." [6]

The label *per se* was attached to boycotts by Justice Goldberg in *Silver v. New York Stock Exchange.* [7] But the doctrine of the Supreme Court had in effect been completely set out in *Klor's.*

Did a specific category of per se offenses mean that in such cases the presumption of injury to competition could not even be refuted by a factual showing that actually no injury had occurred? In *Klor's,* Justice Black concluded that if the presumption could be rebutted, the distinction would have made but little sense in itself. As to the *per se* offenses, he stated, "Congress had determined its own criteria of public harm and it was not for the courts to decide whether in an individual case injury had actually occurred." [8]

---

(1) J.A. Rahl, *Per se Rules and Boycotts Under the Sherman Act: some reflections on the Klor's case*, 45 VA. L. REV. 1168 (1959).

(2) *Id.*

(3) Klor's Inc, v. Broadway-Hale Stores, Inc., 359 U.S. 207, 211 (1959).

(4) *Id.*

(5) *Id.*

(6) Oppenheim, *Selected Antitrust Developments in the Courts and Federal Trade Commission during past years,* 15 ABA ANTITRUST SECTION, 41 (1959).

(7) Silver v. New York Stock Exchange, 373 U.S. 341, 347 (1963).

(8) Klor's Inc. v. Broadway-Hale Stores Inc., 359 U.S. 207, 211 (1959).

c) *Neither Purpose nor Effect of Agreement Relevant. - A Critical Appraisal.*

The *per se* rule regarding boycott is certainly more drastic than the price-fixing rule. A boycott is unreasonable, regardless of its *purpose* or its *effect* on competition at large. (1) Even if the victim of the boycott is just one manufacturer whose business is so small that his destruction makes little difference to the economy, boycott is not to be tolerated. (2) Unlike the price-fixing rule which comes into play only if there is an intent to alter market prices, the prohibition of boycott will not even require " an element of purpose to suppress competition. " (3) Completely disconnected from competition, which it is the policy of the Sherman Act to preserve, the boycott rule formulated in *Klor's* has received severe criticism. Professor Rahl has demonstrated why " a boycott rule which is not geared to a cogent test of effect on competition is ... completely unmanageable. " (4) True, the per se rule is designed to obviate the inquiry into the effect of the challenged practice on competition, which must normally be done pursuant to the Rule of Reason. But we must ask whether, in rejecting any consideration of purpose, the Supreme Court did not go too far. " The Court's rule that all concerted refusals to deal by traders are per se illegal is so broad that it probably goes beyond the boundaries of antitrust policy. " (5) Professors Blake and Jones suggest that with the *Klor's* case the Courts have returned to the position adopted fifty-five years ago: " employing the antitrust laws to assure that individual businessmen are not deprived of freedom

---

(1) Although it cited the *Klor's* case in support of its argument, *United States v. General Motors Corporation* [384 U.S. 127 (1966)] is not as far-reaching as that case. In the *General Motors* case, there was ample evidence in the record to support a finding that the concerted effort to eliminate sales of new Chevrolet cars by discounters was intended to restrain market competition and actually had that effect. The purpose as well as the necessary effect of the boycott was to protect franchised dealers from price competition and thus to deprive consumers of the opportunity to buy in a competitive market.

(2) Klor's Inc. v. Broadway-Hale Stores Inc., 359 U.S. 207, 213 (1959).

(3) *Cf.* J.A. Rahl, *op. cit.*, at 1172.

(4) *Ibid.*, at 1172.

(5) J.T. Chadwell, *Competition and Section 1 of the Sherman Act - Instant Antitrust or Long-run Policy*, 27 ABA ANTITRUST SECTION, 60, 65 (1965).

and opportunity, even though the restriction in question may have no adverse impact upon consumers, the market, or economic efficiency." [1]

C. - Tying Arrangements: the Inadequacies of the Per Se *Formula*

Comparison of the price-fixing rule with the boycott rule shows considerable differences of degree in the per se illegality doctrine. There is no such a thing as a single and uniform *per se* rule. There are as many different *per se* rules as there are offenses to which the latin label has been attached.

The doctrine elaborated by the Supreme Court in regard to tying arrangements in *Northern Pacific Railway Co. v. United States* [2] is another illustration of this truism. At one time the Supreme Court stated, by way of dictum, that "tying agreements serve hardly any purpose beyond the suppression of competition." [3] If this was so, it would be a strong argument for a *per se* rule. But this early statement was qualified in *Northern Pacific Railway*.

Tying agreements "are unreasonable in themselves whenever a party has sufficient economic power with respect to the tying product to appreciably restrain free competition in the market for the tied product and a 'not insubstantial' amount of interstate commerce is affected." [4]

It was held that "the vice of tying arrangements lies in the use of economic power in one market to restrict competition on the merits in another, regardless of the source from which the power is derived and whether the power takes the form of a monopoly or not." [5]

In *United States v. Loew's Inc.*, Justice Goldberg again made clear the reasons why tying agreements should be deemed

---

(1) Northern Pacific Railway Co. v. United States, 356 U.S. 1 (1958).

(2) Blake and Jones, *The Goals of Antitrust: A Dialogue on Policy - Toward a Three-Dimensional Antitrust Policy*, 65 COLUM. L. REV. 422, 431 (1965).

(3) Standard Oil Co. of California v. United States, 337 U.S. 293 (1949).

(4) Northern Pacific Railway Co. v. United States, 356 U.S. 1, 6 (1958).

(5) *Ibid.*, at 11.

pernicious, and thus prohibited. " ... They may force buyers into giving up the purchase of substitutes for the tied product ... and they may destroy the free access of competing suppliers of the tied product to the consuming market. " ([1])

But the reasons for prohibiting tying devices in turn presuppose, as Justice Goldberg concluded, that " the seller, by virtue of his position in the market for the tying product has economic leverage sufficient to induce his customers to take the tied product along with the tying item. " ([2])

How can we best define the approach taken? Is it a true per se rule? Is it a quasi per se rule as was suggested by Justice Douglas in *White Motor* when he stated that tying arrangements are per se violations if certain conditions are met? ([3]) Or is it a rule making for limited factual inquiry?

The role of the Rule of Reason is to ascertain when competition is significantly impaired. The very existence of such conditions as required by the rule on tying implies a substantial adverse effect on competition. " ... It would seem that nearly as much time will be consumed in ascertaining whether the transaction fits the category as would be consumed without any rule, and substantially the same economic ground will have to be covered. " ([4]) For this reason, the label per se should be avoided: the doctrine laid down by the Supreme Court on tying agreements appears rather as a particularization of the general Rule of Reason, to the extent that it specifies the measure of economic analysis necessary to find unreasonable restraint.

Moreover cases like *Jerrold Electronics* ([5]) and *Dehydrating Process Co.* ([6]) prove that the early statement of the Supreme Court in *Standard Oil of California* does not accurately depict business realities. In some instances, tying may be the sole

(1) United States v. Loew's Inc., 371 U.S. 38, 45 (1962).

(2) *Ibid.*, at 45.

(3) White Motor Co. v. United States, 372 U.S. 253 (1963).

(4) See J.A. Rahl, *op. cit.*, at 1173.

(5) United States v. Jerrold Electronic Corp., 187 F. Supp. 545 (E.D.Pa. 1960), *aff'd per curiam*, 365 U.S. 567 (1961).

(6) Dehydrating Process Co. v. A.O. Smith, 292 F. 2d 654 (1st Cir. 1961).

way for a manufacturer not to have his own throat cut. Respectable business justifications are conceivable. This indicates that tying agreements should not be called inherently anticompetitive.

D. - Market Sharing Agreements: False Analogy with Price-Fixing

In its 1955 Report, the Attorney General's National Committee, while stressing that in no Supreme Court case have the facts been limited exclusively to simple market division among competitors, stated that " there is little doubt, either as a matter of principle or of precedent, that agreements among competitors for market division should be and are treated like price control arrangements. " [1] The Attorney General's National Committee did not use the term *per se,* but the comparison with price-fixing agreements seems to imply that *per se* illegality is attributed to market-sharing agreements.

Several times, by way of dictum, the United States Supreme Court has branded market-sharing agreements as *per se* unreasonable. In *Northern Pacific Railway Co.*, it regarded divisions of market as in and of themselves unlawful, and put these agreements in the same category as price-fixing. [2] The authority cited in support of such a classification was, however, not very convincing. The Court relied essentially on *United States v. Addyston Pipe and Steel Co.* [3] which was a case involving a vast conspiracy. Although the defendants in that case claimed that their output did not exceed 30 % of the national production of cast-iron pipe, they supplied about two-thirds of the markets where they did the bulk of their business. [4] There was undoubtedly a showing of a substantial effect on competition. Consequently, it is difficult to refer to *United States v. Addyston Pipe and Steel Co.* to support the

---

(1) REPORT OF THE ATTORNEY GENERAL'S NATIONAL COMMITTEE TO STUDY THE ANTITRUST LAWS, 26 (1955).

(2) Northern Pacific Railway Co. v. United States, 356 U.S. 1, 5 (1958).

(3) United States v. Addyston Pipe and Steel Co., 85 F. 271 (6th Cir. 1898), *aff'd*, 175 U.S. 211 (1899).

(4) REPORT OF THE ATTORNEY GENERAL'S NATIONAL COMMITTEE TO STUDY THE ANTITRUST LAWS, 26 (1955).

proposition that market division is unlawful without any need for inquiry into the effect on competition.

In *White Motor*, the Supreme Court stated that " if competitors agree to divide markets, they run afoul of the antitrust laws ", [1] although it carefully avoided using the Latin label. *Timken Roller Bearing Co. v. United States* [2] was the only case cited by Justice Douglas. But the Attorney General's National Committee has analyzed this latter case as one concerning competitors who, as a group, possessed substantial market power. The *Timken* case " condemned the allocation of market territories between the dominant American producer of tapered roller bearings and British and French firms, the latter controlled jointly by Timken and its British competitor. " [3] Speaking of the *per se* doctrine in this context is as misleading as in *Trenton Potteries* where the cartel members controlled the entire market. That the Supreme Court in *Timken* refused to take into account " current foreign trade conditions " is no valid indication of a *per se* violation in the market division involved. The Supreme Court rejected this argument just as in *Trenton Potteries* it had put aside the defense based on reasonableness of prices. Actually the Court applied the competition policy declared in the Sherman Act and thus implemented the Rule of Reason. The agreement was not declared unlawful on its face, but because, on the facts, it ran foul of the policy intended by Congress. Justice Frankfurter, in his dissent, pointed out that " a 'division of territory' is not so self-operating a category of Sherman Act violations as to dispense with analysis of what on paper is a geographic division of territory. " [4] To the extent that it states that political considerations, apart from competition, are out of place, the majority opinion is not a denial of this view.

Reference to the *Trenton Potteries* decision [5] in order to support the thesis of a *per se* rule for market division agreements

(1) White Motor Co. v. United States, 372 U.S. 253, 259 (1963).
(2) Timken Roller Bearing Co. v. U.S., 341 U.S. 593 (1950).
(3) *Op. cit.*, at 26.
(4) Timken Roller Bearing Co. v. U.S., 341 U.S. 593, 605 (1950).
(5) *Cf.* REPORT OF THE ATTORNEY GENERAL'S NATIONAL COMMITTEE TO STUDY THE ANTITRUST LAWS, 26 (1955).

proves to be misleading, since *Trenton Potteries* was a plain application of the Rule of Reason. In this context, the use of the term *per se* only indicates that any attempt to justify a cartel by a showing of its economic expediency is precluded. It does not suggest that market analysis to support a finding of anti-competitive effect becomes irrelevant.

In *United States v. National Lead Co.*, the Court held:—

> No citation of authority is any longer necessary to support the proposition that a combination of competitors, which by agreements divides the world into exclusive trade areas and supresses all competition among the members of the combination, offends the Sherman Act. (1)

One can agree with this proposition. But it does not exclude the necessity of market analysis and of a showing of a substantial anticompetitive effect. In *National Lead*, the requirement of an actual and adverse effect on competition was met, since the parties had substantial market power, and had agreed upon a division of territories. Again, *National Lead* involved a combination dominating a whole industry. " Every pound " of titanium was " trammelled by privately imposed regulation. " (2)

True, showing the domination of the industry involved is not necessary. As the Court stated in *United States v. Imperial Chemical Industries Ltd.*:—

> With respect to price-fixing, the Supreme Court has written that such a showing is unnecessary [...]. Territorial division is " in restraint of trade ", no less than price-fixing. It involves " the denial to commerce of the supposed protection of competition " [...]. There is no intimation in any decision that elimination of competition is to be given a more favorable judicial consideration when achieved by the route of territorial division rather than by price-fixing, or that proof of industry domination is required in one case though not required in the other. (3)

Market-sharing arrangements are not likely to be entered into unless the contracting parties expect to gain a substantial

---

(1) United States v. National Lead Co., 63 F. Suppl. 513, 523 (S.D.N.Y. 1945), *aff'd* 332 U.S. 319 (1947).

(2) *Ibid.*, 63 F. Supp. 513, 521 (S.D.N.Y. 1945).

(3) United States v. Imperial Chemical Industries, Ltd., 100 F. Supp. 504, 593 (S.D.N.Y. 1951).

degree of power in their own and separate markets, which presupposes that the group as a whole possesses a significant share of the market. [1] This may seem a good argument for a *per se* rule. However, this assumption should be subject to possible rebuttal. To have a market-sharing arrangement, there must be something to share. The assumption made above should not be extended so as to dispense " with analysis of the practical consequences of what on paper is a geographic division of market. " [2] But, in turn, by the time it is demonstrated that competition has been adversely and significantly impaired, a full " rule of reason " inquiry will have been made. [3]. Thus, we must ask whether some decisive advantage is gained by classifying market-sharing arrangements as *per se* offenses.

10. - Conclusions

A. - Free Competition: Undoubted Policy Behind the Sherman Act

American Antitrust Law is built upon absolute faith in the values of competition. As stated in *Northern Pacific Railway Co.*:—

> The Sherman Act was designed to be a comprehensive charter of economic liberty aimed at preserving free and unfettered competition as the rule of trade. It rests upon the premise that the unrestrained interaction of competitive forces will yield the best allocation of our economic forces, the lowest prices, the highest quality and the greatest material progress, while at the same time providing an environment conducive to the preservation of our democratic political and social institutions. But even were that premise open to question, the policy unequivocally laid down by the Act is competition. [4]

---

(1) *Cf.* REPORT OF THE ATTORNEY GENERAL'S NATIONAL COMMITTEE TO STUDY THE ANTITRUST LAWS, 26 (1955).

(2) Justice Frankfurter in his dissent in Timken Roller Bearing Co. v. United States, 341 U.S. 593, 605 (1950).

(3) *Cf.* for price-fixing agreements, J.A. Rahl, *Price Competition and the Price Fixing Rule*, 57 NW. U. L. REV. 146 (1962).

(4) Northern Pacific Railway Co. v. United States, 356 U.S. 1, 4 (1958).

There is no room here for the exemption of cartels which can be shown to be economically desirable, because competition is thought to be the best way to produce rationalization and to provide incentives for product innovations and product development. Through competition, not cartels, the flow of capital and other resources will be guided toward the most productive uses.

B. - European Anticartel Law Represents a Different Philosophy

The Common Market Law, and in varying degrees most of the European anticartel statutes (among others article 59*bis* and 59*ter* of the French Price Ordinance no. 45-1483 of June 30, 1945, Sections 1-8 of the German anticartel law, the British Restrictive Trade Practices Act of 1956), have all questioned the validity of this premise. For these laws, competition is not necessarily the ultimate panacea: in some circumstances, it may be creative of efficiency, while in others destructive of investments. The basic underlying philosophy is at least partly different, and this difference is reflected in the manner in which European statutes have been drafted. Regulation of competition by private agreements in certain cases is considered conducive to beneficial results for the public. A competitive system is a tool to achieve certain aims of economic policy, but only a tool. The last word belongs not to the market, but generally to government agencies which determine, according to certain guidelines, when cartelization may be more suitable and opportune than free economic activity. Different economic, social and political developments are accountable for the divergent approaches.

C. - The Sherman Act Does not Discriminate between Good and Bad Restraints

At the time when the Sherman Act was passed, the law could have evolved in the European direction. The record of the common law was not completely clear. Several trends were discernible. Under one view, price-fixing agreements might be upheld if the prices established were reasonable, and the object of the combine was not the exploitation of the public, but the rectification of intolerable industrial conditions. (1) But the Rule of Reason as it finally evolved under American law does not contemplate any distinction between bad and good restraints of trade. Holding competition to be at the root of the statute's policy, the rule is essentially a rule of construction. (2) Not every restraint of trade, in the literal meaning of that term, is to be forbidden—only those which are intended to, or actually do significantly impair the competitive process.

D. - Restraints on the Freedom of Action of the Individual Business Man not Necessarily an Excessive Impediment to Market Competition. - White Motor *as a Possible Example*

It is important to my subsequent discussion to note that under this approach to the Rule of Reason, a mere restriction on the freedom of action of an individual trader might be excused, but not a significant restraint on market competition. This distinction explains to some extent why judicial usage is anything but clear. " To some, unreasonableness means lacking in affirmative justification. To others, it means substantially injurious to competition. " (3) A case like *White Motor*, which involved vertical territorial restriction between White Motor's dealers, is typical of this kind of confusion. As to the *per se* violations, it was stated that " a trial to show their nature, extent and degree is no longer necessary. " (4) This confirms the view that agreements classified as *per se* unreasonable are held inherently illegal without any inquiry at all into their effect on competition. The nature of the practice, not its factual content, is what is significant. (5) As regards the vertical territorial confinement system at issue, the Supreme Court surprisingly confessed that it did not know " enough of the

(1) See HANDLER, A STUDY OF THE CONSTRUCTION AND ENFORCEMENT OF THE ANTITRUST LAWS, TNEC Monograph no. 38, 4-5 (1941).

(2) See NEAL, THE ANTITRUST LAWS OF THE U.S.A., 13 1962).

(3) J.A. Rahl, *Per Se Rules and Boycotts under the Sherman Act: Some Reflections on the Klor's Case*, 45 VIRG. L. REV. 1174 (1959).

(4) White Motor Co. v. United States, 372 U.S. 253, 260 (1963).

(5) *Cf.* J.A. Rahl, *op. cit.*, at 1174.

economic and business stuff out of which these arrangements emerge " to be certain as to which rule to apply. [1]

> They may be too dangerous to sanction or they may be allowable protections against aggressive competitors or the only practical means a small company has for breaking into or staying in business [...] and within the " rule of reason ". We need to know more than we do about the actual impact of these arrangements on competition to decide whether they have " such a pernicious effect on competition and lack ... any redeeming virtue " and therefore should be classified as *per se* violations of the Sherman Act. [2]

The Supreme Court declined to promulgate a rule applicable to a vertical closed territorial system. But the opinion by Justice Douglas creates the impression that agreements clearly inimical to competition are *per se* illegal, but that outside of these categories the Rule of Reason could serve to justify a restraint of competition in the market. This is not an accurate conception of the Rule of Reason. Undoubtelly the territorial restrictions imposed by White Motor on its dealers were restraints of trade in the literal meaning of that term, since the freedom of action of the dealers was abridged. But was that impairing competition in the market, and any way what the relevant market? One had to determine the importance of interbrand competition as opposed to intraband competition. Were these limitations not the sole way to foster a vigorous interbrand competition? If so, then, far from restraining competition in the market, they were improving it, or even making it possible for the first time. These questions, since they could not be decided in the abstract, called for a rule of reason approach as was suggested by Justice Brennan in his concurring opinion.

It is true that, as the dissenters emphasized, the public policy of the Sherman Act is that the suppression of competition is ex hypothesi a public injury. [3] But of what competition were they speaking? Of the ability of the individual dealers to compete or of market competition? Restrictions like those found in the *White Motor* case can be considered not only as

---

(1) White Motor Co. v. United States, 372 U.S. 253, 263 (1963).

(2) *Id.*

(3) *Ibid.*, at 281.

having an insignificant market impact (in which case, they would not be " undue " or excessive), but also as the only feasible way to compete (and from that standpoint " reasonable " can mean " rational "). This is, for instance, how exclusive franchise agreements, containing no system of territorial confinement, have been evaluated in American law. Although " restraints of trade " in the literal sense 'since the manufacturer is committed not to grant a franchise to any other dealer in the specified area' they have generally been upheld as reasonable.

> The fact that any other dealers in the same product of the same manufacturer are eliminated does not make an exclusive dealership illegal; it is the essential nature of the agreement. [1]

Economic arguments and business necessities can certainly serve to justify an agreement which is not found to produce a significant restraint on competition in the market at large. The proper role of the Rule of Reason is to focus on this inquiry. And, in turn, this inquiry can only be made on a case-by-case basis, and not in the abstract.

E. - Difficulties in Administering the Reasonableness Test Lead to the Development of Per Se *Rules*

The Rule of Reason gives the Courts discretion to draw the line somewhere. This is a burdensome task, since theoretically all market factors bearing on competition are to be considered. Far from being in conflict with the Rule of Reason, the *per se* concept is designed to facilitate the accomplishment of this judicial duty. This was clearly expounded in *Northern Pacific Railway Co.*:—

> ... there are certain agreements or practices which because of their pernicious effect on competition and lack of any redeeming virtue are conclusively presumed to be unreasonable and therefore illegal without elaborate inquiry as to the precise harm they have caused or the business excuse for their use. The principle of *per se* unreasonableness not only makes the type of restraints which are proscribed by the Sherman Act more certain to the benefit of everyone concerned, but it also avoids the necessity for an incredibly

---

(1) Packard Motor Car Co. v. Webster Motor Car Co., 243 F. 2d 418, 421 (D.C. Cir. 1957), *certiorari denied* 355 U.S. 822 (1957).

> complicated and prolonged economic investigation into the entire history of the industry involved, as well as related industries, in an effort to determine at large whether a particular restraint has been unreasonable—an inquiry so often wholly fruitless when undertaken. (1)

Certain authors have much too broad a conception of the Rule of Reason. This is reflected for instance in Professor Schwartz's dissent from the Attorney General's National Committee Report.

> The Rule of Reason—*he said*—affords an opportunity to justify the restraint in a particular case as harmless or even beneficial, but by the same token makes it difficult to forecast the balance of pros and cons ... It [the rule of reason] makes relevant the entire history of the industry, all evidence bearing on the good and bad purposes and consequences of the restraint, political and military exigencies possibly accounting for the restraint, conflicting expert testimony to explain phenomena like price matching. (2)

This is certainly not in accordance with the main tradition of the Rule of Reason which I have tried to explain in this study. The inquiry called for by the Rule of Reason relates only to the purpose or effect of restraining competition.

I have advocated a stricter view of the Rule of Reason than that presented by Professor Schwartz. But, conversely, I think that the *per se* doctrine should also have a more restricted application. The *per se* concept is designed to alleviate extensive inquiries into the actual anticompetitive effect of the challenged practices. This being so, it should not be attached to tying arrangements since the rule applicable to these arrangements, as it has been formulated in *Northern Pacific Railway Co.*, appears rather to be a particularization of the Rule of Reason. It is doubtful whether market allocations should be subject to a mechanical rule precluding the necessity of showing a substantial adverse effect on competition. Price-fixing and boycott seem to be the only instances where a true *per se* doctrine has been applied. The law applicable to these types of agreements, however, is not identical. The price-fixing rule still requires a demonstration of intent to alter market prices, and thus competition; it is still necessary to analyse the purpose of

(1) Northern Pacific Railway Co. v. United States, 356 U.S. 1, 5 (1958).
(2) *Op. cit., supra*, note 186, at 391-392.

the parties and the market in which they are acting. Thus the kind of investigation which the Rule of Reason demands does not entirely disappear; its scope has merely been limited. On the other hand, the boycott rule has absolutely suppressed any need for an inquiry into the purpose of the conspirators, and the effect of their agreement on competition. For having introduced this rule, the Supreme Court has received severe criticism.

The distinction between the rule of reason and the *per se* rules does not constitute as sharp a dichotomy as some authors might indicate. *Per se* rules, except for boycott, are only different degrees of the Rule of Reason. As such, the principles of law applicable to tying arrangements and to price-fixing agreements undoubtedly perform a useful function inasmuch as they particularize the general Rule of Reason. But one can ask whether the term *per se* itself offers any substantial clarification of these principles.

Even though the Rule of Reason does not include all the considerations which Professor Louis B. Schwartz thought it covers, it is easy to perceive the great difficulties inherent in a full-range application of the Rule, as I have defined it. They have been described as follows:—

> ... proof of the nature of the actual competition in an industry and of the effect on it of a challenged practice calls for painstaking study, the gathering of evidence much of which is difficult to obtain, careful analysis often with the aid of experts, and a great deal of work in synthesizing all this so that it can be brought into court and presented in some intelligible way. This is not easy for lawyers. It is hard for the judges too. (1)

First brought up in *Socony Vacuum* as an answer to all the contentions as to the social expediency of cartels, the *per se* doctrine has, under recent law, been given the function of making things easier for everybody by dispensing with these lengthy economic investigations. The law is considered to be both simpler to apply and more certain. That the Courts felt that they were not equipped to cope with the burdens and to face the responsibilities imposed by the Rule of Reason certainly explains the sometimes noticed reluctance on their part to engage in sophisticated judicial economics. But the conflict is not really so

---

(1) J.T. Chadwell, *Competition and Section 1 of the Sherman Act - instant antitrust or long-run policy*, 27 ABA ANTITRUST SECTION 60, 67 (1965).

much between certainty and flexibility. The crucial issue is rather whether " blind devotion to per se violation rules " is not producing " a rigid formulary system of mechanical rules of law which does violence to the facts of the American economic order. " [1] Are the *per se* rules not in fact defeating the objectives of the antitrust legislation? The debate is still open.

F. - Approach to the Legal Definitions of " Restraint of Trade ": Object of this Comparative Study

American antitrust law and European anticartel law are predicated on different premises. Unlike the Sherman Act, Article 85 of the Rome Treaty considers that restraining competition may lead to improvement of production or distribution or to development of technology. In some circumstances, cartelization will thus be deemed preferable to free competition. But even the most liberal conception of the Rule of Reason does not afford such a large choice of economic policy. Therefore, to be fruitful, the process of comparison undertaken here has to be made on another level. We must ask what is the approach of European law to the concept of restraint of trade? What are the tests employed in determining when competition is restrained? This comparison will show that, despite a different context, the debate between *per se* rules and the rule of reason, originally of common law lineage, is not absent from the emerging continental cartel statutes. In a permanent search for categorization, the continental system of law—whether national or supranational—has borne abstract rules of law even in the area of antitrust. Despite the greater leniency toward cartels, the demand for certainty and predictability motivates a trend toward *per se* rules. In order to obviate the complexities of economic analysis, simplified tests of illegality are formulated. By comparison and contrast of these trends, this study will seek to clarify the scope of the Rule of Reason in America, and perhaps forecast the future of both reasonableness tests and *per se* rules in Europe.

---

(1) S. Chesterfield Oppenheim, *Federal Antitrust Legislation: Guideposts to a Revised National Antitrust Policy,* 50 Mich. L. Rev., 1139, 1161 (1951-1952).

CHAPTER II

THE NOTION OF RESTRAINT OF TRADE UNDER SECTION 1 OF THE GERMAN ANTICARTEL LAW

1. - General Characteristics of the German Statute Against Restraints of Competition

Whereas the Rome Treaty tackles the problem of restrictive trade agreements in two basic substantive provisions, the German statute against restraints of competition utilizes a substantially different technique. It has been drafted in the most detailed manner and contains a wide range of both substantive and procedural rules, which deal with a specific situation. (1) Its main characteristic is its pretension to be a self-contained code, but the language used is not as broad as that commonly found in such legislation. Obviously, the attempt was to define, as precisely as possible, the basis on which courts and the administrative enforcement agency would proceed, so that discretionary decisions of economic policy would be confined within narrow limits. If it can be said that Article 85 of the Rome Treaty has, like the Sherman Act, " a generality and adaptability comparable to that found to be desirable in constitutional provisions (2) ", conversely, it is certainly the rigidity and the technicality of the German statute which first strikes the comparative lawyer. Differences of the same kind exist, for instance, between the French and the German law of torts. While the French Civil Code has limited itself to laying down a few broad and general principles, entrusting the courts with their application to all factual situations, the German Civil Code has formulated a series of rules, each of which, again, provides for a particular situation.

---

(1) The German Act against restraints of competition enacted July 27, 1957, contains more than one hundred sections. It has been amended by a statute of September 15, 1965 (See BGBl. 1965, Teil I, 1363). This statute is reproduced in WuW 829 (1965).

(2) I am quoting the words used by Chief Justice Hughes in Appalachian Coals Inc. v. United States, 288 U.S. 344, 359, 360 (1933).

2. - Difficulties and Dangers Involved in a Comparative Study

This basic difference in approach and legislative technique, of course, makes every comparison very difficult. Taking an isolated provision out of the German statute and contrasting it with the Rome Treaty or with the Sherman Act may, for this reason, be misleading and arbitrary in several respects. Two examples will illustrate this danger. Whereas the Rome Treaty, like the Sherman Act, contains a single set of provisions for vertical arrangements as well as for horizontal agreements, the German statute draws a fundamental distinction between the two [1]. A single sentence is employed by Article 85 to outlaw all restrictive practices, and in the same way, the Treaty opens a general gateway for all those agreements which can be shown to be beneficial. In contrast, the German statute lays down separately the conditions in which exemptions may be granted for cartels on terms of trade, discount cartels, crisis cartels, rationalization and specialization cartels, and export and import cartels. To this long enumeration of exceptions is added a further provision which empowers the Federal Minister of Economics to approve the establishment of a cartel, even if none of the statutory exemptions may be invoked, when it appears appropriate in view of the general economic situation and the public interest. [2]

3. - Object of this Study : What is a Restraint of Competition under Section 1 of the German Statute Against Restraints of Competition ?

In the present study, my concern will not be to analyse the whole system of the German Act. To render the comparison fruitful, I must narrow the perspective. Several comparisons

(1) Sections 1-14 of the German law pertain to cartel agreements, while Sections 15-21 relate to vertical arrangements. On the law applicable to certain types of restrictive practices, *e.g.*, exclusive dealing, tying, franchise agreements, see *infra*, this chapter, at 103-106.

(2) See Section 8 of the statute.

between the Rome Treaty and the German statute in the field of horizontal agreements could be made. For instance, it is obvious that the German administrative and judicial practice as to rationalization and specialization cartels will help the EEC Commission to define the range of Article 85(3) more precisely. (1) Before considering such questions, however, the fundamental question must be faced: *what is a restraint of competition?* It is that concept in Section 1 of the German Act, as it has been construed by the courts, the administrative agency and the legal writers, on which I will focus my attention.

4. - Comparison with the British Restrictive Trade Practices Act : the Use of the Word " Competition "

The Sherman Act did not say anything about " competition ". As has been pointed out by Justice Holmes in his dissent in *Northern Securities*:—

> Much trouble is made by substituting other phrases assumed to be equivalent, which then are reasoned from as if they were in the act ... The act says nothing about competition. I stick to the exact words used. (2)

But seven years later, Chief Justice White, in announcing the Rule of Reason as the proper standard to construe the Sherman Act, declared that the policy embodied in the statute was the preservation of competition, (3) and so the decisive word was read into the Sherman Act.

It is remarkable that the more modern British Restrictive Trade Practices Act of 1956 also does not use the word,

(1) See *e.g.* the comparison made by DERINGER between the exemption provided by the German statute for rationalization cartels and that by Art. 85(3) of the Rome Treaty, in MULLER-HENNEBERG and SCHWARTZ, GESETZ GEGEN WETTBEWERBSBESCHRÄNKUNGEN UND EUROPÄISCHES KARTELLRECHT (hereinafter referred to as GEMEINSCHAFTSKOMMENTAR), 312-316 (1963).

(2) Northern Securities v. United States, 193 U.S. 197 (1904).

(3) Standard Oil Co. of New Jersey v. United States, 221 U.S. 1 (1911) and United States v. American Tobacco Co., 221 U.S. 106 (1911).

" competition ". Indeed, in its drafting technique, the British Act appears to be closer to the German statute than to Article 85 and the Sherman Act. Great precision has been used in order to make certain *specified* kinds of restrictive practices *prima facie* contrary to the public interest. The agreements which are registrable under the British Act are not defined in terms of their purpose or their effect on competition. Section 6 subjects to registration agreements between two or more persons *under which restrictions are accepted by two or more parties* in respect of matters *which are enumerated* in the Act. Much care has been taken to describe accurately the agreements which involve the kinds of restrictions on trade at which the Act is aiming: prices, terms of supply, quantities or descriptions of goods, processes of manufacture, persons or areas. (1) By so listing the matters to which restrictions relate, the British Act has, in my view, adopted a *per se* approach. Specific practices are outlawed. The Restrictive Practices Court's power under Section 21 of the British Act to decide that these specified agreements are not against the public interest when certain circumstances prevail does not alter this basic analysis. While tests of public interest codified by Section 21 may be viewed as embodying standards of reasonableness, in this context " reasonable " means economically desirable in regard to certain declared aims, and has little in common with the same word as it is used by the American courts. The British tests are fundamentally the expression of a different economic and social policy. (2) A choice must be made by the British Court between bad and good effects of restraints, an alternative not open to the American courts. If some kind of rule of reason, in the American sense, is to be discovered in the British Act, it has to be looked for somewhere other than in Section 21. In fact, Section 12 of the Act lays down something of a rule of reason of this kind, inasmuch as it enables the Board of Trade, upon

(1) On Section 6 of the British Restrictive Trade Practices Act of 1956, see *e.g.* WILBERFORCE, CAMPBELL and ELLES, THE LAW OF RESTRICTIVE TRADE PRACTICES AND MONOPOLIES, 238-294 (1966) and STEVENS and YAMEY, THE RESTRICTIVE PRACTICES COURT 157-192 (1965).

(2) "The Act is a step toward the promotion of competition, but it is very far from accepting competition as invariably desirable." STEVENS and YAMEY, *op. cit.*, at 44.

the representation of the Registrar, to authorize the latter to remove from the register particulars of such agreements as appear to the Board *to be of no substantial economic significance.*(1) Although they are restrictive, certain agreements may be considered to be unlikely to produce any serious effect on general market conditions. It appears that Section 12 gives the Board of Trade the discretion to make such a determination " in the light of reason ", in the American sense.

This short examination of the British Act will help me to explain my purpose. Read by the American courts into the Sherman Act, the word " competition " is also in Section 1 of the German Act and Article 85. But, in a comparative study, here the problem starts, not ends. Similarities of language are fallacious to the extent that they may induce ignorance of what is really done under rules phrased in apparently identical terms. The word " competition " does not encompass the same concept in the Rome Treaty as it does in the German Act. As a matter of fact, we will see that the German approach toward restrictive horizontal agreements is less remote from the British than from the Rome Treaty regulation. The language " Wettbewerbsbeschränkung " of the German statute (restraint of competition) tends to cover the same restrictions as Section 6 of the British Act. No lengthy inquiry into the effect on general competitive conditions is required, nor is it necessary to scrutinize the intention of the parties to restrictive agreements.

5. - Section 1 of the German Anticartel Law : a *Per Se* Rule ?

Section 1 of the German Act declares ineffective agreements between enterprises, or associations of enterprises, concluded for a common purpose, to the extent that, by means of restraints of competition, they are likely to affect production or

(1) WILBERFORCE et al., *op. cit.*, at 316-317.

market conditions for the commerce in goods or occupational services. [1]

Although a basic provision of the statute as to horizontal agreements, this text is undoubtedly not a model of draftmanship. It is the source of many obscurities, testified to by the uncertainty of judicial opinions, and by harsh controversies among the legal writers.

Several notions are introduced by Section 1 which are not defined by the statute itself, and which thus need further clarification. What is a contract? Which conception of " enterprise " is embodied in the statute? What is competition itself and when is it restrained? When is a contract likely to affect market conditions? After eight years of enforcement, some of these questions are settled, while others are still debated.

For my present purpose, however, the main issue would be: *is every contract whereby a business firm restrains itself from engaging in its trade and thus limits its ability to compete, made ineffective by Section 1*? Or does the statute itself embody a Rule of Reason, or has such a Rule been developed by administrative and judicial practice? From this standpoint, the study of two concepts becomes relevant to my analysis: " *Wettbewerbsbeschränkung* " *i.e.* restraint of competition and " *Marktbeeinflussung* " *i.e.* market influence. Section 1 turns largely on these two notions of restraint of competition, and of likelihood of influencing market conditions.

6. - Relationship Between Substantive Law and Procedural Rules

A preliminary remark has to be made as to the enforcement system of Section 1 of the German law. Although I will not concern myself with the procedural law, it cannot be ignored

(1) Section 1(1) of the German anticartel law reads as follows: "Agreements made for a common purpose by enterprises or associations of enterprises and decisions of associations of enterprises are of no effect insofar as they are likely to influence, by restraining competition, production or market conditions with respect to trade in goods or commercial services ..." I am quoting the translation prepared by the Guide to Legislation on Restrictive Business Practices published by the OECD.

so far as it has an impact on the substantive rules themselves. The general principle announced by Section 1 may not be separated from the several exceptions brought in by the following provisions. This set of rules appears to be the result of a compromise between proponents of a system of interdiction (" *Verbotsprinzip* "), and those who favored a system of abuse (" *Missbrauchsprinzip* "). This vigorous controversy arose during the drafting of the statute by the German Parliament. (1) According to the system of abuse, cartels are generally permitted, and are struck down only when their bad effects outweigh their beneficial aspects; administrative or judicial action takes place *a posteriori.* Following the system of interdiction, restrictive agreements are presumed to be generally pernicious and invalid, but it is possible to allow certain restrictive schemes which are shown to be in the economic interest of the public. (2) Connected with this latter system is the concept of interdiction with the possibility of authorization (" *Verbot mit Erlaubnisvorbehalt* ") of which the best example is perhaps Article 65 of the European Coal and Steel Community Treaty. In this system, restrictive agreements are made ineffective until the parties have obtained an administrative approval, based on one of the statutory exceptions. Suffice it to say that in this type of enforcement system, cartel agreements are generally judged on their face: they are tried in advance of their operation. Consequently, legal analysis is emphasized more than economic inquiry.

Section 1 of the German Act, with its series of exemption possibilities, embodies a complex system. Certain agreements need the express authorization of the Cartel Office to become effective. Others must be registered, but their validity is secured if the agency does not object within a certain period of time. Finally, some of the agreements falling under Section 1 are made valid outright by the subsequent statutory

(1) See LANGEN, KOMMENTAR ZUM KARTELLGESETZ, 55 (1957); Ivo Schwartz, *Antitrust Legislation and Policy in Germany - A Comparative Study*, 105 U. PA. L. REV. 621 (1956-57).

(2) For a criticism of this distinction, see BLAISE, LE STATUT JURIDIQUE DES ENTENTES ÉCONOMIQUES, 259-260 (1964).

exceptions, and are only subject to the supervision of the Federal Cartel Office which will oppose them in case of " abuses ".

This categorization is of interest for my purpose. Procedural and substantive law are here interrelated. To the extent that parties to cartel agreements are required or encouraged to register their contracts, some clear-cut rules have to be formulated as to what they are permitted to do under Section 1. Since it has been thought that no detailed economic analysis could be expected from the business firms involved, some of whom may be small merchants, greater reliance is placed on precise legal criteria. The concern with " *Rechtssicherheit* ", i.e., with providing the utmost legal predictability, has been generally widespread (1): reflected in the technique used to draft the statute, it has also been echoed in the construction of the statutory language.

7. - Two Possible Approaches to the Definition of Restraint of Competition

Are all restrictive schemes between enterprises at the same functional level restraints of competition under Section 1 of the German Act, or is there some kind of rule of reason? This question seems to me essential. Since the Act provides for strictly defined exceptions, the criteria for finding an injury to competition become all the more important. There might be restrictive agreements which do not come within any of the statutory exceptions, but which perhaps do not deserve to be prosecuted because they have only an insignificant effect on market conditions.

For the French law, this question has been phrased in accurate terms by Blaise.

> There are two possible approaches to the problem of restraint of competition. First one can consider competition as a result. The factors bearing on the identification of competition in a branch of industry will be economic. So long as there are, in the relevant

(1) See Shapiro, *The German Law against Restraints of Competition - Comparative and International Aspects,* 62 Colum. L. Rev. 4 (1962).

market, a sufficient number of firms of comparable size competing with each other, the industry will be regarded as competitive. Every restriction of the independence of one firm towards another will not automatically jeopardize the competitive fabric. Whether such a restriction is restraining competition depends on a market analysis. A line must be drawn somewhere, and thus there is an element of discretion. Second, one can adopt an abstract test: the legal independence of decision of each firm in the market. Each firm will then be considered separately. Every restraint imposed on the freedom of action of one firm will be deemed in restraint of competition. (1) (2)

The identical question may be raised as to Section 1 of the German Act. As a matter of fact, the German statute has tried to reconcile the conflicting doctrines explained by Blaise. " *Wettbewerb* " refers to an abstract concept, *i.e.* the contractual independence of the enterprises towards each other, whereas the second element, " *Marktbeeinflussung* ", is a factual one and relates to general competitive conditions in the relevant market.

8. - Competition and Restraint of Competition under Section 1 of the German Anticartel Law

A. - Legislative History

Although of limited help in shedding light on Section 1 of the German statute, the legislative history at least reveals the intended meaning of " *Wettbewerb* ". The Government explanation of its original Proposed Draft of the Cartel Law defines

(1) BLAISE, *op. cit.*, at 208.

(2) The first conception expounded by Blaise was clearly illustrated by NEALE [THE ANTITRUST LAWS OF AMERICA, 15-16 (1962)] in regard to horizontal integration: " A man with two bakeries in Cardiff buys another in Barry and there is no problem. By and by, however, he acquires more bakeries and yet more until the observer has very real doubts whether the bread trade in South Wales is competitive. Somewhere along the way comes the question whether this firm's newest acquisition is to be regarded as in restraint of trade. " On the other hand, Hefermehl has expressed clearly the second possible theory: " In a sense, every restriction of the freedom of the traders competing in the same line of business has an impact on market conditions, if you consider that, before binding themselves collectively, the cartel members

competition as " the striving of a business firm to induce a consumer to enter into a contract with it, by a performance which surpasses that of a competing firm in quality or price. " (1) Approximately the same conception was adhered to by the Economic Committee of the Bundestag, when it described economic competition as " every kind of economic activity which is designed to achieve some advantage in the trade contest at the expense of a competitor. " (2) The Report of that Committee, however, is not free from contradictions, especially where it declares that the number of market participants must be so great that the market price is " given " to the enterpreneurs and is largely independent of their own behavior. (3) Here the Committee was thinking of competition more in the context of a market structure as idealized by the model of pure competition, but, paradoxically, of such a kind as to render useless the striving of individual competitors which it is the reputed object of the statute to preserve.

B. - Definitions of Competition Proposed by the German Legal Literature

Nevertheless, Section 1 really views competition as a type of *behavior* rather than a *market condition.* Restraint of competition is then equated with restraint of individual behavior. This theory has been largely adopted by German legal literature. Although several definitions of competition have

---

could establish independently the prices of their products, and are free in regard to other factors which are relevant to competition. It makes no difference whether you evaluate the contractual restraint of trade against the model of pure competition or against the competitive situation actually existing before the restraint was adopted. The degree of monopolization of the market has increased if the number of suppliers or purchasers who were previously acting autonomously has decreased. From that theoretical standpoint, every restraint affects market conditions." But turning to the second test laid down in Section 1 of the German law, Hefermehl raised the question with which I will concern myself: "If Section 1 does not satisfy itself with the presence of a restriction, but requires moreover a reasonable probability that market conditions will be affected, this shows that this latter test has a separate meaning." See HEFERMEHL in BAUMBACH-HEFERMEHL, WETTBEWERBS- und WARENZEICHENRECHT, 1231 (1960) (My translation).

(1) Reprinted in GEMEINSCHAFTSKOMMENTAR, 1076 (1958) (My translation).

(2) *Ibid.*, at 1175 (My translation).

(3) *Ibid.*, at 1059. *Cf.* FRANKFURTER KOMMENTAR Tz. 20, § 1.

been advanced, all display the same traits. (1) The most frequently cited are those proposed by Günther, Fikentscher, and Meyer-Cording. All stress the individual behavior of *competitors,* rather than *general competitive conditions.*

Günther, President of the German Federal Cartel Office, has defined competition as " the endeavor of a market participant to displace another competitor pursuing the same business by making a contract of sale, lease, exchange or any other bargain. " (2)

To Fikentscher, " economic competition is the unhampered striving of competitors (either suppliers or purchasers) which exerts a reciprocal influence upon other competitors, when they seek to engage in commercial transactions with other parties (customers or suppliers) by presenting the most attractive terms. " (3)

Again, if we follow the definition of Meyer-Cording, " economic competition is that action (or abstention) exhibited by rivals striving to emulates each other in the pursuit of common objectives *viz.* furtherance of sales and exchange enhancing profit. " (4)

---

(1) See also BAUMBACH-HEFERMEHL, *op. cit.,* at 2; FRANKFURTER KOMMENTAR Tz. § 1; in the area of unfair competition, the German Courts have developed a similar definition, see HEFERMEHL in 1 BAUMBACH-HEFERMEHL, WETTBEWERBS und WARENZEICHENRECHT, 3 (1964). No original idea is conveyed by these definitions. The WEBSTER'S NEW WORLD DICTIONARY similarly regards competition as "the effort of two or more parties acting independently to secure the customs of a third party by offering more favorable terms."

(2) "Das Streben eines Markteilnehmers an Stelle eines anderen gleichgerichteten Mitbewerbers ein Kauf-Tausch-Geschäft oder einen Miet-Pacht-oder auf gewerbliche Leistungen gerichteten Vertrag mit anderen Marktpartnern abzuschliessen." See Eberhard Günther, *Einkaufsvereinigungen und Kartellgesetzentwurf,* DER MARKENARTIKEL, 35 (1957) quoted by Ingo Schmidt, *Zum Begriff der Preiswettbewerbs nach § 17 GWB,* WuW 132 (1964) (My translation).

(3) "Wirtschaftlicher Wettbewerb ist das selbständige Streben sich gegenseitig im Wirtschaftserfolg beeinflussender Anbieter oder Nachfrager (Mitbewerber) nach Geschäftsverbindung mit Dritten (Kunden oder Lieferanten) durch Inaussichtstellen günstiger erscheinender Geschäftsbedingungen." See Fikentscher, *Neuere Entwicklungen der Theorie zum Tatbestandsmerkmal der Wettbewersbeschränkung* § 1, 798 WuW (1961) (My translation).

(4) "Wirtschaftlicher Wettbewerb ist ein Verhalten betätigt durch Handlungen (oder Unterlassungen) mit denen mehrere Rivalen um die Wette das gleiche Ziel anstreben, ihren auf Gewinn gerichteten Leistungsaustausch zu fördern." See Meyer-Cording, *Die Grundbegriffe des Wettbewerbsrechts,* WuW 462 (1962) (My translation).

These three authors have the same conception of competition as Joel Dean attributed to the business man: " whatever he has to do to get sales away from his rivals and whatever they do to to take sales away from him. " [1]

Taking for granted that firms in the market behave in that way, these authors assume that the benefits of a free market will flow from this state of rivalry and independence. Autonomous enterprises will normally offer the buyer the option of buying from a rival at better terms. Buyers, as well as sellers, will have many alternatives as the consequence of the independent rival behavior of a certain number of business firms. [2]

C. - Restraint of Competition Defined as Contractual Limitation on the Individual Firms' Freedom to Compete

Under Section 1 of the German Act, in regard to the concept of " *Wettbewerb* ", the stress, then, is put on the freedom of decision of the individual sellers and buyers. Competition will be restrained whenever two of them in the same line abridge their freedom of behavior in the market. [3]

> By diverse measures such as contracts, decisions or recommendations, the actions of entrepreneurs in respect of price, terms of trade, quality or output, hitherto unlimited, are now impeded. Restrictions narrow the freedom of action of the parties in regard to the competitive steps they might take. [4]

Restraint of competition will then lie in any contractual restriction of the liberty possessed by individual traders to compete. " Competition is restricted whenever enterprises in the same market and on the same level contractually limit the freedom of their activity in this market. " [5] Restraint of

---

(1) J. Dean, *Competition - Inside and Out*, 32 HARV. BUS. REV. 64 (1954).

(2) See Meyer-Cording, *op. cit.*, at 462.

(3) See BAUMBACH-HEFERMEHL, *op. cit.* (1960) at 1233; FRANKFURTER, Tz. 25, § 1.

(4) See Meyer-Cording, *op. cit.*, at 469.

(5) MÜLLER-HENNEBERG in GEMEINSCHAFTSKOMMENTAR, 136 (1963) (My translation).

competition thus becomes synonymous with a " legally binding renunciation of one's freedom of decision. " [1]

D. - *Whether Competition is Restrained Can be Decided Abstractly*

Under this definition, then, restraint of competition is achieved in the abstract. Whether a "*Wettbewerbsbeschränkung*" within the meaning of Section 1 exists consequently can be decided regardless of the particular circumstances of each factual situation. Contrary to the American law, each case will not require a close scrutiny of its own facts. [2] For example, if enterprises agree by contract to publish their freely determined list prices, and are committed to adhere to the prices and terms publicly announced, this undertaking will be considered a restraint of competition under Section 1 of the German Act. [3] Under the Sherman Act, this may or may not be an unreasonable restraint of trade, depending on the facts of each case. In *Sugar Institute v. United States*, on similar facts, Chief Justice Hughes stated that " questions of reasonableness are necessarily questions of relation and of degree " and stressed that " in the instant case, a fact of outstanding importance is the relative position of defendants in the sugar industry. " The defendants supplied 70 to 80 % of the sugar consumed, so that " their agreements and concerted action have a direct effect upon the entire sugar trade. " Chief Justice Hughes also stressed, later, that sugar is a thoroughly standardized commodity and that the strong tendency to price uniformity made it " the more important that such opportunities as may exist for fair competition should not be impaired. " [4]

---

(1) See Müller-Henneberg, *Zu den Begriffen "Kartell" und "Wettbewerbsbeschränkung"*, WuW 883 (1963) (My translation).

(2) I am here referring to the formula used by Chief Justice Hughes in Sugar Institute Inc. v. United States, 297 U.S. 553 (1936).

(3) See *e.g.* decision of the B Kart A, December 9, 1959, WuW/E B Kart A 101, WuW 139 (1960); 1959 B Kart Rep. 51-52; letter of the B Kart A, April 6, 1962, WuW/E B Kart A 486, WuW 576-578 (1962); decision of the B Kart A, WuW/E B Kart A 310, WuW 150 (1961); 1958 B Kart A Rep. 39-41. Among the authors, see MÜLLER-HENNEBERG in GEMEINSCHAFTSKOMMENTAR, 142 (1963); HEFERMEHL in BAUMBACH-HEFERMEHL, *op. cit.*, at 1239.

(4) Sugar Institute Inc. v. United States, 297 U.S. 553 (1936).

As far as the notion of " *Wettbewerbsbeschränkung* " is concerned, therefore, the German theory underlying Section 1 comes fairly close to what is meant by " *restriction* " under the British Restrictive Trade Practices Act. The restraint relates to prices, terms of trade, quantities produced, types of products, territory of sales or classes of customers and so on. (1) Some border-line cases may, of course, arise: to what extent for instance does a restriction in respect of advertising between competing firms constitute a " *Wettbewerbsbeschränkung?* " (2)

Generally speaking, then, the question of restraint of competition under Section 1 may be answered abstractly. It will not depend on the percentage of business controlled or the strength of the remaining competition (3) Its determination turns essentially on whether the freedom of action of the competing traders is restrained: other market factors are irrelevant to that analysis. To that degree, it is true that there is no place for a rule of reason, if such a rule means that beneficial, or economically desirable, restraints could escape the purview of Section 1, even when they cannot benefit from any of the statutory exceptions.

---

(1) See *e.g.* MÜLLER-HENNEBERG in GEMEINSCHAFTS KOMMENTAR, 143-145 (1963).

(2) See for discussion, MÜLLER-HENNEBERG, *op. cit.*, 134-135; BAUMBACH-HEFERMEHL, *op. cit.*, at 1244; Meyer-Cording, *op. cit.*, at 472-473; *cf.* judgment of the German Federal Supreme Court, BGH, October 26, 1961 (Export ohne BS), WuW/E BGH 451, WuW 293 (1963). It seems that the German Court held that *every* agreement by which competing firms agree to refrain from advertising will be regarded as a "restraint of competition"; but as far as the market effect of the restraint is concerned, the German Court gives the impression that it would prefer a case-by-case analysis. In a comment, Hefermehl has approved this view. Advertising is an essential means for competing. Thereby purchasers are informed of the sources of supply. Advertising is also designed to increase the number of customers patronizing a producer. Hence, if a firm limits itself in its ability and freedom to advertise, its possibilities of action are restricted and there will be a "restraint" within the meaning of Section 1. But Hefermehl then raises the question whether every restraint of that kind is likely to affect market conditions. JZ 364 (1962). In United States v. Gasoline Retailers Association Inc., the United States Court of Appeals for the 7th Circuit held that an agreement between competitors to stabilize the local retail gasoline market, in an effort to prevent, by the elimination of price advertising at the station sites, gasoline price wars, constituted a price-fixing device which was illegal *per se*, 285 F. 2d 688 (7th Cir. 1961).

(3) I am referring here to some of the tests applied by the United States Supreme Court in United States v. Columbia Steel Co., 334 U.S. 495 (1948).

E. - No General Limitation on the Cartel Prohibition Beyond the Scope of the Exemptions of Section 2-8 of the Statute

On this point, a unique case arose in the Federal Cartel Office involving a trade association of manufacturers of electrical appliances. (1) This trade association sponsored an agreement whereby the parties committed themselves to recommend to their members that they produce, admit and use only electrical appliances complying with the safety standards set up by the association. For that purpose, the association had created a testing office to check the appliances submitted, and issue the association's seal of approval. The Federal Cartel Office held that the recommended measures did not come within the scope of Section 1. To be sure, the agreement was likely to influence market conditions by the withdrawal from trade of certain appliances, and whether this influence was substantial did not matter, for conditions of Section 1 are met even if the market impact is insubstantial (unerheblich). (2) As there was a likelihood of market affect, (3) the purpose of the parties to assure safety was irrelevant. But, apart from this probable "*Marktbeeinflussung*" was every restraint of competition ("*Wettbewerbsbeschränkung*") to be forbidden? The wording of Section 1 being all ambracing, should not some limitation be imposed on its scope? The purpose of Section 1 led to the conclusion that certain limitations were permissible and even indispensable. Not all measures which are likely to produce an effect on the market are forbidden. If statutory safety standards are admissible, why would not the same be true of a self-restriction of the industry, so long as it is not a way to by-pass the purpose of the statute? The right of free economic activity is subordinated to the safety of the individual. It was clear to the Federal

---

(1) Letter of the B Kart A, February 20, 1960 (*Doppelstecker*) WuW/E B Kart A 145, WuW 363 (1960).

(2) See *infra*, this chapter, at 87-88 and 94-96.

(3) See the Government Explanation for its Draft Law reprinted in GEMEINSCHAFTSKOMMENTAR, 1076 (1958); BAUMBACH-HEFERMEHL, *op. cit.*, at 1242.

Cartel Office that this latter benefit should not be endangered merely for the sake of economic performance. The safety standards issued in this instance, were found not to be a mere mask for a market action, and were therefore held beyond the scope of Section 1. Section 1 as viewed by the Federal Cartel Office protects competition in order to preserve economic freedom of action of the individual and thereby achieve the greatest benefit for the economy as a whole, including the ultimate consumers. (1)

However, this decision should probably be limited to its facts, since the Federal Cartel Office subsequently made clear that there was no room for a general limitation on the cartel prohibition beyond the scope of the exemptions of Sections 2-8 of the statute. Horizontal restrictive agreements could not escape Section 1 on the ground that they were indispensable (*notwendig*) or rational (*vernünftig*). A different position, it was thought, could only lead to an undesirable uncertainty. Invalidity of agreements provided for by Section 1 could not therefore be made dependent on such vague criteria as " necessary " or " rational ". (2)

F. - The " Gegenstandstheorie "*: the Restriction as an Express Part of the Content of a Binding Agreement*

The main problem raised in connection with the concept of " *Wettbewerbsbeschränkung* " under Section 1 is whether " competition " as defined by the German authors, must be restricted by an enforceable contract, or whether it is sufficient to have an unexpressed restriction which nevertheless tends to produce a restrictive effect on the market. (3)

(1) For discussion of this case, see MÜLLER-HENNEBERG in GEMEINSCHAFTSKOMMENTAR, 159, 163 (1963).

(2) Decision of the B Kart A, April 10, 1964 (*Teerverwertung*) WuW/E B Kart A 795, WuW 765 (1964) and 1959 B Kart A Rep. 8.

(3) MÜLLER-HENNEBERG in GEMEINSCHAFTSKOMMENTAR 139 (1963); *id., Zu den Begriffen "Kartell" und " Wettbewerbsbeschränkung"*, WuW 891 (1963); Deringer/Tessin, Comment on the Grundig-Consten case, AWD BB 332 (1964).

This issue has been especially debated in relation to common sales agencies or buying pools, joint ventures, and price information agreements. The overwhelming majority of legal writers, mainly for reasons of promoting legal predictability (Rechtssicherheit), intimated that Section 1 requires that the agreements themselves must contain certain expressly restrictive provisions. (1)

The problem was examined several times by the Federal Cartel Office when it had to decide the legality of cooperative purchasing organizations set up by voluntary chain stores (*Einkaufsgemeinschaften von freiwilligen Handelsketten*). (2) In these cases, the question was whether there was a restraint of competition if the basic agreement did not provide for an undertaking on the part of the members to make all their purchases through the organization. The Federal Cartel Office in one instance refused to challenge such a cooperative organization because of the lack of binding commitment on the participants to place all their orders through the "*Handelskette*" and also because they were, in fact, procuring a significant part of their requirements from other sources. (3) This latter circumstance operated, however, to obscure the answer. But all doubt was removed by a letter addressed by the Federal Cartel Office to certain voluntary groups:—

> Common purchasing by several autonomous enterprises does not raise any antitrust objection so long as there is no legal obligation under the agreement to satisfy all your requirements, or a fixed percentage, or to purchase certain determined items only through the common organization. (4)

Commenting on this decision, Benisch thought he could infer that Section 1 reaches only agreements which create an obligation to restraint competition, and not informal agreements which induce behavior in restraint of competition. (5)

---

(1) See *e.g.* BAUMBACH-HEFERMEHL, *op. cit.*, at 1234.

(2) 1960 B. Kart A Report 17 which raises the issue.

(3) See information, WuW 324 (1962).

(4) Letters of the B Kart A of February 8-9 and March 27-28, 1962 (Freiwillige Ketten), WuW/E B Kart A 576, WuW 432 (1963).

(5) See Benisch, Comment, WuW 434 (1963).

As to joint purchasing of marketing organizations, the Federal Cartel Office went so far as to hold in one earlier case that it was sufficient if the participants had merely acted in concert. And, a concerted action could be found, even when the members did not mean to bind themselves legally, but had merely agreed upon a parallel action by a gentleman's agreement. It seems, however, that in later pronoucements the Federal Cartel Office has retreated from this advance position. ([1])

In later cases, the issue of the validity of joint ventures or common buying (or purchasing) agencies has turned essentially on whether the parties had accepted some binding restriction on their competitive freedom. ([2]) What will be decisive is the existence of an obligation on the part of the members to use the common agent exclusively.

The most recent cases reported for 1964 reflect the same trend. ([3]) In one instance, theater owners agreed to designate one of their number as common agent for negotiating films licenses with distributors. This so-called "*Abschlussgemeinschaft*" was examined under Section 1. The Federal Cartel Office held that there would be a restraint of competition only if the theater owners had entered into some binding commitment. This would be the case if each partner, surrendering his own commercial freedom of action, had delegated to the common agent the negotiation of all his firm's requirements. ([4]) In another reported case two public utilities had declared in one agreement their intent to purchase imported gas in common. But, as it was explained to the agency that, beyond this declaration of intention, the parties were not committed to make their pruchases in common, no restraint of competition was found. ([5])

([1]) 1960 BKartA Rep. 16-17.

([2]) 1963 BKartA Rep. 19; 1961 BKartA Rep. 52-53 (*Kieler Fisch Grosshandel*); 1962 BKartA Rep. 23-24 (*Putzträger*); 1963 BKartA Rep. 18 (*Torf*); 1963 BKartA Rep. 34-34 (*Fotogeräte*); 1963 BKartA Rep. 56 (common procurement agency of TV companies).

([3]) See *e.g.* 1964 BKartA Rep. 18 (*Teererzeugnisse*) 1964 BKartA Rep. 38 (Frauen- und Mädchenoberkleidung).

([4]) 1964 BKart A Rep. 45.

([5]) 1964 BKartA Rep. 50.

In view of this administrative practice, and of the almost complete unanimity of the legal writers, it seems correct to conclude that Section 1 reaches only agreements which obligate the participating enterprises to behavior which restrains competition. Agreements which, without diminishing the contractual freedom of action of the parties, create market conditions likely to lessen competition may be considered beyond the scope of Section 1. (1) The agreement must contain some provision restricting the individual freedom of action of competitors. Thus, in Section 1, the word " contract " refers to an agreement intended to create legal relations. (2) I will refer to this doctrine as the " *Gegenstandstheorie* ".

9. - The Likelihood of Influencing Market Conditions : a Limited Rule of Reason for Section 1

The second requirement for banning a cartel is that the agreement is likely to influence market conditions as a result of " restraint of competition ". The legislative history does not reveal the intent of the draftsmen in this respect. According to the Government Explanation, the statute aims only at agreements which restrain competition in the commercial area and regulate commercial activities by private law contracts. The word, " Marktbeeinflussung ", was intended to exclude services provided by the state in its governmental capacity. (3) But

(1) See Deringer/Tessin, *op. cit.*, at 332.

(2) This position is almost unanimous. See MÜLLER-HENNEBERG in GEMEINSCHAFTSKOMMENTAR, 120 (1963); FRANKFURTER KOMMENTAR Tz. 26 Sec. 1 and Tz. 7 § 1; BAUMBACH-HEFERMEHL, *op. cit.*, at 1235 and 1229. An opposite thesis has been advocated by LUKES, DER KARTELLVERTRAG (1959). His opinion stands rather isolated. For a criticism, see *e.g.* P. Ulmer, *Kartellvertrag und Gentleman's Agreement*, WuW 3 (1962).

The German Parliament was aware that the requirements set up in Section 1 were opening a loophole. See the Government Explanation for its Draft Statute, in GEMEINSCHAFTSKOMMENTAR, 1077 (1958). As put by Shapiro, *op. cit.*, at 15, " the cartel's prohibition against anticompetitive agreements could be circumvented by substituting formless agreements for such agreements. " This loophole was only partly corrected by Section 38(2) (*Umgehungsverbot*).

(3) See BEGRÜNDUNG ZU DEM ENTWURF EINES GESETZES GEGEN WETTBEWERBSBESCHRÄNKUNGEN, reprinted in GEMEINSCHAFTSKOMMENTAR 1075 (1958).

the real question is whether, by requiring that restrictive agreements be likely to produce some impact on the market, the legislative intent was to incorporate a codified rule of reason. ([1]) To put it another way, should every restrictive contract between competing firms entered into with a common purpose be prohibited regardless of how insignificant its effect on general competitive conditions may be? Only a negative indication is furnished by the legislative history. A proposal to include in Section 1 the requirement that the influence on market conditions be substantial was rejected, because the Economic Committee felt that this qualifying addition would create uncertainty and signify an appreciable change in the basic provision. ([2]) Such a qualifying clause would perhaps open the door to excessively loose interpretations.

But these pre-legislative debates show clearly that the issue was a choice between a *per se* rule and a " moderate " *rule of reason.* One of the authorities in cartel law who played an essential role in its preparation expressed, a few years before the statute's enactement, the following opinion. What counts really in judging the validity of these agreements, he said, is not that the contracting parties are restraining their own freedom of competing. What is decisive is that they do so with the intent and effect of reducing the opportunities of third parties, and thus ensure a greater chance of success for themselves. ([3]) This implied that *not every* restraint should be made unlawful.

Restraint of competition and market effect are, as a matter of fact, two separate concepts which ought to be distinguished carefully. ([4])

As has been said by Meyer-Cording, "restraint of competition" (*Wettbewerbsschränkung*) is not prohibited for its own sake,

---

(1) DERINGER in AKTUELLE GRUNDSATZFRAGEN DES KARTELLRECHTES 71-72 (1957).

(2) The report of this Committee is reprinted in GEMEINSCHAFTSKOMMENTAR 1156, 1217 (1958). See at 1175.

(3) See Böhm, WuW 153, 177 (1956) quoted by DERINGER in AKTUELLE GRUNDSATZFRAGEN DES KARTELLRECHTES, 72 (1957).

(4) Meyer-Cording, *op. cit.*, WuW 470, 471 (1962); FRANKFURTER KOMMENTAR Tz. 49, § 1.

but because of its possible effect on the market, i.e. on third parties. It may adversely curtail the alternatives left to the market partners and, in that way, impair competition's function of regulating the market. The contracting parties, by restraining themselves, seek to gain influence in the market in order to impose their own terms. The legislature makes the restraints of competition unlawful in order to eradicate the adverse influence on the market which may flow from the restrictions. [1]

This distinction between " *Wettbewerbsbeschränkung* " and " *Marktbeeinflussung* " has been sometimes overlooked. For instance in the second *Textillohnveredelung* case, the Federal Cartel Office left open the question of whether restraint of competition ("*Wettbewerbsbeschränkung*") meant the restrictions on the competitive freedom of the cartel members arising from the cartel agreement, or, alternatively, the effects of the cartel agreement in the relevant market. The Federal Cartel Office did not need to answer this question, because, in that case, both constructions led necessarily to the same conclusion. Both the limitation of the free economic activity of the cartel members and the effects in the relevant market were so significant that the restraint was not justified by the rationalization which it produced. Competition between the participants as to prices, discounts and terms of sales was entirely suppressed. As to the effect of the agreement in the relevant market, the Federal Cartiel Office found that the number of domestic outsiders accounted only for 10 % of the total output and that only 1 % of goods consumed were imported. Although refusing to decide the issue raised in that instance, the Federal Cartel Office drew a clear line between the two concepts of " *Wettbewerbsbeschräkung* " and " *Marktbeeinflussung* ", and as to the latter took into account the share of the cartel in the relevant market. [2]

Thus, Section 1 uses two different concepts, and each of them must be given a useful meaning lest the legislative language be deprived of its proper effect. Recently, for instance, the

---

(1) *Id.*, at 470.

(2) Decision of the B Kart A (Einspruchsabteilung), *Textillohnveredelung* II, December 15, 1962, WuW/E B Kart A 569, WuW 263 (1963).

Federal Supreme Court (*Bundesgerichtshof*) stated that a restriction on production does not, by itself, meet the test of invalidity set up by Section 1. Such a restriction becomes relevant only when it is likely to exert an influence on the market. " This may be inferred from the purpose of this Section which is to prevent restraints of competition because of their effects on the market (*Aussenwirkungen auf dem Markt*) and not for the mere reason that the freedom of action of the contracting parties towards each other is restrained. " [1]

The distinction between restraints of competition and likelihood of influencing market conditions has been expressed in another way by a German expert. He denominated as " formal " restrictions (" *formale Wettbewerbsbeschränkung* ") those restraints of the individual freedom of trade between competing firms which are not likely to produce any market effect. On the other hand, for restrictions which are capable of altering the market situation and cutting off buyers' (or sellers') access to other alternatives, he proposed the term, " material " restrictions (" *materielle Wettbewerbsbeschränkung* "). This author had already attempted to rationalize in this way the rule of reason applied by German Courts to the Military Government Decartelization Laws. [2]

Theoretically, the preceding statements are certainly, it is submitted, the only reasonable way to explain the use by the German statute of two separate concepts. But a practical issue remains: how far have the Courts and the enforcement agency been prepared to give Section 1 its full meaning in exploiting the possibilities of the statutory language, and in developing their own rule of reason, limited though it might be.

At the time of the enactment of the statute, some doubts were expressed as to the ability of the Courts to make complex economic determinations. [3] Such objections have, of course,

(1) Judgment of the BGH, July 1, 1964 (*Flussspat*), WuW/E BGH 605, 610, WuW 653, 658 (1964).

(2) See Fikentscher, *Neuere Entwicklungen der Theorie zum Tatbestandsmerkmal der Wettbewerbsbeschränkung*, § 1, WuW, 799-801 (1961).

(3) See BIEDENKOPF, AKTUELLE GRUNDSATZFRAGEN DES KARTELLRECHTES, 24 (1957).

also been expressed in America against a generalized application of the Rule of Reason. [1] In his dissent in *Standard Oil Co. of California,* Justice Jackson, speaking of the qualifying clause of Section 3, confessed that he regarded it " as unfortunate that the Clayton Act submits such economic issue to judicial determination. It not only leaves the law vague as a warning or guide, and determined only after the event, but the judicial process is not well adapted to exploration of such industry-wide questions. " [2]

10. - " Probable Market Effect " Test and Analysis of the Case-Law

Analysis of the German case law reflects great reluctance on the part of the German courts to engage in economic investigations of a broad scope. Feeling perhaps that they are ill equipped for that purpose, the courts have avoided lengthy inquiries by adopting a highly formalistic approach. The policy announced by the enforcement agency when evaluating the task awaiting it after the enactement of the Act against Restraints of Competition was not encouraging. The Federal Cartel Office stated that all restrictions limiting a firm's freedom as regards prices, quality and terms of trade were, as a rule, likely to influence the general market conditions. [3]

I shall now examine whether this *per se* approach announced by the Federal Cartel Office in the early days of the Act received the ratification of the courts.

A. - Gasglüköper

In *Gasglühkörper,* the Federal Surpeme Court had to construe the word " *Marktbeeinflussung* " for the first time. But the

(1) See Oppenheim, *Federal Antitrust Legislation: Guideposts to a revised national Antitrust Policy,* 50 MICH. L. REV. 1161 (1951-1952).

(2) Standard Oil Co. of California v. United States, 337 U.S. 293, 322 (1949). See the observations made by Justice Frankfurter in his majority opinion, *Ibid.,* at 310 and note 13.

(3) 1959 B Kart A Rep. 8 and Fikentscher, *op. cit.,* at 801.

particular facts of the case enabled it to avoid facing the problem squarely. This case involved an agreement between two firms engaged in the manufacture of neon lamps, whereby the plaintiff, who was suing for breach of contract, had allowed the defendant to use certain machines, equipment and trade-marks in the manufacture of neon lamps. In addition, the plaintiff was committed to discontinue manufacturing such lamps, and forbidden to acquire any stock in any firm doing so. In return the defendant had to pay to the plaintiff a certain share of the profits. Contrary to the Court below, the Federal Supreme Court found a *common purpose* underlying the Gasglühkörper agreement, stating that, to make this finding, one had to examine the entire contract thoroughly, and consider the economic intentions of the parties, the circumstances which led to the conclusion of the agreement and the development of the relationship between the parties. The Court stressed that, in order to be encompassed by Section 1, the contract must not be aimed at influencing market conditions. Effect, not intent, is the test. The language of Section 1, as well as its legislative history, gave the Court its main argument. The Government explanation to which the Court referred revealed that the draftsmen wanted to settle the ancient controversy as to whether the intent to influence market conditions is a part of the definition of a cartel. (1) The Court confirmed the Government view, and held that the market effect was sufficiently probable in this case. To support its conclusion, the Court noted simply that both parties to the agreement were important (*namhafte*) firms in the manufacture and distribution of the products concerned, and had a substantial share of the relevant market. Under these circumstances, the Court did not pass explicitly on the question of whether the market share of the parties was to be scrutinized for purposes of Section 1. (2)

Interpretation of this decision is far from unanimous. Fikentscher thought that one could read into it a holding that the substantiality of the restraint of competition is irrelevant. The

---

(1) See GEMEINSCHAFTSKOMMENTAR, 1175 (1958); *cf.* FRANKFURTER KOMMENTAR, Tz. 49, § 1.

(2) Judgment of the BGH, October 26, 1959, WuW/E BGH 359, WuW 295 (1960).

words " likely to influence market conditions " are no support, he wrote, for the application of a rule of reason in the American conception. The degree of influence on market conditions likely to be exercised by the agreement is irrelevant: even a slight (*gering*) influence would be sufficient. (1)

B. - Kohlenhandel

But in *Kohlenhandel*, however, the Federal Supreme Court, in what might be a first step by the Court in developing its own rule of reason, seemed willing to reject such a narrow interpretation. The case arose under Section 38(2) of the Cartel Law which prohibits trade associations' recommendations which result, through uniform conduct, in an evasion of Section 1. To be illegal, the recommendation must be likely to influence market conditions by means of " restraint of competition ". Since no parallel action had been produced by the recommendation, the Courts below found no violation. The dealers who followed the price recommended by their local trade association represented just 5 % of the relevant market, and their action was not likely to influence the market conditions. In its turn the Federal Supreme Court held that a substantial effect on market conditions was not required by the statute. But, contrary to the petitioners, the Court did not think that the analysis of the Court of Appeals implied recognition of a quantitative test. It said that whether the recommendation had been carried out by a sufficient number of dealers, was relevant only in determining the question of whether the members of the trade association, by conforming to the recommendation, had been able to influence the market in any way. To decide this factual question, the Court below had correctly inquired whether the coal purchasers could still cover their requirements from dealers who did not adhere to the recommended prices. Thus, the mere reduction in the number of independent competitors did not suffice to show an influence on market conditions. (2)

---

(1) See Fikentscher, Comment on *Gasglühkörper*, WuW/E BGH 368, WuW 346 (1960).

(2) Decision of the BGH, January 14, 1960, Kohlenplatzhandel, WuW/E BGH 369. WuW 347 (1960). See the judgment of the Court of Appeal, OLG Hamburg, August 24, 1959, WuW/E OLG 290, WuW 64 (1960).

Benisch expressed the view that this interpretation of Section 38(2) could be extended to Section 1 itself. The same notion of " *Marktbeeinflussung* " could hardly be construed differently in the two instances. Thus a cartel agreement would not be likely to influence market conditions within the meaning of Section 1, if purchasers could easily cover their needs without patronizing the cartel members. And consequently a cartel agreement covering a market share of only a small percentage might not violate the Act. That the Court examined the actual effects on the market conditions in that case shows by analogy, said Benisch, that Section 1 does not spell out a *per se* prohibition of every " restraint of competition " (*Wettbewerbsbeschränkung*). The opposite interpretation would indeed deprive the market effect test of any meaning. Only the view suggested by the Court would be consistent with the purpose of the statute which is to forbid restraints of trade likely to affect competition as the regulating factor of a market economy. Small agreements with insignificant effects on the market would be beyond the scope of Section 1. ([1]) However justified this analogy between Section 1 and Section 38 may be, it must be noted that Section 1 does not require an actual effect on the market, but satisfies itself with a kind of reasonable probability test.

This conception was adopted by the District Court of Mannheim when it stated that the likelikood of influencing market conditions is absent so long as the requirements of purchasers can be satisfied otherwise, to wit, so long as other alternatives are still available to purchasers. ([2])

C. - *The* Spar *case*

The most important decision of the Federal Supreme Court on the point in issue was the *Spar* case. The charter of the *Spar* chain association of wholesalers and retailers included

([1]) See Benisch, Comment, WuW/E BGH 374, WuW 352-353 (1960). This judgment of the German Federal Supreme Court has also been discussed by Lieberknecht, GRUR 353 (1960); Deringer, BB 43 (1960); Buntig, BB 384 (1960); von Beringe, DB 289 (1960); Lea, AktG, 95 (1960); Benkendorff, WRP 146 (1962).

([2]) Cited by Klaue, *Zwei Jahre Rechtsprechnung zum GWB*, WuW 393 (1960).

a provision whereby "only such dealers can be admitted as members of *Spar* who are not in competition with each other, or who have delimited the area of their economic competitive activity toward each other. Before obtaining membership in this organization, wholesalers are required to delimit the field of their activity against nearby wholesalers." Such delimitation had been agreed upon between the parties—two out of about 400 wholesalers in Berlin. In litigation between them, one party argued that the provision to which they had alhered contravened Section 1. The other replied that the clause in question was not embraced by Section 1 because in any event the likelihood of influencing market conditions was lacking, the two wholesalers in the city alone having signed it. The Appellate District Court of Frankfurt rejected this contention, holding that, by the agreement in question, at least in case of further growth of the organization, the wholesalers could achieve a stronger position towards the retailers established in their territory than under free competition between them. Denying that a substantial influence on market conditions would be required (there were numerous other wholesalers in the food market, not belonging to *Spar*), the Court of Appeals stressed that the gist of the statute was to catch as many restrictive agreements as possible within the net of Section 1 in order to enable the Federal Cartel Office to exercise supervision. ([1])

The Federal Supreme Court affirmed. The petitioner contended that the Court of Appeals had based its findings on a further growth of *Spar* in the future, but that it had not made sufficient findings as to present conditions, and consequently that the impact on market conditions was quite uncertain. The impact on market conditions must be more discernible, it was argued. The Federal Supreme Court held, on the contrary, that the division of market between the wholesalers met the requirements of Section 1. The relevant market was the wholesale market for food in the Berlin area. Even in the presence of the relatively large number of 400 competitors, the confinement of two efficient and competitive wholesalers each to a territorially defined part

---

(1) Judgment of the Court of Appeals of Frankfurt, OLG Frankfurt, March 3, 1960 (SPAR), WuW/E OLG 337, WuW 793 (1960).

of the market constituted a strong limitation of business activity. The possibility of adverse effects of these measures on the relationship between wholesalers and their purchasers within the Berlin area could not be entirely precluded. The Federal Supreme Court rejected any quantitative test. Every influence on market participants (*Marktbeteiligten*) which is perceptible according to general economic experience is likely to influence market conditions within the meaning of Section 1. A purely theoretical likelihood of influencing market conditions is, however, not sufficient. The Court below had thus applied a correct legal standard, especially since even in its assigned territory, the *Spar* wholesaler was not completely free but was committed to give preference to the *Spar* retailers. Pursuant to the regulation, the effects of the agreement in question could reach beyond the competition between the wholesalers, parties to the agreement, and be perceptible on the competition at the retailer level, namely between *Spar* retailers and other retailers. To be sure, out of 400 wholesalers in the Berlin area, only two were members of the *Spar* organization at the time of the suit. But the *Spar* retailers themselves had no freedom of choice: they depended, without any alternative, on their assigned *Spar* wholesaler. (1)

D. - Critical Appraisal of the Spar *case*

Some writers have expressed dissatisfaction with this judgment because it is not clear that the Federal Supreme Court gave to the term "*Marktbeeinflussung*", i.e. the market effect test, its full meaning. Dörinkel, for instance, wrote that only an extensive construction of Section 1 could enable insignificant restraints of trade to escape. There was no doubt that a large number of restraints were so insubstantial that they do not deserve to be prosecuted. As an example, this author cited the American rule of reason, which permits such judicial discretion. Undoubtedly, the German Act contains a series of exemptions, but these cover limited situations and as a consequence their requirements are hard to satisfy. In *Kohlenhandel* the Federal

(1) Judgment of the BGH, June 7, 1962 (SPAR), WuW/E BGH 486, WuW 680 (1962). *Cf.* FRANKFURTER KOMMENTAR, Tz 50, § 1.

Supreme Court had strengthened the hope that some flexibility would be injected into Section 1 by way of judicial interpretation. But the language used by the Court in the present case is likely to embrace horizontal arrangements, regardless of their economic significance. It has been said that, by reading the word " perceptible " into the statute, the Court has weakened the term " influence ". In order to give a fairer interpretation to the statute Dörinkel suggested a return to the purpose of Section 1, which was to prohibit not all restraints of trade, but only those which jeopardize the efficiency of the competitive process itself, adversely affecting its inherent tendency toward a higher performance, by endangering the best possible supply of consumers. For that author, the decisive criterion should be whether the alternatives on the other side of the market (*Marktgegenseite*) are removed or *reduced.* (1)

This conception, which appears to be sounder, has been adopted by two lower courts. In an action for breach of contract where a price-fixing agreement was involved, the District Court of Düsseldorf decided that the agreement obviously constituted a " restraint of competition ", since both parties gave up their freedom to determine independently of each other the price of the product in question, and this restraint was likely to influence market conditions. As to this latter test, the District Court stated that it was not the situation of the parties to the agreement which must be considered, but rather that of outsiders and purchasers (*Partner auf der Marktgegenseite*). Market conditions are influenced, said the Court, when the opportunities of purchasers to obtain better conditions by threatening to switch to other commercial partners are reduced. (2) This doctrine was also relied upon by the District Court of Dortmund when confronted with a market division agreement between home delivery milk dealers in a small community.. The agreement was found to be unlikely to influence market

(1) See Dörinkel, Comment on the *Spar* case, GRUR 43 (1963). This is also the conception advocated by the FRANKFURTER KOMMENTAR, Tz. 49, § 1 und MÜLLER-HENNEBERG in GEMEINSCHAFTSKOMMENTAR, 156 (1963).

(2) Judgment of LG Dusseldorf, August 15, 1961, WuW/E LG/AG 186, WuW 446 (1962).

conditions. The situation of the competitors and of the purchasers, not of parties to the agreement, was decisive. The appropriate question was whether by reason of the agreement the situation of other milk dealers had become more difficult, and the opportunities of the purchasers to negotiate better terms of sales by threatening to buy from other dealers had been affected. Neither was true here . The District Court emphasized that other alternatives were left to the buyers. (1)

E. - The Bockhorner Klinker *case*

The doctrine of the Federal Surpeme Court in the *Spar* case was applied by the Kammergericht (Court of Appeals) of Berlin in *Bockhorner Klinker.* Several producers of bricks and tiles had formed a common sales agency. Each partner was committed to place his entire output at the disposal of the agency, which was given power to establish prices and other terms of trade. The defendants did not deny that their agreement was a " restraint of trade " (" *Wettbewerbsbeschränkung* ") within the meaning of Section 1, but they argued that, since their market share was insignificant, they were not in a position to influence market conditions. There was some dispute as to the relevant product line and the necessity of taking into account the competition from substitute products. Relying on *Kohlenhandel* the defendants contended that a market share of at least 5 % was a necessary requirement for a cartel to come within the purview of Section 1 and to meet the test of " likelihood of influencing market conditions ". Saying that the *Kohlenhandel* case had not set up such a general standard, the Court of Appeals rejected this contention, and followed the *Spar* doctrine. In that case the market share was still more insignificant (0,5 %), the alternatives of the purchasers were even more favorable, and, nevertheless, the Federal Supreme Court had found a violation of Section 1. The Court of Appeals ruled that " die Vorschrift des [Artikeln] 1 GWB soll jede Beeinträchtigung des freien Wettbewerbs unterbinden, die sich praktisch auswirken kann."(2)

(1) Judgment of L. G. Dortmund, October 16, 1961 (*Milchhändler*), WuW/E LG/AG 189, WuW 623 (1962).

(2) Decision of the Kammergericht (Court of Appeal of Berlin), October 16, 1964 (*Bockhorner Klinker*), WuW/E OLG 709, 713, WuW 235, 239 (1965).

In other words, every contract in restraint of trade which *can* have in any way an actual effect on the market must be forbidden. It is quite clear that this decision destroyed any possibility of a serious market effect test. Restraints of trade are unlawful in and of themselves, without the necessity of a actual showing of their adverse effect on competition in the market. The risk, then, is great that conjecture becomes a substitute for thorough market analysis.

11. - Conclusions

A. - A Formalistic Approach to the Definition of Restraint of Trade under Section 1

In regard to horizontal agreements, the German law starts with a very narrow notion of competition which is equated with the individual freedom of action of the firms. " *Wettbewerbsbeschränkung* " under Section 1 of the German Act is not adequately translated as " restraint of competition ". " *Wettbewerbsbeschränkung* " denotes that competing parties are restricted in their freedom to carry on their business as they otherwise would. These restrictions may pertain to prices, quality, service, output, advertising, sales territory, customers or terms of sale.

A majority of the legal writers are of the opinion, and the administrative practice agrees, that the restriction must be stipulated by an enforceable contract, and be part of its explicit terms(*Gegenstandstheorie*). (1) On this view, there would be no plausible reason for declaring ineffective agreements which were not meant to produce any legal effect. (2) Under this doctrine, a common sales agency would completely escape the ban against cartels, provided that the business firms creating it were sufficiently careful not to bind themselves to do all, or

(1) See *e.g.* FRANKFURTER KOMMENTAR, Tz. 26, § 1.

(2) See *e.g.* MÜLLER-HENNEBERG in GEMEINSCHAFTSKOMMENTAR 120 (1963).

part of, their business through the agent. [1] If an arrangement in fact produce a lessening of competition in the market, but is free from any restrictive clause, it will not be caught by Section 1 of the German Act. The legality of a joint venture under Section 1 turns solely on the presence or absence of agreements not to compete (*Wettbewerbsverbote*) in the basic contract.

The German Act, however, does not reach every agreement as defined above. Restraints of trade can be struck down only if they are likely to affect market conditions, a test which can be applied only by a case-by-case analysis. [2] This illustrates that the German Act preserves the individual freedom of trade of competing firms not for its own sake, but because it is a necessary condition of competition viewed as a fabric. " There may be freedom without competition, but is is impossible to have competition without freedom. " [3]

The German Act opposes restraints of trade only to the extent that they may impede the normal working of a free market. Unlike the Sherman Act, Section 1 of the German Act does not require actual harm to occur. The market effect test contained in Section 1 is merely a reasonable probability standard. [4] In effect, the policy of the statute, as far as horizontal agreements are concerned, is to reach the restraints of trade in their incipiency before they ripen into full blown restraints. Section 1 of the German Act thus deals more with probabilities than with certainties. [5] and from that point of view, may be compared to Section 7 of the Clayton Act.

The legislature may have assumed that, when two competing firms have gone so far as to bind their freedom of trade by contract, there must be a rather strong purpose behind it. Presumably they would not do this if the agreement was not

---

(1) See Kurt Market, *Gemeinschaftsunternehmen und Antitrustrecht,* AWD BB 243 (1964).

(2) See FRANKFURTER KOMMENTAR, Tz. 52, § 1.

(3) See MÜLLER-HENNEBERG, *op. cit.*, 129 (1963).

(4) See FRANKFURTER KOMMENTAR, Tz. 51, § 1.

(5) *Cf.* Brown Shoe Co. v. United States, 370 U.S. 294, 323 (1962).

of some utility to them. This view has been expressed by Hefermehl:—

> As a rule one can take for granted that the participants will only contractually limit their ability to compete if they expect to achieve, through this cooperation, more influence over the market. Otherwise they have no incentive to restrain themselves. They will prefer to behave as rivals. But this is only a rebuttable assumption. (1)

Suggesting that minority groups should not be permitted to combine, Handler advocated the same idea: " Moreover, these combinations are normally not established unless competition in the industry as a whole can be affected. " (2)

Thus it could be thought appropriate to forbid such action, without demanding more than a likelihood of market effect, and in that way free the courts and the enforcement agency from entering into a complex and detailed economic analysis.

The test of likelihood of market effect could be the starting point of a limited Rule of Reason. (3) Its original purpose was certainly to avoid bringing insignificant restraints within the purview of Section 1. By requiring a market analysis, the test implies a case-by-case approach. Nevertheless, the scope of this test has been considerably narrowed by the Federal Supreme Court in the *Spar* decision, under which the expectation of any kind of perceptible effect is enough.

The truth is that this requirement has thus almost been read out of the statute. Minority groups cannot possibly escape Section 1 by showing they still face an effective outside competition. Their sole resource is to claim the benefit of one of the statutory exceptions. But Section 1 itself is essentially concerned with the elimination of competition among the group. Moreover there is no room under Section 1 for a demonstation that a particular restriction is likely to promote rather than to

---

(1) See BAUMBACH-HEFERMEHL, *op. cit.*, 1231 (1960) (My translation). *Cf.* NEALE, THE ANTITRUST LAW OF THE U.S.A. 430-431 (1962).

(2) HANDLER, A STUDY OF THE CONSTRUCTION AND ENFORCEMENT OF THE FEDERAL ANTITRUST LAWS, TNEC Monograph no. 38, 34 (1941).

(3) See FRANKFURTER KOMMENTAR, Tz. 25, § 1.

supress competition; it is sufficient to find that traders have limited their independence. Although Sections 2 to 8 of the German Act provide for possible exemption of cartel agreements which are deemed economically desirable, these exemptions must be construed strictly. (1)

As a matter of fact, the whole system of enforcement organized under the German Act fits this policy very well. If they want the benefit of an exemption, cartel members must communicate their agreements to the Federal Cartel Office, which may issue an authorization or simply not raise any objection. Everything being based on a contract and probabilities, it is possible to judge the agreements on their face. Since the test of likelihood of market effect has been deprived of much of its importance by the Federal Supreme Court, the Courts and the enforcement agency can obviate the difficulties of scrutinizing the actual effects of restraints of trade, as the Sherman Act requires in thoses cases which are subject to a full range application of the Rule of Reason. Under the guise of predicting the influence that restraints might have on market conditions, the German Courts seem to have satisfied themselves with mechanical formulas.

In contrast, under the Sherman Act, matters of form are to be subordinated to matters of substance. " The substance is the interference with competition; when this is established, the courts are often inclined, as the cases will show, to be cavalier in their treatment of formal matters—the forms for example, of agreements or combinations or price formulas—and impatient of the defences relying on formal ingenuities. " (2) The tendency in the German anticartel law is almost the reverse. The " *Gegenstandstheorie* " and the *Spar* doctrine show how much the German courts and the writers have been legalistic in their approach to antitrust. It has been said that because, of its detailed nature, the German anticartel law is preoccupied primarily with the manner in which competition is restrained, while, in contrast, the

---

(1) See Frankfurter Kommentar, Tz. 35-36, § 1.

(2) See Neale, *op. cit.*, 22 (1962).

American antitrust laws focus on the anticompetitive results of economic activity. (1)

True, the American law has borne *per se* violation rules which present some similarity with the German approach inasmuch as the first question which must be raised is whether a given practice is of a particular form. Nevertheless, *per se* offenses are those which, *experience* has shown, warrant a conclusion that an inquiry into effect upon competition would be irrelevant. These practices are deemed *inherently* anticompetitive because of the excessive burden placed upon the free play of market forces, The distinctive feature of *per se* rules is not a matter of form. Thus, despite the development of *per se* rules under which most of the cases brought under the Sherman Act are now adjudicated, this evaluation seems entirely correct.

B. - Other Uses of the Word " Competition ". Section 18 as an Example of a Different Competitive Test

If Section 1 of the German Act uses the term " competition " in a very formal way, however, this is not always the case throughout the statute. For example, in the field of horizontal agreements, the statute provides for an exemption in favor of specialization cartels, but permission may be granted only of the proposed specialization does not exclude competition in the market. (2) On the other hand, a market-dominating enterprise (*Marktbeherrschendes Unternehmen*) is defined by Section 22 as an enterprise *which is not exposed to any substantial competition* in a certain type of goods or commercial services. (3)

Still more important differences appear in the field of vertical arrangements. Section 18 of the German Act which regulates exclusive dealing and distributorship agreements, as

(1) Ulmer, *Wettbewerbsbeschränkende Absprachen im Rahmen von Unternehmenszusammenschlüssen*, WuW 164, footnote 7 (1960), Shapiro, *op. cit.*, at 4. at 4.

(2) Section 5(2) of the German Law against restraints of competition; See DERINGER in GEMEINSCHAFTSKOMMENTAR, 288, 290.

(3) On this provision, see BARTHOLOMEYCZIK in GEMEINSCHAFTSKOMMENTAR 631 (1963).

well as tying arrangements, does not aim so much at the protection of the restricted enterprise as at the preservation of competition as the regulator of the economy. (1) (2) These kinds of agreements affect, of course, the competitive ability of the enterprise which is committed not to supply another dealer in a determined area, not to purchase its requirements from another producer, or to buy a second product tied with a first one. But the main concern of the German Act in that area is not to protect the contractual freedom of one of the parties. In respect of exclusive dealing or tying, for instance, the statute seeks to keep outlets open to competitors of the manufacturer. The German Act goes beyond the freedom of economic action of the parties to the arrangement: it is preoccupied with the market effect of the practices, with keeping alive competition in the market. Exclusive dealing can only be challenged by the Federal Cartel Office if it restricts the dealers without reasonable consideration, and provided that, by the amount of such restrictions, competition *in the market* for these goods or other commercial goods is substantially restrained.

Section 18 of the German Act thus combines tests of injury to private persons (unreasonable limitation of the economic freedom of a contracting party) and of injury to the public (substantial restraint of competition in the market). This latter test originated in a proposal of the *Bundesrat*, finally adopted

---

(1) Section 18 of the German Law reads as follows:—

(1) The Cartel Office can invalidate, either immediately or effective at some future date, agreements between enterprises relating to goods or commercial services and can prohibit the consummation of other similar agreements insofar as such agreements

a. restrain one of the parties in its freedom to use the delivered goods, other goods or commercial services; or

b. restrain one of the parties in the purchase or sale of other goods or other commercial services from or to third parties; or

c. commit one of the parties to accept other goods or commercial services that are not normally related either technically or by custom of the trade, *and* thereby unreasonably restrict the freedom of economic action of a party to the agreements or any other enterprise and insofar as, by the amount of such restrictions, competition in the market for these or other goods or commercial services is substantially restrained.

(2) See SCHWARTZ in GEMEINSCHAFTSKOMMENTAR, 522 (1963); FIKENTSCHER, *Sonstige Verträge im Gesetz gegen Wettbewergsbeschränkungen*, in FESTSCHRIFT FÜR ALFRED HUECK, 543 (1959); Shapiro, *The German Law against Restraints of Competition, Comparative and International Aspect*, 62 COLUM. L. REV. 211, 219 (1962).

despite the criticism expressed by the Economic Committee of the *Bundestag*. (1) This Committee felt that the proposed test would, in each case, require lengthy and complex economic analysis as to the market effect produced by the group of restraints. This debate is a good illustration of the reluctance shown by the German legislature to organize real economic tests: the very same arguments generally directed against the Rule of Reason were used. The search was rather for mechanical and easy-to-apply formulas.

An Act of September 16, 1965, has amended Section 18. (2) The private injury test has been abandoned. Under the new Section 18, the cartel office can interfere and challenge the enumerated restraints in two cases: either if they *unreasonably restrict the access of other enterprises to a market*, or if competition in the market for these or other goods and commercial services is substantially restrained by the amount of such restrictions.

This fundamental distinction between Section 1 and Section 18 of the German Act has generally been regarded mainly as a matter of procedural law. Section 1 would embody a system of interdiction (*Verbotsprinzip*) under which the embraced agreements would be ineffective until the members obtain the permission of the administrative agency. On the other hand Section 18 would consider the restrictions involved there as initially lawful but would subject them to later invalidation by the cartel office in certain determined conditions (*Missbrauchsprinzip*). This difference, however, in the enforcement procedure should not obscure the differences in the substantive law. Section 1 and Section 18 represent two different kinds of competitive tests. In forbidding every contractual limitation of the freedom of decision between competitors, Section 1 comes very close to a *per se* rule, whereas the restrictions involved in Section 18 are subject to a *rule of reason*. There is not very much room for examination of the market effect under Section 1 as presently

(1) See GEMEINSCHAFTSKOMMENTAR 1186 (1958).

(2) GESETZ ZUR ÄNDERUNG DES GWB, September 15, 1965, BGBl 1965, Teil I, 1363. This statute is reproduced in WuW 829 (1965). See also the excerpts of the Report issued by the Economic Committee, WuW 834 (1965).

construed. On the other hand, the restrictions enumerated by Section 18 *standing alone* are not *per se* unlawful. There is no competition between the supplier and the purchaser so that the restraint imposed by one on the other cannot *in itself* be equated with a restraint of competition. Under Section 18 restraint of competition does not signify a contractual restriction of the individual freedom of trade. Those protected by Section 18 are *outsiders* to the arrangements.

Such differential treatment does not exist under either the Sherman Act or the Rome Treaty. Competition has but one meaning in both statutes.

CHAPTER III

A RULE OF REASON FOR ARTICLE 85(1) OF THE ROME TREATY

1. - Recent Developments of the EEC Antitrust Law: the *Grundig-Consten, Technique Minière* and the *Italian Government* Cases

As I have pointed out in the introduction, the first draft of this dissertation was written prior to the Court of Justice pronouncements in three landmark cases—*Grundig-Consten v. EEC Commission, Société Technique Minière v. Maschinenbau Ulm GmbH,* and *Italy v. EEC Council and EEC Commission.* At that time, only the Commission had begun to expound its doctrine and thus the basic substantive issues were still debated. This was especially the case with the concept of restraint of competition. (1)

Now that the Court of Justice itself has announced its doctrine, the controversy as to the existence of a Rule of Reason under Article 85(1) is no longer merely theoretical. Although its decisions do not put an end to all controversies which have arisen from the application of Article 85(1), it is possible to discern several trends in the construction of the Treaty. Regarding a Rule of Reason under Article 85(1), the positions advocated by the EEC Commission and by Advocate General Roemer and those taken by the European Court present three substantially different theories. The last word belongs of course to the Court, which has in fact adhered to a sort of

(1) A tremendous amount of literature has been devoted to EEC antitrust law. However, most of it is preoccupied with procedural problems, and of the remainder very little is relevant to this study.

See the bibliography established by the Court of Justice of the European Communities, PUBLICATIONS JURIDIQUES CONCERNANT L'INTÉGRATION EUROPÉENNE, Publication du Service de Documentation de la Cour de Justice des Communautés Européennes. This bibliography, started in October, 1962, lists *inter alia* all the books, articles, studies, judicial and administrative decisions regarding the common market antitrust law. The *CCH Common Market Reporter* also contains a list of the publications in English on the same topic, 2 CCH COMMON MARKET REPORTER, § 900. Deringer—*WuW/EWG-Wettbewerbsrecht,* WuW 871 (1965)—has a selective bibliography of the most important studies on Article 85 and 86 of the Rome Treaty. In this dissertation, I will only refer to the authors who have expressed views on the precise questions with which I am dealing.

compromise between the conflicting views urged by the enforcement agency and the Advocate General.

Far from making this dissertation obsolete, these three cases which bore directly on the issue of the rule of reason emphasized the immediate relevance of my topic. I had to accommodate the latest developments of European law. Nevertheless, they did not require a fundamental change in the presentation of this study. It is still essential to gain a initial understanding of the doctrines expressed by the Commission in its decisions, to try to discover why in fact the enforcement agency largely rejected any kind of rule of reason, to explain the misunderstandings concerning the Rule of Reason, and to measure the impact of the German theories. This I will first do without considering the decisions of the Court of Justice. I will in the same way articulate my argument in favor of a Rule of Reason for Article 85(1) of the Rome Treaty. I will then analyse the doctrine propounded by the European Court of Justice. This manner of exposition will also enable me to follow more or less chronologically the developments of the law and to determine to what extent the theories suggested by Advocate General Roemer and partly adopted by the Court constitute a departure from the literal approach which had been taken by the EEC Commission.

2. - Substantive Test of Restraint of Competition and Jurisdictional Requirement under Article 85(1) of the Rome Treaty

The test upon which the ban against cartels is predicated is whether the agreement is intended to restrain competition or has that effect. Like the Sherman Act, Article 85 contains an interstate commerce clause: " juridiction is dependent upon showing that the restraint affects commerce between two or more of the member nations. " [1] In American law:—

> The phrase " restraint of trade " which ... had a well-understood meaning at common law, was made the means of defining the

(1) James A. Rahl, *Antitrust Problems of Doing Business Abroad,* Remarks made at the Chicago Bar Association, March 11, 1965, at 22 of the mimeographed text.

> activities prohibited. The addition of the words " or commerce among the several States " was not an additional kind of restraint to be prohibited by the Sherman Act but was the means used to relate the prohibited restraint of trade to interstate commerce for constitutional purposes ... so that Congress, through its commerce power, might suppress and penalize retraints on the competitive system which involved or affected interstate commerce. (1)

The Rome Treaty has separated the substantive test of restraint of competition and the jurisdictional requirement. In American law, the dollar volume of interstate commerce affected by a restraint is immaterial. No showing of " adverse " effect is needed; any kind of substantial effect will be sufficient. (2) Similar problems have been discussed in relation to Article 85(1). (3) The present study does not concern itself with this

---

(1) Apex Hosiery v. Leader, 310 U.S. 469, 495 (1940).

(2) See James A. Rahl, *op. cit.*, at 12 and 14.

(3) See *e.g.*, Deringer, *op. cit.*, WuW 871-872 (1962); 1961 BKartA Rep. 62; Ellis, *L'interprétation du Mot «Affecter» dans l'Article 85(1) du Traité CEE par Rapport aux Mots «Empêcher», «Restreindre» ou «Fausser le Jeu de la Concurrence»*, RECUEIL DALLOZ, 221-228 (1963); submissions of Advocate General Maurice Lagrange in the case 13-61, de Geus v. Bosch, Court of Justice of the European Communities, April 6, 1962, VIII RECUEIL DE LA JURISPRUDENCE DE LA COUR, 139-141 (1962); decisions of the EEC Commission in the following cases: Faïence, WuW 54 (1964) and 1 CCH COMMON MARKET REPORTER, § 7023; Grundig-Consten, *Official Journal of the European Communities*, 2545 (1964) and 1 CCH COMMON MARKET REPORTER, § 7026; Blondel, *Official Journal of the European Communities*, 2194 (1965) and 2 CCH COMMON MARKET REPORTER, § 9049; Hummel-Isbecque, *Official Journal of the European Communities*, 2581 (1965) and 2 CCH COMMON MARKET REPORTER, § 9063; Jallate, *Official Journal of the European Communities*, 37 (1966) and 2 CCH COMMON MARKET REPORTER, § 9083. The problem as to whether it is necessary under article 85(1) to show an adverse effect on interstate commerce can be considered as solved after the decisions of the European Court of Justice in the cases 56 and 58/64, Consten and Grundig v. E.E.C. Commission (2 CCH COMMON MARKET REPORTER, § 8046) and in the case 56/65, Société Technique Minière v. Maschinenbau Ulm GmbH (2 CCH COMMON MARKET REPORTER, § 8047). Advocate General Roemer had espoused the thesis whereby a showing of adverse effect on interstate commerce would be necessary in order for a restrictive agreement to come within the purview of Article 85(1). The EEC Commission, on the other hand, had strongly emphasized that the test of "effect upon interstate commerce" had only a jurisdictional function. The recent pronouncements of the Court of Justice have at least terminated this controversy. In both instances the Court has ruled that the purpose of the concept of " agreements liable to affect trade between Member States " is to separate the respective fields of application of Community law and of national law on cartels. Thus the fact that an agreement helps to bring about a considerable increase in the volume of trade between Member States is not sufficient to preclude the possibility that such agreement can " affect " trade within the meaning of article 85(1). An agreement will meet the jurisdictional test if there is a sufficient degree of probability that it may have some influence, direct or indirect, actual or potential, on the flow of trade between Member States.

question. The issue on which I will concentrate my attention concerns restraints of competition. How significant must the restraints be in order to be caught within the net of Article 85(1)?

3. - The American Rule of Reason as Viewed in Europe

Although it encompasses all restrictive agreements and concerted practices between enterprises, the prohibition of the Rome Treaty is qualified by an exculpatory clause, Article 85(3), which enables the EEC Commission to grant exemption to those cartels which satisfy four distinct requirements. (1) The agreement must contribute to improvement of production or distribution or to technological or economic progress. (2) The public must share in the benefits of the improvement. (3) The restriction must be indispensable for the achievement of these results. (4) The restriction may not be such as to afford the enterprises involved the possibility of eliminating competition in respect of a substantial proportion of the commodity concerned.

Labouring under an erroneous conception of the American Rule of Reason, eminent authorities in the field of European law have doubted whether the American approach toward the concept of restraint of competition could be transferred to Article 85(1) of the Rome Treaty. They assumed that the Rule of Reason allowed the American Courts to indulge in some reckoning of the ultimate social or economic debits and credits to determine which agreements are beneficial. (1) Relying on the codified criteria set up in Article 85(3), they inferred that in the Rome Treaty Article 85(3) established the metes and bounds of such evaluation, and that under Article 85(1) itself any exercise of discretion was precluded. (2)

---

(1) See the formula used by Justice Brennan in United States v. Philadelphia National Bank, 374 U.S. 321, 371 (1963).

(2) See the references cited *supra* in the introduction, at 4 and footnotes (1) and (2) and at 5 and footnote (1).

The German delegation to the EEC expressed this widely held view when it stated:—

> Article 85(1) contains no standard either for measuring the significance of a restraint of trade against the strength of the remaining competition or for balancing the beneficial or pernicious effects of restraints. Such a process of evaluation is involved in Article 85(3). A judgment as to the significance of the restraint and as to its effects is allowed only within the limits set out in Article 85(3). (1)

4. - The Sherman Act Does not Permit a Consideration of the Economic Advantages Resulting from Restrictive Agreements

As we have seen, the United States Supreme Court has insisted that decisions of this type are value choices of such magnitude that they are beyond the ordinary limits of judicial competence. (2) The Rule of Reason avoids the formidable problem of balancing benefits and detriments of restraints. Article 85(3) is not the equivalent of the Rule of Reason. The Rule of Reason does not permit the sustaining of agreements which, although clearly detrimental to competition, are shown to bring about an improvement of production or distribution, or other benefits to the public. (3) It does not take into account such considerations of policy. They are unrelated to the main purpose of the Sherman Act which is to prevent purchasers or

---

(1) See 1961 BKartA Rep. 62 (my translation). A similar view was advocated by the EEC Commission before the European Court of Justice in the *Grundig* case. See 2 CCH COMMON MARKET REPORTER, par. 8046 at 7641, and this chapter *infra* at 160.

(2) See the statement of Justice Brennan in United States v. Philadelphia National Bank, 374 U.S. 321, 371 (1963). Although it was made in relation to Section 7 of the Sherman Act, I think that this statement can be applied equally to Section 1 of the Sherman Act. For the " essential difference between the Sherman Act approach and the Clayton Act is simply that the Clayton Act requires a lower standard of proof of the same kind of facts", *cf.* Adelman, *Acquire the Whole or Any Part of the Stock or Assets of Another Corporation*, ... A.B.A. ANTITRUST SECTION 111, 118 (1953). Accord: James A. Rahl, *Anti-merger Law in Search of a Policy*, Proceedings of the Fourth Annual Corporate Council Institute, 77 (1965).

(3) See GEORGE W. STOCKING, WORKABLE COMPETITION AND ANTITRUST POLICY, 136-137 (1961).

consumers from being deprived of the advantages which they derive from a freely competitive system. [1] The role of the reasonableness standard, as I have defined it, is to ascertain when a restraint of trade has actually produced, or is intended to produce, an excessive anticompetitive effect on the market. To justify a restraint under the Rule of Reason, it is not necessary to show that it has improved anything; one need only show that no harm has been done to competition. This inquiry relates to the quantitative significance of the restraint, and not to economic or social benefits which may flow from it. [2] By opening the way to the validation of certain rationalization and specialization cartels, [3] Article 85(3) goes much further than the Rule of Reason. Article 85(3) presents similarities with

---

(1) See HANDLER, A STUDY OF THE CONSTRUCTION AND ENFORCEMENT OF THE FEDERAL ANTITRUST LAWS, TNEC Monograph no. 38, 8-9 (1941); Apex Hosiery v. Leader, 310 U.S. 469, 500, 501 (1940).

(2) See Eugene V. Rostow, *Report of the Attorney General's Committee in Perspective,* in CCH ANTITRUST LAW SYMPOSIUM, 70 (1956).

(3) See H. v. der Groeben, *Competition Policy as Part of Economic policy in the Common Market,* Address to the European Parliament, Strasbourg, June 16, 1965, 2 CCH COMMON MARKET REPORTER, § 9036. I am referring to the German text published in WuW 691 (1965). On Article 85(3), see *e.g.,* Arno Sölter, *Die Ausnahmevorschrift des Artikel 85 Abs. 3 EWG-Vetrag,* WuW 665 (1961). Recently the EEC Commission has published two horizontal agreements of this type in regard to which the contracting parties have requested an exemption under Article 85(3) or a negative clearance. Pursuant to Article 19(3) of Regulation no. 17, the Commission has invited any interested third parties to state their views, and their possible objections to an exemption. The first one is a specialization and sales agreement filed by the *Alliance of French Machine-Tool Makers.* The ten firms which are shareholders in this corporation have signed a standard contract through which they have given the Alliance the exclusive right to sell their products out of France. Each firm has agreed not to manufacture or sell machines that might compete with machines manufactured by another shareholder. This is therefore a division of fields connected with an export agreement. These small and medium size firms argue that the agreement furthers economic progress by giving them sales possibilities to which they would otherwise not have access. See notice of the EEC Commission, *Official Journal of the European Communities,* 2566 (1966) and 2 CCH COMMON MARKET REPORTER, § 9122. An agreement registered by the *Transocean Marine Paint Association* is another instance of cooperation for standardisation and research. The alleged purpose of this arrangement is "to enable its members to combine their experience to perfect and manufacture according to uniform processes special paints to be added to the line of marine paints manufactured and sold by each, and also to rationalize the sale of these products through identical packaging bearing the same mark and thus to increase competition with the large international marine paint consortia." 2 CCH COMMON MARKET REPORTER, § 9124 and notice of the EEC Commission, *Official Journal of the European Communities,* 2962 (1966). See also the application for an exemption or a negative clearance filed by a French non-profit trade organization (*Socemas*), 2 CCH COMMON MARKET REPORTER, § 9101 and *Official Journal of the European Communities,* 1173 (1966).

the Rule of Reason only to the extent that it precludes any approval of restrictive agreements by which groups of enterprises obtain a monopolistic position. But even in this respect, the American law is stricter. It is of no consequence under the Sherman Act that the cartelizing firms may not yet have achieved a complete monopoly. It is sufficient if the cartel really tends to create such a monopoly and to deprive the public of the advantages which flow from free competition. (1) A much lesser degree of retraint is necessary to find an agreement unreasonable than to bar a possibility of exemption under Article 85(3). Even though the precise effect accorded to the factor of market power in loose-knit confederation cases is unclear, it seems that under the Rule of Reason minority groups are not permitted to eliminate competition among themselves. (2)

> Such arrangements inevitably lessen to some extent the competition to which the public looks for its protection. They are often the first step in a program of monopoly control. Each group when separately considered may not affect the competitive texture of the industry, but with the formation of each additional group, competition becomes more and more attenuated until it disapears. (3)

5. - The Need for a Rule of Reason under Article 85(1) of the Rome Treaty

The four tests formulated by Article 85(3) are obviously not easy to satisfy. It is possible to conceive a restrictive agreement which will not be able to obtain the approval of the EEC Commission because it does not result in the benefits described in Article 85(3), but which on the other hand does not deserve to be prosecuted because it does not significantly impair competition. (4) I take, for instance, the case of the

(1) See Fashion Originator's Guild of America, Inc. v. Federal Trade Commission, 312 U.S. 457, 466 (1941).

(2) Handler, *op. cit.*, at 34.

(3) *Id.*

(4) *Cf.* the submissions of the Advocate General in the cases 56/64 and 58/64, Consten and Grundig v. EEC Commission, 2 CCH Common Market Reporter, §§ 8046 at 1662-1663.

common selling agency held unlawful by the Court of Appeal of Berlin in *Bockhorner Klinker.* (1) The share of the market possessed by the firms was totally insubstantial. Such an arrangement is likely neither to serve nor to injure the public. It does not make things worse; it does not make them better. This illustrates that it becomes essential to decide the issue whether Article 85(1), like the Rule of Reason, requires a factual showing of illegality or whether it embodies an abstract proposition of law such as the *per se* rule.

To determine whether an agreement between enterprises has as its purpose or as its effect the restraint of competition within the Common Market inevitably involves a certain degree of judicial or administrative discretion. (2) This is a factual question which necessitates economic analysis, unless *per se* rules are formulated or unless the model of pure competition is adopted as guide. (3)

6. - The EEC Commission's Doctrine: Regurgitation of the German Theories

Just as German law strongly influenced the enforcement system codified by Regulation No. 17, so it has inspired the EEC Commission in its approach to the substantive concept of restraint of competition. The German theories are faithfully echoed in a recent statement made by the EEC Commission before the European Court of Justice:—

> The restraint of competition must be " appreciable ". This is the case if the agreement alters appreciably the market situation of enterprises not party to the agreement or of consumers—*i.e.* affects appreciably their opportunities for procuring supply and marketing merchandise. Accordingly, limitation of the freedom of action of the parties to the agreement as purchasers or potential purchasers does not by itself amount to restraint of competition. The measure

(1) See Chapter II, *supra,* at 98-99.

(2) See remarks by R. Joliet in La Fusion des Communautés Européennes, Collection Scientifique de la Faculté de Droit de Liège, 196 (1965).

(3) *Cf.* the excerpt of Baumbach-Hefermehl, Wettbewerbs- und Warenzeichenrecht, 1231 (1960) translated and quoted *supra,* Chapter II, note (2) at 77-78.

of the impact of an agreement on the market situation is the extent to which the situation of enterprises not party to the agreement or of consumers is altered by the existence of the agreement. There is, however, no rule defining the extent to which the situation must be affected. Article 85(1) contains no such quantitative criterion. (1)

The quotation of this statement in the 8th General Report of the Community constitutes a genuine declaration of policy. The purpose is to provide business firms with a set of guidelines regarding the applicability of Article 85. As in the German law, this trend toward abstract rules is motivated by a preoccupation with "*Rechtssicherheit*". A recent speech of Commissioner Von der Groeben has already attempted to justify this approach. (2)

In effect, the EEC Commission has taken over the two concepts utilized by Section 1 of the German anticartel law, *i.e.*, "*Wettbewerbsbeschränkung*" and "*Eignung zur Marktbeeinflussung*". One will recall that the notion of "restraint of competition" under Section 1 is an abstract concept which is determined by reference to the individual firm's contractual independence of decision, regardless of other market factors. The probable market effect test would seem to require, on the other hand, some market analysis on a case-by-case basis, but as a matter of fact has been given a rather mechanical application. The 8th Report reveals the impact both of the *Spar* case (3) and of the German writers. (4) The EEC Commission refused to read the word "undue" into Article 85(1), in order to secure control of the largest possible number of restrictive agreements. This refusal seems also to have been motivated by the desire to avoid having to exercise a discretion which would have provided businessmen with an additional defence. Cartelizing firms would otherwise not only have

---

(1) 8th GENERAL REPORT ON THE ACTIVITIES OF THE COMMUNITY, EEC Commission, June 1965, at 73.

(2) See H. von der Groeben, *op. cit.*, WuW 695 (1965).

(3) Judgment of the German Federal Supreme Court, BGH, June 7, 1962 (*Spar*), WuW/E BGH 486, WuW 680 (1962) and *supra* Chapter II at 94-98.

(4) See *e.g.* MÜLLER-HENNEBERG in GEMEINSCHAFTSKOMMENTAR, 156 (1963); FRANKFURTER KOMMENTAR, Tz. 49/51, § 1.

claimed the benefit of the exemption; in case their agreement would not fulfill the requirements of Article 85(3), they could also have asserted that it did not ignificantly harm competition.

Similarly, the German Courts had repudiated the view that the market impact of a restraint of trade need reach a certain proportion. The use of the word " perceptible " by the German Federal Supreme Court in the *Spar* cas was explicitly designed to escape using the terms " significant " or " substantial " which are peculiar to American antitrust law. The attitude of the German courts could at best find some support in the legislative history of the Act since the legislature had rejected a proposal to include the word " substantial " into Section 1 because of its inherent vagueness. (1) But the parallel position of the EEC Commission lacks such justification.

In regard to exclusive dealing arrangements, for instance, the theory developed by the EEC Commission would imply that such a contract would be in and of itself within the purview of Article 85(1). There would be no place under Article 85(1) for an inquiry as to whether " the challenged practice menaces competition in the distribution process by actually foreclosing competitors from access to a substantial share of the consuming market. " (2)

This approach, which is not warranted by the language of the Treaty, has already led, as we will see, (3) to objectionable results in the field of exclusive franchise arrangements. It is my thesis that the German anticartel law has no more relevance in the construction of Article 85 of the Rome Treaty than any other antitrust statute. To demonstrate this, I must first trace the influence of the German theories on the EEC case law.

---

(1) See Chapter II, *supra*, at 87-88.

(2) REPORT OF THE ATTORNEY GENERAL'S NATIONAL COMMITTEE TO STUDY THE ANTITRUST LAW, 144 (1955); *cf.* Standard Oil Co. of California and Standard Stations Inc. v. United States, 337 U.S. 293 (1959) and Tampa Electric Co. v. Nashville Coal Co., 365 U.S. 320 (1961).

(3) See this Chapter, *infra*, at 146-152.

7. - The Construction of Article 85(1) Proposed by German Writers: Restraint of Competition Equated with " *Wettbewerbsbeschränkung* " under Section 1 of the German Statute

While Section 1 of the German anticartel law invalidates contracts which by a " restraint of competition " (" *Wettbewerbsbeschränkung* ") are likely to affect market conditions, Article 85(1) of the Rome Treaty outlaws agreements and concerted practices which have as their *object* or *effect* the prevention, restraint or distortion of competition within the Common Market and which are likely to affect trade between member states.

This alternative test of liability in Article 85(1) has generally been construed to mean simply that the restraint of competition must be either intended or effected. Article 85(1) is violated if there is an anticompetitive result or else an intent to bring about such a result. (1) As the conspirators must be regarded as intending the consequences of their action, intent will be inferred when there is an anticompetitive effect (2) On the other hand, Article 85(1) can cover an agreement even if no actual effect has been achieved provided that the action is likely to have consequences harmful to competition. The purpose alone is an offence only if the intended effect would be unlawful if it actually happened. (3) The intent itself, even though not

---

(1) See *e.g.* 1961 BKartA Rep. 61; Deringer, *op. cit.*, WuW 867 (1962) and the references cited.

(2) This is why it is difficult to perceive how an actual restraint of competition could be produced without intent, as the German Federal Cartel Office [1961 BKartA Rep. 61] and Deringer, *ibid.* seem to believe.

(3) *Cf.* Everling in Wohlfarth-Everling-Glaesner-Sprung, Die Europaïsche Wirtschaftsgemeinchaft, Kommentar zum Vertrag, 244 (1960). In *Grundig-Consten v. EEC Commission* (2 CCH Common Market Reporter, § 8046), the European Court of Justice ruled that "for purposes of applying Article 85(1), it is not necessary to take into consideration the actual *effect* of an agreement where its purpose is to prevent, restrict or distort competition." (CCH translation.) This construction of the Treaty is unassailable. However, the *Technique Minière* case (2 CCH Common Market Reporter, § 8047) reveals an objectionable tendency to limit the inquiry to the purpose of the agreement, or at least to ascertain first the anticompetitive object. There, the Court said: —

"The alternative rather than cumulative nature of this condition—as shown by the conjunction 'or'—makes it necessary first to consider the actual purpose of the agreement, taking into account the economic context within which it is to be expressed in the agreement, can be inferred either from its content, or from the surrounding circumstances or from the way in which the agreement has been carried out. (1)

However, the most difficult problem is to ascertain when competition is prevented, restrained or distorted. In short, what is a restraint of competition under Article 85(1) of the Rome Treaty? No definition has been elaborated in American antitrust cases which are decided on a factual basis under the Rule of Reason. Abstract definitions have indeed been carefully and deliberately avoided. Only German legal writers to whom definitions of restraints are familiar (2) have concerned themselves with this problem, and naturally they have regarded it as appropriate to look at the German law for guidance.

Kleemann was one of the first to equate restraint of competition within the meaning of Article 85(1) of the Rome Treaty and " *Wettbewerbsbeschränkung* " under Section 1 of the German

---

applied. The alterations of competition referred to in Article 85(1) must result from all or some of the *clauses* of the agreement itself. If, however, an analysis of these clauses does not reveal a sufficient degree of injury to competition, then the effects of the agremeent must be examined." (CCH translation.)

This approach might well be consonant with the language of the Treaty, but it seems to me that it defeats its policy, because it provides an easy way of avoiding any economic investigation into the effects upon market competition produced by the agreement. In my view, the decisive test of Article 85(1) is one of effect. Article 85(1) prohibits restrictive agreements as soon as they have, or are meant to have, a significant effect on competition. The analysis should always turn on the effect, whether actually produced or merely intended. As I will try to demonstrate, Article 85(1) is not satisfied by any kind of effect: it must be significant or at least perceptible. In the same way, not every kind of restrictive purpose is sufficient to bring an agreement within the prohibition; Article 85(1) covers only an intent to produce a significant anticompetitive effect. The terms of an agreement, however much they restrict the contracting parties' freedom of trade, do not by themselves necessarily reveal an anticompetitive purpose. This is especially obvious in the case of exclusive franchises. Agreements of this type undoubtedly restrict the manufacturers' freedom of action. However, one may not for that reason infer automatically a significant anticompetitive purpose or effect, for, as the European Court has itself acknowledged in *Technique Minière,* such an agreement may not be in restraint of competition within the sense of Article 85(1) "where the agreement appears to be necessary for an enterprise to penetrate a territory where it was not doing business" (the CCH COMMON MARKET REPORTER does not translate the full force of the Court's misgivings in the French counterpart). See *infra* this chapter, my analysis of the EEC Commission decisions and of the opinions handed down by the European Court of Justice.

(1) 1961 BKartA Rep. 61 and Deringer, *op. cit.,* WuW 868 (1962).

(2) See Chapter II, *supra,* at 78-81.

law. To him, restraint of competition could only mean restriction on the freedom of decision (" *Einschränkung der Entschluss-freiheit* ") accepted by the contracting parties. However, a difference between Section 1 of the German Act and Article 85 of the Rome Treaty caused this author some embarrassment. Section 1 of the German Act provides no basis for counteracting parallel behavior of businessmen which stems from common discussions and understanding, if no legal agreement has been reached. On the other hand, Article 85 bans restraints of competition brought about by concerted practices and this could suggest that Article 85 can be violated even if no binding agreement has been entered into. The test suggested by Kleeman does not fit such an hypothesis since, in such a case, none of the participants would be bound and limited in his own freedom of action. Nevertheless, this author continued to press his view, thereby unduly belittling a basic difference between the German law and the EEC law. Moreover he thought that the requirement of a likelihood of prejudicial market effect set up by Section 1 of the German Act could be usefully adopted in the interpretation of Article 85 : only those agreements which are likely to influence interstate commerce to some perceptible degree would come within the range of the Treaty. (1) Kleeman is confusing the notion of restraint of competition and the jurisdictional requirement, which are two separate questions. However substantial the effect on interstate commerce must be, one has first to determine how significant the restraint of competition must be. This author would consider any restriction of the individual firm's independence of decision as being in restraint of competition, regardless of its concrete effects on the market conditions. No rule of reason would be conceivable under Article 85(1) of the Rome Treaty.

Although more sophisticated, the theory developed by Deringer is not fundamentally divergent from Kleeman's views. He too thinks that restraint of competition should be interpreted in the light of German law. For him competition implies both freedom of unilateral action by every enterprise and the

(1) Kleeman, Die Wettbewerbsregeln der EWG, 38-43 (1962).

possibility of choosing one's market partner. ([1]) This theory can readily be traced to the construction given to Section 1 of the German Act. In the German anticartel law the notion of competition serves primarily to describe what can be the subject of the restraint. ([2]) Under Section 1, " *Wettbewerbsbeschränkung* " (literally, restraint of competition) is equivalent to every contractual limitation of the individual's freedom to exercise his business as he pleases. ([3]) The other concept used by Section 1—the likelihood of influencing market conditions—has been construed by certain writers and by a few courts to be present when the possibilities of choice of market partners are curtailed: as a result of the agreement, outsiders must be impeded in marketing their own products or consumers must have reduced facilites for patronizing other suppliers. ([4]) ([5]) According to Deringer, restraint of competition (isolated from the Article 85 formula of " effect or purpose ") conveys only these two ideas. In a later note, he makes clear that the limitation of individual freedom of trade must be contained in

---

([1]) Deringer, *op. cit.*, WuW 800 and 865 (1962).

([2]) See MÜLLER-HENNEBERG in GEMEINSCHAFTSKOMMENTAR, 129 (1963).

([3]) See Chapter II, *supra*, at 78-82.

([4]) See *e.g.* judgment of L. G. Dusseldorf, August 15, 1961, WuW/E LG/AG 186, WuW 446 (1962) and judgment of L. G. Dortmund, October 16, 1961 (Milchhändler), WuW/E LG/AG 189, WuW 623 (1962). These judgments are discussed *supra*, Chapter II, at 97-98. Among the authors, see MÜLLER-HENNEBERG, in GEMEINSCHAFTSKOMMENTAR, 156 (1963); FRANKFURTER KOMMENTAR, Tz. 49, § 1; Meyer-Cording, *Die Grundbegriffe des Wettbewerbsrechts*, WuW 462 (1962); see *supra*, Chapter II, at 81-91 and 96-98.

([5]) The availability of alternatives in sources of supply and demand precisely is one of the conditions of a *workable competition* judged by reference to a market *structure*. Wilcox expressed the view that " competition among sellers, even though imperfect, may be regarded as effective or workable if it offers buyers real alternatives sufficient to enable them, by shifting their purchases from one seller to another, substantially to influence quality, service and price " (WILCOX, COMPETITION AND MONOPOLY IN AMERICAN INDUSTRY, TNEC, Monograph no. 21, 76th Cong., 2d Sess. 1940). In PUBLIC POLICIES TOWARD BUSINESS (p. 103), the same author writes similarly that " a market may be regarded as workably competitive when it is characterized by conditions that afford to buyers and sellers real opportunities to protect themselves, each against the other. " Workable competition " does not require that traders be present in such numbers and limited to such a size that none of them has a appreciable influence on supply, demand, or price; it does require that traders be sufficiently numerous to offer to buyers and to sellers, respectively, a considerable number of genuime alternatives in sources of supply and demand, so that, by shifting their purchases or sales, they can substantially influence quality, service and price."

the agreement itself (1). Thus the *Gegendstandstheorie* would as a logical consequence be transferred to Article 85(1) of the Rome Treaty. Deringer's theory would preclude any kind of rule of reason in the application of Article 85(1). He considers that whenever the number of firms which were acting independently has decreased, the degree of monopolization (*der* "*Monopolisierungsgrad*") has increased. (2) Article 85(1) would leave no room for assessing the strength of remaining competition.

The German test has also been adopted by a French scholar. "Every restriction of the individual firm's independence of decision must be regarded as being in restraint of competition." (3)

The analytical method of these authors, it is suggested, is misleading in its concentration on individual concepts and in its failure to view the various elements of the prohibition as a whole. Such an approach defeats the spirit of the Treaty.

A German critic of the views has pointed out that these sophisticated theories fall short of really preserving competition as the regulator of a free market system. Under them insignificant cartels will be hit while conspiracies of impressive magnitude, if purely informal, will be immune. The *Penn-Olin* case (4) gave him the opportunity to stress this inherent weakness of the German law. He objected to the attempt made by some writers to extend the concept of *Wettbewerbsbeschränkung* and the *Gegenstandstheorie* to Article 85(1) of the Rome Treaty on the ground that the two statutes were differently worded. (5)

---

(1) Deringer-Tessin, *EWG-Kartellrecht: Keine Freistellung fur Alleinvertriebsverträge mit absolutem Gebietschutz,* Comment on the Grundig-Consten case, AWD BB 332 (1964); Deringer, *Exclusive Agency Agreements with Territorial Protection under the EEC Antitrust Law,* 10 ANTITRUST BULL. 601 (1965).

(2) Deringer, *op. cit., supra,* note (1) at 109, WuW 865 (1962), referring to BAUMBACH-HEFERMEHL, WETTBEWERBS- und WARENZEICHENRECHT, 1231 (1960). This passage of the latter author (reproduced and quoted *supra,* Chapter II, note (2) at 77-78) does not, however, provide any support for the thesis advocated by Deringer.

(3) See BLAISE, LE STATUT DES ENTENTES ÉCONOMIQUES, 223 (1964) (my translation).

(4) United States v. Penn-Olin Chemical Co., 378 U.S. 158 (1964).

(5) Kurt Markert, *Gemeinschaftsunternehmen und Antitrustrecht,* AWD BB 243 and note 19 (1964).

8. - Arguments Against the Application of the German Theory to Article 85 of the Rome Treaty

A. - Linguistic Discrepancies Between Article 85(1) and Section 1 of the German Statute: Test of Anticompetitive " Object " or " Effect "

First, Section 1 of the German Act and Article 85 have different notions of restraint of competition. Where the German Act resorts to two concepts (" *Wettbewerbsbeschränkung* " and " *Marktbeeinflussung* "), the Rome Treaty mentions only restraint of competition. Where the German Act is satisfied by a contractual restriction and by a mere likelihood of market effect, the Rome Treaty requires an actual effect on competition at large or else an intent to bring it about. The equation of the German Act with Article 85(1) would deprive the alternative test of " object " or " effect " of any significance. In German law the " restraint of competition " (" *Wettbewerbsbeschränkung* ") has to be part of a binding agreement and thus is always intended, while on the other hand probability of market effect, not intent, is the test. (1)

B. - Inadequacies of the Gegenstandstheorie *in Interpreting Article 85. The Ban on Concerted Practices*

Second, while the German statute is built on the formality of the contract (conceived more as a written and binding piece of paper than as an informal gentleman's agreement), (2) the same is obviously not true of Article 85. Much more so than Section 1 of the German statute, Article 85 aims at substance

(1) See Chapter II, *supra,* at 92. According to Section 1 of the German Statute, there must be a reasonable probability of market effect. Thus the intent to affect market conditions is not sufficient. However when this intent exists, this may raise presumption that the market is likely to be affected. See BAUMBACH-HEFERMEHL, *op. cit.,* at 1242. In this way, Article 85(1) goes further than Section 1 of the German Statute. Accord, Deringer, *op. cit., supra,* note 1 at 109, WuW 867, 868 (1962).

(2) See *supra,* Chapter II, at 84-87.

and not a form. [1] By including *concerted practices* as a possible source of restraint of competition, the EEC Treaty has been generally regarded as borrowing from the American concept of *conspiracy*. [2] As the German Federal Cartel Office put it,

> In regard to the term concerted practices, as in the Anglo-American case-law defining conspiracy..., it will not be necessary that the enterprises concerned intend to enter into binding contractual relations; on the other hand it will not be sufficient that several enterprises show a consciously uniform behavior if there has not been an understanding. What is decisive is rather that several enterprises reach an understanding concerning their future economic behavior and act according to this plan, whether they act in uniformity or whether they act differently according to pre-determined patterns. [3]

Like a conspiracy, a concerted practice does not demand a contract in due form [4]: all that is required is a meeting of the minds. [5] Under Article 85(1), as under Section 1 of the Sherman Act, no express agreement, written or oral, is necessary to support a finding of concerted practice. [6] If we

---

(1) A similar formula has been applied by Chief Justice Hughes to the Sherman Act, Appalachian Coals, Inc. v. United States, 288 U.S. 344, 377 (1933).

(2) See on this question Deringer, *op. cit., supra*, note 1 at 109, WuW 798-799 (1962); OBERDORFER-GLEISS-HIRSCH, COMMON MARKET CARTEL LAW, 7-9 (1963); Gabriel, *Aufeinander abgestimmte Verhaltensweisen unter wettbewerbspolitischem Aspekt*, WuW 802 (1961); Gleiss, *Der Begriff der aufeinander abgestimmten Verhaltensweisen in Art. 85 EWG-Vertrag*, WuW 485 (1964); Heinrich, *Die "conscious parallelism" Doktrin des U.S. - Antitrustrechts und der Begriff "aufeinander abgestimmte Verhaltensweisen" in Art. 85 EWG-Vertrag*, WuW 95 (1965).

(3) 1961 BKartA. Rep. 61 (my translation).

(4) See NEALE, THE ANTITRUST LAWS OF THE U.S.A., 83 (1963), and *e.g.* James A. Rahl, *Conspiracy and the Antitrust Laws*, 44 ILL. L. REV. 743 (1953) and Turner, *The Definition of Agreement under the Sherman Act: Conscious Parallelism and Refusals to Deal*, 75 HARV. L. REV. 655 (1961-62); also references cited in OPPENHEIM, FEDERAL ANTITRUST LAWS, 224 footnote 4 (1959).

(5) In this respect, it is suggested that it is completely unrealistic to speak of notification of concerted practices, as does Regulation no. 17 [*Official Journal of the European Communities*, 204 (1962)]. If conspirators choose not to enter into an express and formal agreement, they do so precisely to escape discovery. Most of the restrictive schemes which fall under the category of concerted practices will probably not meet the requirements of Article 85(3). If this was not so, there would be no reason for the conspirators not to organize their action in a more formal and open way. However, it is interesting to note that Section 6(3) of the British Restrictive Trade Practices Act of 1956 subjects to registration any agreement or arrangement, whether or not it is intended to be enforceable. It seems that the purpose of this provision is to force gentlemen agreements into the open or to compel conspirators to drop their concerted practices. On this provision, see *Basic British Slag Ltd. v. Registrar of Trading Agreements*, and *Colvillies Ltd. v. Registrar of Trading Agreements*, L.R. 3 R. P. 178 (1962).

(6) See, among recent cases, the opinion of Circuit Judge Barnes in Esco Corp. v. United States, 340 F. 2d 1000, 1008 (9th Cir. 1965).

transfer the American notion of conspiracy to Article 85(1) of the Rome Treaty, as the German Federal Cartel Office suggests, it will be likewise sufficient that concerted action be contemplated and that firms conform to the arrangement. (1) This being so, it is difficult to perceive how the German theory of " restraint of competition " could be adequately used under Article 85(1), since it requires not only an express agreement but even a legally binding contract containing provisions which restrict the firm's freedom of action. (2) Article 85(1) and Section 1 of the Sherman Act have much wider scope than Section 1 of the German Act.

C. - Unlike the German Act, the Rome Treaty Does not Discriminate between Horizontal and Vertical Restraints of Trade

Third, the German statute establishes a basic distinction between vertical and horizontal agreements. In case of horizontal agreements, the statute extends to every contractual limitation of the traders' freedom of action while in the case of exclusive dealing arrangements, for instance, it is concerned with the restraint of competition in the market. (3) If the German system is to be transferred to Article 85(1), then this division should at least be respected. But Article 85(1) only recognizes a single notion of competition and thus the German distinction cannot be used in the interpretation of the Rome Treaty.

D. - The Prevention of Dominant Positions by Article 85(3)

Fourth, in order to be able to obtain an exemption under Article 85(3), an agreement restraining competition must not be such as to give the parties the power to exclude competition in respect of a substantial part of the goods concerned. Articles 85(1) and 85(3) both refer to the market effects of the

(1) Esco Corp. v. United States, 340 F. 2d 1000, 1008 (9th Cir. 1965).

(2) See *supra*, Chapter II, at 78-87.

(3) See *supra*, Chapter II, at 103-106.

restrictive agreement: between the test of " restraint of competition " and the test of Article 85(3) there is only a difference in degree.

Obviously, in Article 85(3) " competition " cannot mean the competitive freedom of individual traders in the German sense. However, certain leading authorities have suggested that Article 85(1) " is aimed not at the aggregate effect of the cartel agreement on the market, but at the exclusion of competition between the parties to the agreement themselves. " (1) On the other hand, the test of Article 85(3) goes " not to the extent of the competitive restraint as a matter of the internal relations between the parties, but to the effects upon the market. " (2) Such views imply that *every* suppression of competition between competing firms *inter se* is unlawful under Article 85(1), whatever its significance on the market and the strength of the remaining competition, while Article 85(3), in its negative requirement, would be directed at the market share of the cartelizing enterprises. Insignificant restrictive agreements would fall under the scope of Article 85(1), whereas cartels of some economic importance would never be in a position to obtain the approval of the EEC Commission. A cartel found to have a share of 25 % of a market could never meet the requirement of Article 85(3). Both Article 85(1) and Article 85(3) would thus receive a very narrow construction. This doctrine which is also inspired by the theories regarding Section 1 of the German Act must be rejected.

The clause of Article 85(3) can in my view best be compared with the nearly identical provision of Article 65 of the Coal and Steel Community Treaty. (3) The power to exclude competition is part of the definition of monopoly power developed

---

(1) See the submissions of Advocate General Roemer before the Court of Justice of the European Communities in the case 13/60, VIII Recueil de la Jurisprudence de la Cour, 239 (1962); 1 Common Market Law Reports, 127 (1962).

(2) Oberdorfer-Gleiss-Hirsch, *op. cit.*, 64.

(3) Article 65(2) of the ECSC Treaty provides that the High Authority shall authorize agreements to specialize in the production of, or to engage in the joint buying or selling of, specified products if it finds :—

...(c) that it [the agreement] is not capable of giving the enterprises concerned the power to determine prices or to control or limit the production or marketing of a substantial part of the products in question within the Common Market or of protecting them from effective competition by other enterprises within the Common Market.

by the United States Supreme Court in cases under Section 2 of the Sherman Act. [1] Power to control market prices and power to exclude competition are the hallmarks of monopoly. But this definition is valid for single firms as well as for cartels. Regarding Article 65(2) (*c*) the European Court of Justice has held that power to fix prices means power to fix prices arbitrarily without taking market conditions into account. [2] Cartels are prevented from achieving such a monopolistic power. This is also the purpose of Article 85(3). The difference between restraining competition and the power to exclude competition

---

(1) REPORT OF THE ATTORNEY GENERAL'S NATIOMAL COMMITTEE TO STUDY THE ANTITRUST LAWS, 43 (1955); Standard Oil of New Jersey v. United States, 221 U.S. 1 (1911); American Tobacco v. United States, 328 U.S. 781 (1946); United States v. Griffith, 334 U.S. 100 (1948); United States v. E.I. Du Pont de Nemours, 351 U.S. 377 (1956).

(2) In "*Geitling*" *Ruhrkohlen-Verkaufsgesellschaft m.b.H. and others v. High Authority* (case 13/60), the Court of Justice of the European Communities has distinguished price-fixing agreements where the group, although establishing prices in common, is not in a position to fix them independently from outside competition and price-fixing agreements which enable the group to dictate market prices arbitrarily. Two tests have been applied by the Court to ascertain the power to fix market prices. 1) *A test of structure.* The market share of the enterprises may be such as to raise the presumption that in the relevant market they have the power to dictate prices. Since the Court did not think this test was entirely sufficient it developed: 2) *A test of behavior.* One has here to investigate whether in past transactions the cartel took into account market factors to set its prices or whether it possessed a certain margin of discretion. See case 13/60, Court of Justice of the European Communities, July 17, 1962, VIII RECUEIL DE LA JURISPRUDENCE DE LA COUR, 169, 266 (1962); 1 COMMON MARKET LAW REPORTS, 113 (1962). On this important case, see *e.g.* M. Bye, *L'arrêt 13-6 du 18 Mai 1962 sur les Comptoirs de la Ruhr,* DROIT SOCIAL, 257 (1963) and BLAISE, *op. cit.,* at 382-393. In his submissions Advocate General Roemer has surprisingly rejected any reference to the American antitrust cases in his construction of the notion of "power to fix prices", because these cases had been decided under Section 2 of the Sherman Act and related to single enterprises dominating a market. Roemer claimed that price-fixing agreements are *per se* unlawful in American law [See VIII, RECUEIL DE LA JURISPRUDENCE DE LA COUR, 238 (1962)]. His opinion is erroneous. True, price-fixing schemes are *per se* offenses. But the issue was one of economic analysis. A case like *Appalachian Coals* shows that the United States Supreme Court has applied the same analysis to a loose-knit arrangement [Appalachian Coals Inc. v. United States, 288 U.S. 344 (1933)]. The Court held that the Sherman Act did not forbid cooperation among a small group, within a large competitive industry, where entry was easy and uncontrolled, in order to end "injurious [competitive] practices" and to improve the group's competitive position "*where the group must still meet effective competition in a fair market and neither seeks nor is able to effect a domination of prices.*" [REPORT OF THE ATTORNEY GENERAL COMMITTEE TO STUDY THE ANTITRUST LAWS, 23 (1955), emphasis supplied.] Whether or not Appalachian Coals has been superseded by the *per se* rule is irrelevant because it could still serve as an illustration of an economic analysis. But in effect, and despite Roemer's erroneous comparison, the European Court of Justice applied a definition very close to the American theory.

is essentially one of *degree.* The limits to the power which can be obtained by cartelization are indicated by Article 85(3): a monopolistic position shall prevent the enforcement agency from exempting a cartel under Article 85(3). As to the words " substantial proportion of the goods concerned " in Article 85(3), they have in my view the following meaning. Because of the existence of particular isolated markets, the group making the cartel agreement can enjoy a monopolistic position only in a limited area of the Community territory. This, however, might not be sufficient reason to refuse an exemption. The goods distributed in the area where the group is dominant must in turn constitute a substantial proportion of the total amount of the goods of this type distributed within the Community as a whole. Thus Article 85(3) sets up two different tests in the same sentence. Monopoly power will not necessarily preclude an exemption; and only those cartels which dominate a vast part of the Common Market are prohibited absolutely. But this does not solve the preliminary problem: how much restraint is necessary to come within the scope of Article 85(1)? By requiring an actual effect on competition, Article 85(1) implies at least that something must be changed in the economic structure. A restraint which has but a theoretical impact is not covered. " Competition " in Articles 85(1) and (3) means market competition. In order to be covered by Article 85(1), a cartel must in the first place have an impact on market conditions. This does not mean that the group making the agreement needs to be in a position to *control* the market prices or a substantial part of the commodity. But it does mean that the group must be able to exercise an effective *influence* over the market.

E. - Market Competition Is the Policy Behind Article 85(1); e.g., *Price Information Agreements, Joint Ventures and the* Grundig-Consten *Understanding on the Trade-Mark Gint*

The competition which Article 85 of the Rome Treaty seeks to protect is the same as the competition with which the policy of the Sherman Act is concerned: it is competition at large as the regulating factor of the free market and it is not necessarily synonymous with the freedom of action of the individual traders. Restraints, actual or intended, prohibited by Article 85(1) are only those which are so substantial as to affect market conditions. (1)

Under the Rome Treaty as well as under the Sherman Act, not every restraint of trade in a literal sense amounts to a restriction of competition in the market. (2) It is possible to conceive an agreement between competitors which contains certain restrictive features and which nevertheless will not be regarded as producing a significant anticompetitive effect on the market. (3) On the other hand, there are schemes which, although free from any explicitly restrictive provision, can be found to have as their purpose or effect the hampering of the competitive process. An example is the open competition plan held unlawful in *American Column and Lumber Co. v. United States* which had as its avowed purpose merely the dissemination of production and market condition statistics. (4) There was no definite agreement between the participants to abridge their freedom to produce and to establish prices according to their own judgment. But in its actual operation, the plan provided reports giving the view of each member on future market conditions and furnished significant suggestions respecting both future prices and production. The effect of this was to induce members to cooperate in restricting production and in demanding higher prices. To that extent, the plan was as effective as an explicit and binding agreement to fix prices and curtail production, and was held to constitute an unlawful restraint of competition.

The broad and general language used by the Rome Treaty shows that its framers meant to deal with competitive realities,

---

(1) *Cf.* Apex Hosiery v. Leader, 310 U.S. 469, 500-501 (1940). This case, however, applies too narrow a test in that it speaks only of market *prices.*

(2) See Niederleithinger, Comment on the Judgment of the District Court of Mannheim (*Voma-Exquisit*), AWD BB 62 (1965). See *infra,* this chapter at 152-154.

(3) See for instance, the common selling agency agreement held unlawful by the Courts of Appeals of Berlin in the *Bockhorner Klinker* case, judgment of the Kammergericht, October 16, 1964, WuW/E OLG 709, WuW 235 (1965). For discussion of this case, see *supra,* chapter II, at 98-99.

(4) American Column and Lumber Co. v. United States, 257 U.S. 377 (1921).

and not mere words. (1) To defeat this policy by an excessively legalistic formalism would be easy. For instance, the legality of a joint venture under Article 85(1) will not be dependent, as under Section 1 of the German Act, (2) upon the presence of an express agreement not to compete between the collaborating firms. The test will be whether the effect on competition is significant. It must be determined whether the joint venture has the same effect as a market-sharing agreement. A theory like that which underlies Section 1 of the German Act would lead the enforcement agency to catch only all the small fry and to lose sight of the most dangerous concerted practices. Contracts of no substantial economic significance would come within Article 85(1) as long as they contained some restrictive provisions; on the other hand, informal agreements distorting competitive conditions would be able to escape, provided they did not legally restrict the firms' independence of decision.

After the decision of the EEC Commission in the *Grundig-Consten* case, a proponent of the " *Gegenstandstheorie* " objected to the doctrine applied by the EEC Commission in regard to the use of the trade-mark Gint. (3) In his view, there was in this agreement no express provision which restrained the freedom of either Grundig or Consten. It will be recalled that Grundig, a German firm, had given Consten, a French company, the exclusive right to distribute its products in France and had transferred to the French company the right to register the supplementary trade-mark Gint. (4) The competitive importation by unauthorized French firms of the genuime products bearing such marks could in this way be stopped by an action for infringement of the trade-mark. It is true that the agreement pursuant to which Consten had registered the trademarkt Gint in France did not contain any provision restricting other firms' ability to compete. But the purpose of the agreement was to

(1) These words are used by Justice Clark in Times Picayune Pub. Co. v. United States, 345 U.S. 594, 615 (1953).

(2) See Kurt Market, *op. cit.*, at 243 and note (19).

(3) Deringer, *Exclusive Agency Arrangements with Territorial Protection under the EEC Antitrust Laws*, 10 ANTITRUST BULL. 602 (1965).

(4) Decision of the EEC Commission, Sept. 23, 1964, *Official Journal of the European Commnities*, 2545 (1964) and 1 CCH COMMON MARKET REPORTER, § 7026.

make more effective the exclusive rights of distribution granted to Consten: the parties obviously intended to take advantage of the territorial rights derived from the trade-mark registration. Consten was in effect protected against parallel imports by French pirates who bought Grundig products in Germany. [1] The EEC Commission correctly found that the purpose of the agreement was to implement the closed territorial system of distribution organized by Grundig; its effect was likewise to suppress any intra-brand competition. Whether this arrangement provided for restrictions of the contracting parties' freedom of action was not really relevant. What was decisive was rather the actual and intended effect on third parties. [2] Deringer, advocating the German theories, expressed his apprehensions:—

> If the effect alone of contracts were decisive, almost all forms of business cooperation, to the extent that they related to commerce between the Member States, would run the risk of being prohibited by Article 85(1) of the Treaty and invalid under Article 85(2) of the Treaty, even if they contained no kind of obligations of the parties. [3]

The error of this author was to equate the notion of " *Wettbewerbsbeschränkung* " under Section 1 of the German Act and the concept of " restraint of competition " under Article 85(1) of the Rome Treaty. But as Article 85(1) has a much

---

(1) This case should be compared with United States v. Guerlain, Inc. (and Parfums Corchay and Lanvin Parfums), 155 F. Supp. 77 (S.D.N.Y. 957) in which a similar factual situation was involved. The registration of the trade-mark by the American Company was also the means used to prevent parallel imports. See Oppenheim, The Federal Antitrust Laws, 1010-1011 (1959) and the references cited. It is necessary to stress that I am not relying on this case as an authority but only for comparison with the facts at issue in the *Grundig-Consten* case. For in Guerlain, after a successful prosecution of these points in the District Court, and before argument of the appeals in the Supreme Court, the Government moved in the Supreme Court to vacate the judgments in order that, on remand, it might move for dismissals. [See 358 U.S. 914 (1958)]. On remand the District Court held that the decision of the Department of Justice to abandon suits was a decision of policy within its discretion and the motion to dismiss was granted but, inasmuch as defendants would thereby be deprived of an opportunity to prevent an appeal, dismissal would be with prejudice. See United States v. Guerlain, Inc.; United States v. Parfums Cordoy, Inc.; United States v. Lanvin Parfums, Inc., 172 F. Supp. 107.

(2) See the submissions of the Advocate General in the cases 56 and 58/64, Consten-Grundig v. EEC Commission, 2 CCH Common Market Reporter, §§ 8046 at 7669.

(3) Deringer, *op. cit.*, 602.

wider ambit than the German Act, those who support such ideas run the risk of finding out one day that Article 85 of the Rome Treaty was a " sleeping giant ". (1)

9. - The Test of " Purpose " or " Effect " in Article 85(1). - Its Use in the American Cases

The lack of legislative history makes it difficult to retrace the origin of the formula " purpose of effect ". (2) It is used neither by the German GWB nor by Article 65 of the Coal and Steel Community Treaty. (3) Among the European statutes, only Article 59*bis* of the French Price Ordinance No. 45-1483 of June 30, 1945, is phrased in nearly identical words, since it strikes down " every concerted action... which has the object or may have the effect of interfering with full competition... ". But the test seems to be not whether an actual restraint has occurred but whether it is probable, or even merely possible. And thus the similarity is not complete. (4)

Without asserting unequivocally that the origin of the test laid down by Article 85 is to be found in American antitrust law, I can at least point to the identity of standards. Apart from the *per se* violations, Section 1 of the Sherman Act, as construed under the Rule of Reason, strikes down a restraint only if it actually has an adverse effect on competition or is intended to have such an effect.

This test was part of the Rule of Reason formulated by Chief Justice White in *Standard Oil* (5) and *American Tobacco.* (6)

---

(1) Statement of Justice Burton in respect to the original Section 7 of the Clayton Act, United States v. E.I. Du Pont de Nemours, 353 U.S. 586, 611 (1957).

(2) Indications regarding the discussions which led to the present language of Article 85 are contained in Ellis, *op. cit., supra,* note (3) at 111.

(3) Article 65(1) forbids agreements between enterprises, (...) and all concerted practices *tending,* directly or indirectly, to prevent, restrict or distort the normal operation of competition within the Common Market. It is very difficult to determine whether the verb " to tend " is taken to refer to the effect or to the object of the agreements or to both. See however, BLAISE, *op. cit.*, 174.

(4) On this question, see BLAISE, *op. cit.*, 26-27 and 173.

(5) Standard Oil of New Jersey v. United States, 221 U.S. 1 (1911).

(6) United States v. American Tobacco, 221 U.S. 106 (1911).

In this latter case, the Chief Justice spoke of inherent nature, effect or evident purpose.

In *White Motor Co. v. United States,* Justice Douglas restating the doctrine of the Court said that:—

> Horizontal restraints like " group boycotts, or concerted refusal by traders to deal with other traders " ... are naked restraints of trade with no purpose except stifling of competition. A vertical territorial limitation may or may not have that *purpose* or *effect.* (1)

The very same theory was also applied by the District Judge in *United States v. Imperial Chemical Industries* when he referred to the settled law that

> Joint manufacturing ventures, even in domestic markets, are not made unlawful *per se* by the Sherman Act, but become unlawful only if their purpose or their effect is to restrain trade or to monopolize. (2)

This alternative test for unlawfulness of " wrongful purpose " or " harmful effect " is typical of the American antitrust law and is often repeated. (3) Whenever an American Court refers to the object of a conspiracy, it is referring to its purpose or intent. (4) " Object " is not necessarily synonymous with the terms of an explicit agreement. The Court will scrutinize the objective pursued by the concerns beyond the terms of the agreement. Far form being satisfied by the letter of a contract, the Courts will look at the ultimate motives of the enterprises involved. This is done, for instance, under the *primary purpose* doctrine applied in the field of trade-mark and patent licensing.

In *Denison Mattress Factory v. Spring-Air Company,* the United States Court of Appeals, having to consider the legality

---

(1) White Motor Co. v. United States, 372 U.S. 253, 263 (1963).

(2) United States v. Imperial Cheminal Industries, 100 F. Supp. 504, 557 (SDNY 1951).

(3) See for instance Mason City Tent v. Clapper, 144 F. Supp. 754, 768 (D.C. W.D. Missouri 1956) where the court said: " A conspiracy of combination having as its *object* or *effect* a restraint of interstate trade and commerce, whether accomplished by legal or illegal means falls within the orbit of the Sherman Act and is condemned thereby. " Emphasis supplied.

(4) This is for instance the sense in which the Court spoke of the " objects " of the agreements in United States v. National Lead Co., 63 F. Supp. 513 (SDNY 1945). Affirmed 332 U.S. 319 (1947).

of trade-mark licensing arrangements which provided for a division of trade territory between the licensees, ruled that:—

> If the *primary purpose*, however disguised, is to stifle competitors and to create a monopoly, then the agreement or contract is struck down. However, the cases seem to follow the principle that if the *primary purpose* of the contract is lawful, *e.g.*, to protect one in the fruits of his labor, and if the arrangement was actuated by or could be explained on the basis of legitimate *business justification* as opposed to the desire to increase market control through economic leverage, then the court will generally hold *any incidental restraint of trade, not harmful to the public, to be lawful.* (1)

Thus a lawful purpose may save a restraint of trade if no significant impact on the market is found. When no actual anticompetitive effect has been produced and when only the purpose remains to be calculated, business considerations will be taken into account. Although the *terms* of the contracts in *Denison Mattress* were clearly *restrictive,* since trade territories were allocated among the contracting parties, the Court did not confine its analysis to this. It looked, beyond the letter of the agreement, to the primary purpose of the contract. In *Denison Mattress,* the Court concluded that division of territory was not the ultimate purpose of the contract, and consequently upheld the restrictions contained in the licences. The same " ancillary-primary " test was also applied recently by the FTC in the matter of *Carvel* and led to the same conclusion. (2) Restraints of trade were there permitted because the covenant embodying them was held merely ancillary to the principal purpose of a lawful contract. Rooted in the old *United States v. Addyston Pipe and Steel Co.*, (3) this doctrine was also relied upon by the United States Supreme Court in *Timken.* (4) But there the trade-mark provisions of the agreements were, on the contrary, found subsidiary and secondary to the central purpose of allocating trade territories.

---

(1) Denison Mattress Factory v. Spring Air Company, 308 F. 2d 403, 408 (5th Cir. 1962). Emphasis supplied.

(2) In the matter of Carvel Corp., FTC Docket no. 8574 (decision of the Commission, July 19, 1965), 3 CCH Trade Regulation Reporter, § 17 298.

(3) United States v. Addyston Pipe and Steel Co., 85 Fed. 271 (6th Cir. 1898); aff'd 175 U.S. 211 (1899).

(4) Timken Roller Bearing Co. v. United States, 341 U.S. 593 (1950).

Under Article 85 of the Rome Treaty as under the Sherman Act, ascertaining the purpose of an agreement or measuring its anticompetitive effect is essentially a factual question. When deciding the legality of the use of the trade-mark, Gint, by Grundig, the EEC Commission indeed adopted an American approach. (1) It pointed out the that the function of this supplementary trade-mark was solely to protect the exclusive representatives against " parallel imports ". Clearly, the EEC Commission looked at the purpose of the contracting parties, disguised under an apparently innocent arrangement, and found that this trade-mark agreement was not needed to identify the goods that alreardy bore the mark Grundig. Although " the said agreement contained no restriction, either expressed or tacit, of the contracting parties ", (2) it was treated as a violation of Article 85(1) because it was *designed*, by securing the highly effective protection of a trade-mark, (3) to serve as a complementary instrumentality to prevent competition. A subjective analysis of the intention of the parties supported the finding of the EEC Commission. The origin and the history of the trade-mark Gint were listed to show a central purpose harmful to competition. This case shows that in Article 85 of the Rome Treaty, the concept of " object " is the same as that of intent or purpose in Sherman Act cases.

10. Review of the EEC Commission Decisions: Approach to the Problem of Restraint of Competition

A French writer has claimed that Article 85(1) should be taken as an abstract proposition of law with a definite content, while a certain margin of discretion should be involved in the

(1) See this chapter, *supra*, at 131-133.

(2) See DERINGER, *op. cit.*, at 601. On the relationship between the German anticartel law and the trade-mark law, see FIKENTSCHER, *Die Warenzeichenlizenz im Recht der Wettbewerbsbeschränkungen* in DIE WARENZEICHENLIZENZ, 412, 462 (1963).

(3) On the relationship between trade-mark law and the EEC Treaty, see among others, M. Waelbroeck, *Trademark Problems in the European Common Market*, 54, TRADEMARK REP. 333 (1964) and Heiseke, *Die warenrechtliche Problematik der Entscheidung der EWG-Kommission im Falle Grundig-Consten*, NJW 1409 (1965).

evaluation of the conditions set up by Article 85(3). (1) The significance of a restraint would not be judged in relation to the particular market under investigation; Article 85(1) would spell out a *per se* rule. This writer thought in terms of the approach to Section 1 of the German Act. One will recall that in German law the notion of " restraint of competition " can be defined abstractly, while the test of market effect provides the basis for a limited rule of reason. In my view, this approach cannot be adopted towards Article 85(1) of the Rome Treaty. For the same reason that it seems inconceivable to refuse to construe reasonably the concept of restraint of trade, it is hardly defensible to say that Article 85(1) enunciates a test which can be mechanically applied. It is common sense that one cannot protect competition by declining to determine in a case-by-case analysis when it is restrained. A review of the cases decided so far by the EEC Commission may enable us to say which of these conflicting approaches has been followed by the enforcement agency. (2)

---

(1) BLAISE, *op. cit.*, at 223.

(2) I will review all the cases decided so far by the Commission. Some of them do not elucidate in any way the concept of restraint of trade. The negative clearence granted to the *Dutch Engineers and Contractors Association* (Commission decision of October 22, 1964, *Official Journal of the European Communities*, 2761, 1964) raised mainly the issue of the extraterritorial application of Article 85. This case involved an agreement providing for cooperation and pooling with respect to large construction contracts to be fulfilled outside the Common Market. The distributorship agreement for which *Mertens and Straet* were granted a negative clearance (Commission decision of June 1, 1964, Official Journal of the European Communities, 1426, 1964), did not provide for any restriction whatsoever of the firm's freedom of trade. More interesting are the few horizontal agreements which the Commission has disposed of by preliminary notice to the parties under Regulation no. 17, Article 15(6) that the Commission considers the agreements involved to be illegal and not subject to exemption, followed by termination of the agreements by the parties (See EEC Commission, Eighth General Report on the Activities of the Community, June 1965 at 70-72 and 2 CCH COMMON MARKET REPORTER, §§ 9012, 9018, 9024 and 9066). It is impossible however to determine exactly the economic situation which was under investigation, merely through the press releases from the EEC Commission official spokesman. Thus it is very difficult to draw any certain conclusion as to the construction of Article 85(1) which was adopted by the Commission. One of these cases, however, is pending before the European Court of Justice. It concerns the "*Noordwijks-Cement Accord*". By a letter of January 3, 1966, the EEC Commission gave preliminary notice of illegality to a price-fixing and market sharing cartel operated by Belgian, German and Dutch cement producers (see 2 CCH COMMON MARKET REPORTER, § 9085). Pursuant to Article 15(6) of Regulation no. 17, the Commission informed the firms concerned that their agreement fell under the prohibition of Article 85(1) and was not eligible for an exemption under Article 85(3). The purpose and effect of this notice was to put an end to the immunity against penalties which the firms

A. - The Convention Faïence: *a Collective Exclusive Dealing Agreement*

The first case which was formally decided by the EEC Commission involved a horizontal agreement which was terminated by a mere recommendation to cease and desist. (1) This cartel agreement can be characterized as a collective exclusive dealing agreement. (2) Under the so-called "Convention Faïence", manufacturers of tiles united with distributors of the same products. The manufacturers were committed to supply only recognized customers, who in turn undertook to purchase all their requirements of the products listed in the agreement from the member-manufacturers.

At the manufacturing and distribution level, the agreement was sponsored by the trade associations of the respective groups.

---

obtain after filing their agreement. After such a preliminary notice, the enterprises are again subject to fines if they persist in their violation. In that case, appeal has been brought by the firms against this letter which is alleged to be a decision within the definition of the Treaty (see the cases 8-66, 9-66, 10-66 and 11-66 pending before the European Court of Justice, *Official Journal of the European Communities*, March 23, 1966, no. 52 at 738 and April 2, 1966, no. 63 at 913-915). This case, which will be the first concerning a horizontal agreement to be decided by the Court, is obviously of great significance not only because of the large number of firms involved (about 50), but also because of the legal issues raised. It is to be expected that the Court of Justice will have to construe the test spelled out in Article 85(1). As far as my thesis is concerned, the question is whether the Court will adopt a mechanical approach toward Article 85(1) or whether it will impose on the Commission the duty to collect economic data to show that competition has been substantially restrained. Is this latter condition a prerequisite for the application of Article 85(1)? In this thesis, I discuss this question mainly in connection with vertical agreements, but only because the European antitrust policy until now has placed primary emphasis on such arrangements. Naturally, my discussion will also apply to horizontal agreements.

(1) Recommendation of the EEC Commission of July 24, 1963, Faïence, WuW 54 (1964) and 1 CCH COMMON MARKET REPORTER, § 7023. According to Art. 3(3) of REGULATION, no. 17, the EEC Commission may, before making a decision finding a violation of Art. 85, address to the enterprises involved a recommendation to cease and desist. The main characteristic of this procedure is the absence of publicity. Unlike decisions (Art. 21 of REGULATION no. 17), recommendations must not be published. By modifying their behavior as requested by the EEC Commission, the enterprises are able to avoid publicity. In the *Faïence* case, the recommendation was, however, published by a German periodical (WIRTSCHAFT UND WETTBEWERB).

(2) It is interesting to note that an identical agreement was held unlawful by the United States Supreme Court as early as 1902. [Montague and Co. v. Lowry, 193 U.S. 38 (1902)]. NEALE, *op. cit., supra*, at 67. This type of agreement seems fairly common in the Common Market: Building materials and sanitary ware agreements mentioned in the 8th GENERAL REPORT ON THE ACTIVITIES OF THE COMMUNITY, EEC Commission, June, 1965, 70-72.

The EEC Commission noted that the agreement stipulated a certain market behavior for both manufacturers and dealers. The effect was found to be anticompetitive within the Common Market. The freedom of choice of the contracting parties was abridged because recognized customers were refused access to other sources of supply, a limitation which was not insignificant, and conversely, the member manufacturers saw their outlet possibilities reduced since they were prevented from supplying dealers outside the cartel. But there were perhaps still other determinative grounds, for the agreement had an adverse effect on third parties. By the cartel, independent manufacturers in other countries of the EEC were foreclosed from selling to the important outlets represented by the 900 recognized dealers, while the cartel deprived outside distributors of possible sources of supply, and this produced in the language of the Commission, a *perceptible influence on the market conditions.*

The reasoning of the Commission reveals the German influence upon its theory of " restraint of competition ". It was emphasized first that the agreement abridged the freedom of trade of both the manufacturers and the dealers who were members of the cartel, and that this was accomplished by a contract creating obligations. The EEC Commission did not end its analysis there. It pointed to the effect on market conditions, using the German terminology, *fühlbare Beeinflussung der Marktverhältnisse,* and found preemption of outlets by the manufacturers and of sources of supply by the dealers as the essence of the retraint. The restriction of the freedom of the cartel members was thus merely the source of the anticompetitive result. But the approach was typical of the German system—looking first at the contractual restriction put on the liberty of the parties and then at the market effect. The reasoning of the EEC Commission was more legalistic than economic. The Commission did not investigate the industry as a whole to scrutinize the market power of the cartel, or to show that the agreement had raised barriers to entry. No statistical evidence was adduced. " Faïence " was a good case for the EEC Commission: this is precisely why the lack of a more extensive market inquiry may be regretted. Such an investigation would have supported more strongly the conclusion that the purpose of the agreement was exclusionary and the effect harmful to competition. As it stands, however, this case demonstrates that the application of Article 85(1) cannot be decided abstractly. On the contrary, such a decision calls for a factual analysis.

B. - Groxfillex*: a Case of Prohibittion on Reexport to the Common Market; the Notion of Perceptible Restraint of Competition*

A negative clearance [1] granted to Grosfillex indicated that the EEC Commission might adopt a rule of reason approach. Although it found that an enterprise was limited in its ability to compete within the Common Market, the Commission held that this was not sufficient make the agreement violative of Article 85(1). Because of the peculiar facts of the case, the restriction could not produce any discernible effect upon the market conditions.

A French producer of plastic products, Grosfillex, had given an exclusive franchise to a Swiss firm, Fillistdorf, for the distribution of its products in Switzerland. In turn this distributor had undertaken not to sell outside his assigned territory (which amounted to a close territory), and to refrain from handling competitive products (which was an exclusive dealing term). The firms purchasing from the exclusive distributor were not prohibited, however, from re-exporting to the Common Market. The EEC Commission held that, under the circumstances of the case, competition within the Common Market was not restrained in a " perceptible " way, nor was such restraint the purpose of the contract. This holding was based upon two grounds. First, re-export from Switzerland to the Common Market was unlikely because the goods would be subject to two tariffs. Secondly, there were in the relevant market for plastic products a substantial number of producers of similar

(1) Pursuant to Article 2 of Regulation no. 17, the EEC Commission has the power to give a so-called " negative clearance ", indicating that on the facts disclosed to it, it does not think that a given agreement comes within the prohibition of Article 85(1).

Common Market. Moreover, competitive conditions existed at the distibution level. [1]

Obviously, the re-export probibition imposed on Fillistdorf was in " restraint of trade " in the literal sense, since Fillistdorf was restricted in its freedom to sell where it pleased. But the facts of the case were such that this covenant could not have any serious effect on general competitive conditions within the Common Market. The term " perceptible " undoubtedly found its origin in the decision of the German Federal Supreme Court in the *Spar* case. [2] Under Section 1 of the German Act, only those restrictions which are likely to affect market conditions are unlawful. Section 1 resorts, as already explained, to two separate tests. Under Article 85(1) of the Rome Treaty, however, this qualification is completely superfluous and even misleading if the starting point is that of the American Rule of Reason—that not every agreement not to compete is tantamount to a restraint of competition.

C. - Vitapro*: An Example of An Ancillary Covenant not to Compete*

The *Vitapro* case, where the EEC Commission granted another negative clearance, related to what are treated in American antitrust terms as covenants not to compete ancillary to a sale of business and good will. [3] [4] Nicholas Frères, a French firm, had acquired the assets of Vitapointe Laboratories which

(1) Decision of the EEC Commission of March 11, 1964, *Official Journal of the European Communities*, 915 (1964); 1 CCH COMMON MARKET REPORTER, § 2412; 3 COMMON MARKET LAW REPORTS 237 (1964). On this decision, see the following comments: Kirschstein, WuW/E EV 92, WuW 560 (1964); Gleiss-Hirsch, *Das erste Negativtest der EWG-Kommission*, NJW, 1604 (1964); Tessin, *EWG-Kommission erteilt erstes Negativtest,* AWD BB, 114 (1964); Fulda, *The First Antitrust Decisions of the Commission of the EEC*, 65 COLUM. L. REV., 625 (1965).

(2) See Kirschstein, *op. cit.*, WuW 561 (1964).

(3) Decision of the EEC Commission, July 30, 1964, *Official Journal of the European Communities* 2287 (1964); 3 COMMON MARKET LAW REPORTS, 505 (1964). For a comment, see Fulda, *op. cit.* and Kirschstein, WuW/e EV 109, WuW 89, 90 (1965).

(4) See Fulda, *op. cit.*, at 630 referring to United States v. Addyston Pipe and Steel Co., 85 Fed. 271 (6th Cir. 1898), *aff'd* 175 U.S. 211 (1899).

held various patents, trade-marks and designs in the hairdressing line. Vitapointe had a licensing and exclusive dealership agreement with Vitapro, a British corporation, for the distribution of Vitapointe products in Great Britain and other territories outside the Common Market. The agreement for which negative clearance was granted was one by which Nicholas sold to Vitapro part of the assets bough from Vitapointe *viz.* the clientele of Vitapointe in third countries (especially the countries of the Commonwealth), the right to use the Vitapointe trade-name in that area as well as various patents, trade-marks and designs registered in these countries in the name of Vitapointe. This sale of business and good will contained several restrictive covenants. Vitapro agreed not to use the trade-name " Vitapointe "outside the assigned territory. Nicholas undertook on his part to refrain from using the same trade-name in the assigned territory of the other party. Moreover, both parties were committed not to manufacture or to sell for five years any other product used for hairdressing in the territory reserved to the other. This undertaking, however, did not cover products bought from a third party or manufactured and sold pursuant to a licensing agreement with a third party.

This arrangement might have been analysed as the disguising of a division of market between Vitapro and Nicholas as a sale of business and good will. This was a question of fact—what were the firms really doing? The EEC Commission found that the main purpose of the arrangement was to sell the assets of Vitapointe for exploitation in third countries. This *purpose* in itself was, of course, lawful. But the Commission went on to look at the *effect* of the transaction. Two provisions—the two prohibitions imposed on the British corporation, Vitapro—restricted the ability of this firm to compete within the Common Market. First, Vitapro was prohibited from manufacturing and selling hairdressing products within the Common Market. But this prohibition was limited to a five-year period, and products bought from third parties, or manufactured under a licence from a third party, were excepted. Secondly, Vitapro was barred indefinitely from using the assigned trade-mark within the Common Market, apparently because of the division of business of the former Vitapointe firm.

The EEC Commission found no anticompetitive effect within the Common Market since the hair products which these two covenants embraced were in competition within the Common Market with a large number of similar products, and since Nicholas was not among the largest enterprises in this sector, and at any rate, was facing vigorous competition from numerous firms selling hairdressing products.

The reasons relied upon by the EEC Commission are similar to those considered in *Grosfillex.* Although the covenants imposed on Vitapro had the effect of excluding this firm as a competitor within the Common Market, this exclusion could not, under the circumstances of the case, substantially affect competition. The relevant market was not limited to the products bearing the trade-mark " Vitapointe ". Numerous other firms were competing vigorously in the relevant line of business.

This is a genuine rule of reason analysis. In *Vitapro* as in *Grosfillex,* the EEC Commission seemed to adhere to the American proposition, that not every restraint which a trader accepts on his ability to compete is likely to cause a substantial lessening of market competition.

D. - Grundig-Consten*: a Vertical Division of Territory Between Grundig Dealers*

Those who agree with Justice Holmes that " great cases, like hard cases, make bad law ", (1) may find some support in the most important decision so far of the EEC Commission. (2)

(1) In his dissent in Northern Securities v. United States, 193 U.S. 197, 400 (1904).

(2) Decision of September 23, 1964, *Official Journal of the European Communities,* 2545 (1964); 1 CCH COMMON MARKET REPORTER, § 2743. On the EEC Commission decision, see *e.g.* De Keyser, *Territorial Restrictions and Export Prohibitions under the United States and the Common Market Antitrust Laws,* 2 COMMON MARKET LAW REVIEW, 271, 299 (1964-1965); Deringer-Tessin, *EWG-Kartellrecht: keine Freistellung fur Alleinvertriebsverträge mit absolutem Gebietsschutz,* AWD BB 329 (1964); Deringer, *Exclusive Agency Agreements with Territorial Protection under the EEC Antitrust Laws,* 10 ANTITRUST BULL. 601 (1965). The decision of the Commission has been challenged by Grundig and Consten before the European Court of Justice. See the cases no. 56/64 and 58/64, Grundig and Consten v. EEC Commission, 2 CCH COMMON MARKET REPORTER, § 8046. For a discussion of the Court's opinion, see *infra* this chapter at 156-166.

Grundig-Consten had all the attributes of a great case. Thanks to a closed territorial system of distribution, Consten, a French dealer, who had been granted by Grundig, a German manufacturer, an exclusive distributorship in France, had been able to sell the products under agreement at a much higher price than German wholesalers. Such a system in effect deprived consumers of the benefits expected from a common market. Another French firm, UNEF, had proceeded to buy directly from German wholesalers and to undercut the recognized exclusive agent, and was therefore sued by Consten for unfair competition. In its defense, it claimed that the distribution system initiated by Grundig was in volation of Article 85(1), and complained to the EEC Commission. The Court of Appeal of Paris suspended judgment pending the decision of the European authority. The EEC Commission held the distribution system to be illegal under Article 85(1) and decided not to grant any exemption under Article 85(3).

This case illustrates that private agreements between firms to regulate competition can completely defeat the policy which the Rome Treaty is designed to foster in the interest of all European consumers: private barriers were, as a matter of fact, replacing tariff barriers. On the merits, it is doubtful whether the decision could have been otherwise. Grundig, as well as Consten, had a bad case. The distribution system at stake, with its completely closed territories, could only enable each distributor in his specified area to charge higher prices, and it undoubtedly had this purpose. The role played by UNEF, the outsider, showed the importance of intrabrand competition.

On the other hand, the reasoning of the EEC Commission is not completely clear. At least, three kinds of restraints of trade were found: the exclusive franchise given to Consten for France, the exclusive dealing clause on the part of Consten, and his undertaking not to sell outside his assigned territory. While all the arguments of the Commission were directed essentially against the closed territorial system, the decision itself condemned the agreement as a whole. While it was the entire system of Grundig distribution (the export prohibition to France was contained in the agreements with the German wholesalers) which was detrimental to competition, the contract between Grundig and Consten alone was attacked by the Commission. (1) Unlike the Department of Justice in *White Motor Co. v. United States*, (2) the EEC Commission was not challenging the whole group of contracts between a manufacturer and his dealers. These factors both obscure and weaken the scope of the case. It is difficult to ascertain whether the EEC Commission held that every restraint of intrabrand competition by virtue of a closed territorial system violates Article 85(1), or whether only the particular arrangements at issue were bad because they were intended to prevent any intrabrand competition and actually had that effect (great emphasis was placed by the Commission upon the differences between the German and the French prices for Grundig products). Later cases involving exclusive franchises and the general approach of the EEC Commission toward the concept of restraint of competition indicate, however, that every contract by which an enterprise limits itself, in its competitive freedom, or more generally in its trade, will be considered to fall under Article 85(1). The decision of the Commission in *Grundig-Consten* deserves further criticism because it failed to determine, for purposes of Article 85(1), whether the distribution system set up by Grundig was not in fact the only possible way to promote *interbrand* competition. By *regulating* the competition between the sellers of the affected product, the challenged system might in fact have served to make possible a vigorous competition between that product and competing brands. (3) No evidence was adduced, for instance, to show the market share of Grundig in France. The Commission did not make any sophisticated market analysis. To that extent, its decision is an illustration of a *per se* approach.

---

(1) Deringer-Tessin, *op. cit.*, at 332.

(2) White Motor Co. v. United States, 373 U.S. 253 (1963).

(3) *Cf.* White Motor Co. v. United States, 372 U.S. 253 (1963) and Sandura Co. v. FTC, 339 F. 2d 847 (6th Cir. 1964).

E. - Blondel, Hummel *and* Jallate*: a Literal and Mechanical Approach to the Definition of Restraint of Trade. Exclusive Dealing Promises and Exclusive Franchises Inherently Violate Article 85(1). The Prospect of a Group Exemption Regulation*

Three decisions issued by the EEC Commission in the area of exclusive franchises confirm this doctrine regarding the meaning of " restraint of competition ". These are the *Blondel, Hummel* and *Jallate* cases. [1] In these three cases, the firms, which had registered their contracts, were granted an exemption under Article 85(3). In my view, this, however, is not the decisive point. Granted that the restraints were finally approved by the enforcement agency, what seems more interesting is the reasoning followed by the Commission in asserting in the first place that such agreements came within Article 85(1). In that respect, all three decisions are built on the same pattern and depart from the approach initiated by the *Grosfillex* and *Vitapro* negative clearances. Each case concerned an agreement by which a manufacturer in one Member State appointed a dealer in another Member State and granted him an exclusive selling right (*exclusive franchise*). Such agreements fall, according to the EEC Commission, within the scope of Article 85(1) since they have as their purpose the restraint of competition within the Common Market; it was even stressed that this was their *primary* purpose.

The position of the EEC Commission regarding these restrictive clauses had, of course, been known for a long time. [2]

(1) Blondel, decision of July 8, 1965, *Official Journal of the European Communities* 2194 (1965) and 2 CCH Common Market Reporter, § 9049; Hummel-Isbecque, decision of September 17, 1965, *Official Journal of the European Communities* 2581 (1965) and 2 CCH Common Market Reporter, § 9063; Jallate, decision of December 17, 1965, *Official Journal of the European Communities* 37 (1966). On the *Blondel* case, see comments by Suetens in Cahiers de Droit européen 243 (1965) and by Kirschstein, WuW/E EV 120, WuW 866 (1965); on the *Hummel-Isbecque* case, see the comment by Schibel in AWD BB 356 (1965).

(2) See official notice on contracts for exclusive representation concluded with commercial agents, *Official Journal of the European Communities* 2921 (1962) and 1 CCH Common Market Reporter, § 2694.

But these pronouncements demonstrate that the EEC Commission has now applied to vertical restraints of trade the German theory concerning horizontal restrictive agreements. Under Section 1 of the German Act, " restraint of competition " means every restriction which a firm accepts on its freedom and ability to compete. Only those restrictions which are likely to affect, in some discernible way, market conditions are, however, covered by Section 1. An exclusive franchise is not held *per se* anticompetitive under Section 1 because of the restraint it imposes on the manufacturer. Such an agreement is regulated by Section 18 of the German Act and can be challenged by the cartel office only if it causes a substantial lessening of market competition for *this type* of commodity. (1)

From that standpoint, their importance is capital. The Commission's doctrine is but partially accurate. Only the freedom of one party, the manufacturer, was restrained, to the extent that he was prevented from appointing another dealer in the territory assigned. No limitation was imposed on the dealers, who remained free to sell outside the territories for which they had been granted an exclusive right. None of the parties saw their freedom abridged towards any of their actual or potential competitors—which is precisely one of the tests of Section 1 of the German Act. In the judgment of the EEC Commission, the effect on market conditions is that other dealers are barred from the opportunities to be directly supplied by the manufacturer. Thus the EEC Commission merely recites the definition of a typical exclusive franchise and then considers it as inherently anticompetitive for purposes of Article 85(1).

This undoubtedly represents an appreciable departure from the approach initiated in *Vitapro* and *Grosfillex,* for, in determining the applicability of Article 85(1), the EEC Commission did not consider whether similar products were available. In each case, however, rigorous interbrand competition was present. This was indeed one of the reasons for the enforcement agency's conclusion that the agreements could come through the gateway of Article 85(3): they did not enable the enterprises concerned

---

(1) See *supra,* Chapter II, at 103-106.

to eliminate competition in a substantial part of the market for that commodity. But as far as Article 85(1) was concerned, the European authority confined itself to declaring in broad and general terms that:—

> Products similar to the DRU [the manufacturer] products can enter into and move within the market concerned so that there is free competition at the production stage; however, for the items in question, the products of the various manufacturers are identified by their characteristics. Such identification, which is emphasized by the use of a trade-mark, permits customers to show their preferences; for this reason, competition at the distribution stage is of particular importance for items under the same trade-mark. Thus, since Blondel alone can obtain its supplies directly from DRU, not only is the freedom of the parties restricted, but the position of third parties, particularly dealers other than the licensee, who might wish to import the products under contract, is appreciably modified. (1)

The identical reasoning appears in the *Hummel* and *Jallate* cases which by itself tends to show that the Commission is applying a pre-conceived doctrine without considering the particular facts of each situation. This is precisely characteristic of a *per se* approach. But following a strictly formal method, the EEC Commission could not avoid the trap of illogicality. To find a restraint of competition one has to ascertain the relevant market in relation to which the significance of the restraint will be gauged. For purposes of Article 85(1), the Commission suggests that the relevant market is that for the particular brand, rather than that for products of the same type. Examining, however, whether the tests of Article 85(3) are satisfied, it modifies its conception. But the relevant market must be defined in the same way for purposes of both Article 85(1) and Article 85(3). Therein lies the Commission's misconception.

Even limiting the relevant market to the particular brand involved (which at least should be justified by an analysis of the specific facts of each case rather than by a mere formula repeated from case to case), the decisions do not show how the agreements

(1) Blondel, decision of July 8, 1965, *Official Journal of the European Communities* 2194 (1965) (unofficial translation by 2 CCH COMMON MARKET REPORTER, § 9049).

restrained competition. This was not a case of closed territorial arrangements between the manufacturer and its dealers which would amount to a horizontal cartel among the dealers. The dealers remained free to sell where they pleased, and to compete with other distributors of the same brand. Far from being a restraint of competition, the exclusive franchise arrangement, despite the restrictive clause which is inherent in its nature, might well have been the sole feasible way for the manufacturer to have his product marketed in new areas.

It is submitted that the German theory of " restraint of competition " regarding horizontal agreements, applied by the EEC Commission to vertical arrangements, accounts for these controversial developments. " Restraint of competition " is construed as every restriction imposed on the trader. The market effect is looked for, as under Section 1 of the German Act, in the situation of third parties; in these three cases, it was equated with the mere definition of the exclusive franchise. What might be defensible under Section 1 of the German Act becomes highly debatable when transferred to vertical restraints. Two business firms in the same line and at the same functional level do not abridge their competitive freedom towards each other without some serious reason such as the expectation of achieving more influence over the market. Thus, one can be satisfied with a likelihood of market impact. But there is a difference when a person unilaterally abridges his freedom of trade towards a firm on a subsequent level. The wisdom of the German Act consisted precisely in drawing the line between these two fundamentally different kinds of situation. This line has been overlooked by the EEC Commission.

A tendency is revealed by these cases to consider as an intended restraint of competition every restrictive clause of an agreement. More reasonably, in the *Grosfillex* case, the EEC Commission had declared that the purpose of the agreement was for Grosfillex to have an exclusive dealer in a territory outside the Common Market. By itself, such a restrictive clause does not establish that the purpose of the contracting parties was to affect competition as a regulator of a free market. To find such an intent requires at least study of the motives of the parties. In none of these cases has there been such an analysis.

There was no need to read a reasonableness test into Article 85 (1); it was already there to the extent that the formula " object or effect of restraining competition " is similar to the test applied under the Amerian Rule of Reason. Exclusive franchises could be caught under Article 85(1) only by adhering to a formal definition of competition, which, as a result, defeats the policy embodied in the ban against cartels: it is no longer competition which is protected, but an oversimplified version of it. Instead of scrutinizing market conditions to see whether competition has been affected, the enforcement agency has, rather, taken the attitude of judging the contracts on their face. In American antitrust law, the rule regarding exclusive franchises has virtually been one of *per se* legality. (1) Through sophisticated steps which are time-consuming and represent an excessive bureaucratic burden, the EEC Commission will reach the same result. After a policy announcement, whereby the Commission held *in abstracto* that exclusive franchises were covered by Article 85(1), (2) the EEC Commission has been swamped by thousands of notifications. (3) The European authority has tried to find a way out. The recent Regulation No. 19/65 is precisely designed to empower the EEC Commission to grant exemptions to classes of restrictive practices such as the exclusive franchises, without the necessity of examining specifically each case to see whether the four tests of Article 85(3) are met. (4) The explanation of the EEC Council for this class exemption regulation

---

(1) See *e.g.* Packard Motor Car Co. v. Webster Motor Co., 243 F. 2d 418, 420 (D.C. Cir. 1957) and Schwing Motor Co. v. Hudson Sales Co., 138 F. Supp. 899 (D.Md. 1956), *aff'd per curiam*, 239 F. 2d 176 (4th Cir. 1956), *cert. denied*, 355 U.S. 823 (1957).

(2) See this Chapter, *supra*, note (2), p. 146.

(3) See the 8th General Report on the Activities of the Community, EEC Commission, June 1965, at 62.

(4) Regulation no. 19/65. Application of Article 85(3) of the Treaty to Group of Agreements and Concerted Practices, issued by the EEC Council March 2, 1965, *Official Journal of the European Communities*, 533 (1965) and 1 CCH Common Market Reporter, § 2717. On this regulation, see *e.g.* Deringer-Tessin, *Gruppenausnahmen im EWG-Kartellrecht fur Alleinvertriebs- und Lizenzverträge*, WuW 447 (1965). The Italian Government brought suit against the EEC Commission and the EEC Council to seek an annulment of the Regulation no. 19/65 (2 CCH Common Market Reporter, § 9072). The constitutionality of this Regulation was sustained by the European Court. See the case no. 32/65, Italy v. EEC Council and EEC Commission, 2 CCH Common Market Reporter, § 8048. For a discussion of the Court's opinion, see *infra*, this Chapter at 173-183.

was: " because of the large number of notifications submitted pursuant to Regulation No. 17, in order to simplify the task of the Commission, it must be put in a position to declare through a regulation that the provisions of Article 85(1) are inapplicable to certain groups of agreements and concerted practices. " (1) The purpose of the three decisions issued by the EEC Commission is presumably to prepare a regulation exempting certain specified groups of restrictive agreements. (2) The exempting regulation will have to specify the clauses which may not appear and those which must appear in the agreement. (3) This rule-making approach is nothing other than a *per se* approach; that is to say, to declare lawful or unlawful certain kinds of contracts according to their terms without examining specifically their market effect and without analyzing the purpose of the parties.

The same may be said about exclusive dealing arrangements and is even more obvious in this area. An exclusive dealing contract standing alone restrains the freedom of the dealer to patronize other suppliers, and at the same time prevents competitors of the supplier from marketing their own products through *this* dealer. In the *Jallate* case, the EEC Commission held that such agreement, *per se*, falls under Article 85(1) (4) The contract between Maison Jallate and Vandeputte contained an exclusive purchasing clause under which the licencee had agreed not to deal in any similar products of another brand.

> This clause makes access to the Belgian market more difficult for other manufacturers of safety shoes, since the marketing of this product calls for special technical knowledge and hence there is some restriction on the number of dealers who can undertake this. (5)

(1) Justification of the Council, *Official Journal of the European Communities*, 533 (1965). This is the translation of 1 CCH COMMON MARKET REPORTER, § 2717.

(2) See H. von der Groeben, *op. cit.*, WuW 695 (1965); Kirschstein in his comment on the *Blondel* case, WuW/E EV 120, WuW 866 (1965); press release from the EEC, Official Spokesman of the Commission, Brussels, January, 1966, 2 CCH COMMON MARKET REPORTER, § 9086.

(3) See Article 1 of REGULATION, no. 19/65. See the Proposed Regulation on the Application of Article 85(3) of the Treaty to Certain Groups of Bilateral Exclusive Dealing Agreements and concerted Practices, *Official Journal of the European Communities* 2863 (1963) and 2 CCH COMMON MARKET REPORTER, § 9125.

(4) Jallate, decision of December 17, 195, *Official Journal of the European Communities*, 37, 38 (1965).

(5) I am quoting the translation of the CCH COMMON MARKET REPORTER, § 9083.

But when deciding to grant an exemption pursuant to Article 85(3), the Commission noted:—

> In spite of Vandeputte's obligation to purchase exclusively from Maison Jallate, other manufacturers still have access to the Belgian market, including a choice of exclusive dealers. (1)

The two statements are obviously in conflict: the second shows that the restraint of competition was merely theoretical. Such doctrine transferred to an American context would simply result in reading the qualifying phrase (" where the effect may be to substantially lessen competition or tend to create a monopoly ") out of Section 3 of the Clayton Act. The economic theory which inspires the EEC Commission in the application of Article 85(1) is the model of pure competition. Wherever the Commission found a restriction of one firm's freedom of trade, it presumed a market effect without really examining whether it had actually occurred.

11. - The *Voma-Exquisit* Case

A. - Another Illustration of the Literal Approach

Among the cases decided by the national courts, the judgment of a German district court (rendered even previously to the last three EEC decisions) is worth mentioning to the extent that it reflects the same approach and the same tendency to transfer to the Rome Treaty concepts derived from the German law. (2)

Plaintiff, a German import-export firm, purchasing in Great Britain Japanese electric massage instruments and reselling them under its own trade-mark, had been granted an exclusive franchise by its British supplier for Germany and France. On June 14, 1962, the German firm, in turn, entered into an exclusive distributorship agreement with a French firm

---

(1) *Ibid.*

(2) Judgment of the District Court of Mannheim, L. G. Mannheim, January 22, 1965, Voma-Exquisit, WuW/E LG AG 236, WuW 588 (1965); AWD BB 60 (1965) with an annotation by Niederleithinger. English translation in 4 COMMON MARKET LAW REPORTS, 231 (1965) and 2 CCH COMMON MARKET REPORTER, § 8030.

which was to act as sole distributor for the whole French territory. This French dealer undertook not to handle competing products, and was committed to buy a minimum amount of massage instruments each year. No notification had been filed with the EEC Commission. In September, 1962, the French firm stopped buying from the German importer as similar instruments had been introduced on the French market at considerably lower prices. Sued for damages for breach of contract, the French firm alleged as a defense that the agreement was a violation of Article 85(1) and therefore void. This contention was accepted by the German Court.

The agreement was viewed as resulting in a restraint of competition within the Common Market. The contracting firms were restricted in their freedom of action. Plaintiff, located in Germany, was prevented from supplying other distributors in France, while defendant in France was barred from handling competitive products. Thereby the alternative market partners of each of the firms were excluded. Plaintiff was precluded from acting as a supplier for all competitors of defendant in France, and defendant was not available as a distributor in France for competitors of plaintiff.

This restraint of competition was perceptible in the relevant market, *i.e.*, the market for electrical massage instruments in the Member States, although it did not affect the entire economy. As this kind of massage instrument could not be procured from other sources—they were made in Japan and had just been introduced in Europe—the undertaking of plaintiff not to appoint any other distributor in France resulted in giving defendant a monopoly of the sale of such product in the French market. A stronger restraint would be inconceivable. Electrical massage instruments from other manufacturers could not be regarded as homogeneous products. Moreover, at the time of the conclusion of the contract, there were no competitive products in France. The Court recalled, then, the doctrine announced by the German Federal Supreme Court in the *Spar* case that every influence on the market participants which is perceptible according to general economic experience meets the requirements of Section 1 of the German Act. Referring to the EEC Commission pronouncement in *Grosfillex,* the Court expressed the view that Article 85 would be violated only by a perceptible restraint of competition, and that such a restraint existed.

B. - Criticism of the View that Every Technical Restraint Is Necessarily a Limitation on Market Competition

Like the Commission in *Blondel, Hummel* and *Jallate*, the District Court of Mannheim thought that every contractual limitation of the competitive freedom of an enterprise is synonymous with restraint of competition, thus applying to the Rome Treaty the German definition of *Wettbewerbsbeschränkung* under Section 1 of the German Act. Like the Commision, the German Court had overlooked the peculiarities of Section 1 of the German Act and that a different theory had been codified by the German statute itself as to the vertical arrangements of the kind involved here. Following the German pattern, it first pointed out the restriction imposed on the parties and then looked for the market effect—the restraint of competition having then to be found perceptible in order to satisfy the doctrine laid down in the *Spar* case and adopted by the EEC Commission for its own usage.

A German commentator noted after this decision—he wrote before the three recent decisions of the EEC Commission—that restraint of competition has not the same meaning in Article 85(1) as in Section 1 of the German Act. Article 85(1) requires an ascertainment of the effects produced by the restrictive contract on competition in the market. Not every limitation of one firm's freedom of trade amounts to a restraint of competition. This view, he suggested, had been taken by the EEC Commission in *Grosfillex.* However restrictive of the manufacturer's freedom of action, an exclusive franchise may for him be the sole way to break into new markets. To that extent, the agreement makes competition possible for the first time. To such a case Article 85(1) should not be applied. (1)

(1) See Niederleithinger, *op. cit.*, at 62.

12. - The Doctrine Developed by the European Court of Justice

A. - The Rule of Reason under Article 85(1): Not a Mere Academic Discussion

Three cases decided by the European Court of Justice after this dissertation was first written have shown that the debate about the rule of reason in the interpretation of Article 85(1) of the Rome Treaty was not a mere academic discussion.

First, the decision of the EEC Commission in the *Grundig-Consten* case was appealed by those firms on the contention, among others, that the Commission had applied an erroneous legal standard to the construction of Article 85(1), and especially to the concept of restraint of trade. (1)

Second, the Court of Appeal of Paris, resorting to the referral procedure of Article 177 of the Treaty, raised several questions with the European Court of Justice in regard to an exclusive franchise agreement which included an exclusive dealing term, but did not contain any territorial confinement provision. (2) The facts are very similar to the *Voma-Exquisit* case decided by the District Court of Mannheim; but unlike the German Court, the Court of Appeal of Paris did not assume that such an agreement falls automatically under Article 85(1) merely because a German manufacturer was prevented from appointing another dealer in France and a French dealer was prohibited from selling in France similar products bought from another manufacturer. This case directly raised the issue of the existence of a rule of reason under Article 85(1). If the Court of Appeal of Paris had applied a doctrine similar to the one set out by the

---

(1) Grundig-Consten v. EEC Commission, case no. 56/64 and 58/64, July 13, 1966 2 CCH COMMON MARKET REPORTER, § 8046.

(2) Judgment of the Court of Appeal of Paris of July 7, 1965, La Technique Minière v. Maschinenbau Ulm GmbH, reproduced in CAHIERS DE DROIT EUROPÉEN, 350 (1965) with an annotation by P.F. Ryziger, and in DROIT SOCIAL, 483 (1965) with an annotation by P.-H. Teitgen. A summary of this judgment is given in 2 CCH COMMON MARKET REPORTER, § 9074. The judgment of the European Court of Justice is reproduced in 2 CCH COMMON MARKET REPORTER, § 8047, Société Technique Minière v. Maschinenbau Ulm GmbH, case no. 56/65, June 30, 1966.

Commission in the *Blondel*, *Hummel-Isbecque*, and *Maison-Jallate* cases [1], there would have been no need to refer any question to the Court of Justice.

Third, the Italian Government challenged the validity of Regulation no. 19/65 authorizing the Commission to grant group exemptions. [2] This Regulation was based upon the premise that an exclusive dealing agreement, for instance, comes within the purview of Article 85(1), whatever its economic significance may be. I think, on the contrary, that Article 85(1) requires market analysis to support a finding of anticompetitive purpose or effect. This case also raises, although indirectly, the issue of the rule of reason, since the Council and the Commission of the EEC had made an assumption *in abstracto* that economic analysis is unnecessary in considering an entire class of vertical agreements, many of which must plainly be of no anticompetitive significance.

These three cases naturally deal with a series of both substantive and procedural problems, many of which are not relevant to my thesis. There will certainly be numerous discussions of them in the near future. [3] In this study, however, I will analyse them only in regard to the existence of a rule of reason under Article 85(1).

B. - Grundig-Consten v. EEC Commission

I. - Arguments Expounded by Grundig and Consten

Grundig and Consten objected to the decision of the EEC Commission [4] on the ground that it had considered only *in the abstract* a contractual agreement without examining its economic repercussions on the market. Such a *per se* prohibition would be incompatible with Article 85(1) which " requires in each case, a knowledge of the factual circumstances in order

(1) See this Chapter, *supra*, at 146-152.

(2) Italy v. EEC Council and EEC Commission, case no. 32/65, July 13, 1966, 2 CCH Common Market Reporter, § 8048.

(3) On these three cases, see Deringer, *Alleinvertriebsverträge im Wettbewerbsrecht*, NJW 1585 (1966); Kirschstein, *Beurteilung von Alleinvertriebsverträge nach EWG-Kartellrecht*, WuW 777 (1966) and Le Tallec,, *Die Wettbewerbsregeln in der EWG nach der Rechtsprechung des Gerichtshofes*, AWD BB 437 (1966).

(4) For a discussion of the Commission decision, see *supra*, this Chapter at 143-145.

to establish whether competition is restricted to an appreciable extent." [1] The Commission, it was alleged, prohibited the contract without inquiring into its possible effect on the market. Specifically, the Commission limited its investigation to a single type of tape-recorder which, in 1963, represented only 1.9 % of the total turnover between Grundig and Consten. [2]

The petitioners contended that the Commission decision had considered only Grundig products and had thus misinterpreted the concept of competition which, far from being limited to products of different brands, extends to competition between similar products of different brands. [3] The Commission, before declaring Article 85(1) applicable, should have investigated the economic effects of the contract on competition between the various brands in order to obtain an over-all perspective of the economic situation. [4] "The prohibition can only apply to agreements that produce a perceptible, significant change in the market conditions for such products." [5] Petitioners and the German government, an intervenor on their side [6] emphasized

---

(1) Grundig-Consten v. EEC Commission, case no. 56/64 and 58/64, 2 CCH COMMON MARKET REPORTER, § 8046 at 7627 (CCH translation).

(2) *Ibid.*, at 7635.

(3) *Ibid.*, at 7639.

(4) *Ibid.*, at 7640.

(5) *Ibid.*, at 7639 (CCH translation).

(6) According to Article 37 of the Protocol on the statute of the Court of Justice of the European Community (1 CCH COMMON MARKET REPORTER, § 4731) Member States may intervene in cases before the Court. Germany and Italy intervened to support the case of Grundig and Consten, but expounded substantially different views. In regard to the application of Article 85(1) to vertical arrangements such as territorial restrictions, exclusive franchises or exclusive dealing promises, three different views were presented, as was pointed out by Maschinenbau Ulm GmbH in *Technique Minière* (2 CCH COMMON MARKET REPORTER, § 8047 at 7690). According to the Commission, exclusive vertical arrangements are presumed to be illegal but may subsequently be given a general exemption. According to the Italian Government, these arrangements are not covered by Article 85(1) at all. According to the German Government, the prohibition of Article 85(1) is applicable, but only under certain extremely limited conditions. It was to make this point that the German Government intervened and opposed the Commission's decision. This may appear to contradict with what I have said about the German influence on the development of the Commission's attitude (see *infra*, this chapter at 116-118). But this is only a surface contradiction. I never asserted that the German Government itself was responsible for the development of the Commission case law. I only endeavored to show the influence of the concepts developed by the German anticartel law itself. But in my view, the Commission has misinterpreted the German anti-cartel law (see *supra*, this chapter at 149). If the German law had been wholly adopted in the interpretation of the Rome Treaty, a rule of reason would have been applicable to exclusive vertical arrangements (see *supra*, chapter II at 103-106) and, in the second place, these arrangements would not have been subject to registration.

the need to avoid a *per se* prohibition and to apply Article 85(1) on the basis of a rule of reason. (1) In their view, " the narrowness of the exceptions provided for in paragraph 3, particularly the difficulty involved in proving the negative conditions, makes a more 'reasonable' interpretation of paragraph 1 mandatory. " (2) They pointed out that the closed territorial system of distribution, although it restricted the competitive freedom of the parties, had made it possible to increase competition between the different brands within the Common Market. (3)

Grundig and Consten also challenged the Commission decision on the ground that the closed territorial system of distribution, and especially the insulation of the French market, against which the entire reasoning of the Commission was directed, did not result from the agreement between Consten and Grundig which alone was being attacked. The territorial restrictions which isolated the French market, *i.e.*, the export prohibitions to France, were contained in the contracts concluded between Grundig and its German wholesalers. These contracts had not formally been challenged by the Commission. (4)

Petitioners finally opposed the decision on the ground that the Commission had considered the entire agreement as being in violation of Article 85(1). (5) They said that the Commission did not adduce sufficient reasons why the exclusive franchise and the exclusive dealing term were also inherently invalid under Article 85(1) of the Treaty.

II. - The Commission's Theory

In regard to the concept of restraint of trade, the EEC Commission advocated before the European Court of Justice the theory that it had already expressed in its decisions. Restraint of competition means that the restrictive agreement perceptibly limits the freedom of action of the parties or alters the position

(1) *Ibid.*, at 7640.
(2) *Ibid.*, at 7641 (CCH translation).
(3) *Ibid.*, at 7640.
(4) *Ibid.*, at 7634, and at 7628.
(5) *Ibid.*, at 7626.

of third parties. [1] Although the enforcement agency read the word " perceptible " into Article 85(1), it refused to draw the logical consequences from this construction of the Treaty. In its view, the applicability of Article 85(1) does not depend on the share of the relevant market held by the companies making the agreement. [2] The Commission did not think that, in order to ascertain whether the restriction was perceptible, it was its duty to make a thorough economic investigation of the facts of the case. On the contrary, the Commission confined itself to a merely legal analysis of the provisions of the agreement: " All the enterprises established in France are limited in their choice, since they are not able to purchase [Grundig's] products from other dealers, particularly from German dealers " [3]. Thus the European authority was satisfied with a consideration of the terms of the contract alone in finding a violation of Article 85(1).

The Commission argued that " for the Grundig firm's products, the possibility of strengthening competition at the production level does not exclude restriction at the trading stage. It is only within the framework of Article 85(3) that the improvement of horizontal competition could be taken into account."[4] In other words, the fact that interbrand competition might be improved is no valid reason for not holding a restriction of intrabrand competition to be a violation of Article 85(1). The Commission emphasized that Article 85(1) should be applied to every restriction of intrabrand competition.

> There must be competition not only between the producers and distributors of different brands, but also between dealers supplied by a single producer. These different kinds of competition complement each other. (...) Competition between different brands is not very effective because there is no way for consumers to make a comparison. (...) Competition between distributors of the same brand stimulates and rewards the individual efforts of the dealer because it works on identical products. [5]

(1) *Ibid.*, at 7640.

(2) *Id.*

(3) *Ibid.*, at 7641.

(4) *Ibid.*, at 7626 (CCH translation).

(5) *Ibid.*, at 7639 and 7640 (CCH translation).

But once more the Commission failed to establish a clear distinction between the three different kinds of restraints of trade involved in the Grundig-Consten agreement—the territorial restrictions, the exclusive franchise and the exclusive dealing term. Obviously, these three different sorts of restraints should not be treated in the same way. While the territorial restrictions eliminate any intraband competition, this is not the case with exclusive franchises which, on the contrary, maintain a possibility of intrabrand competition from fellow dealers or distributors outside the assigned territory. The exclusive dealing term may be deemed anti-competitive only if it substantially restricts other manufacturers' access to the consuming market.

Regarding a Rule of Reason in the interpretation of Article 85(1), the Commission objected strongly to the construction of Article 85(1) urged by petitioners, supported by the German Government, and advocated by Roemer. Apparently, the Commission understood a Rule of Reason to be a principle under which the application of Article 85(1) should be effected by drawing up " a sort of total economic study of the advantages and drawbacks of the restrictions of competition. " (1) The Commission went on to say that:—

> The system set up by article 85 is different from the American system for which the " rule of reason " standard was developed. Since the American antitrust rules provide no exceptions, the authorities applying them were forced to temper the manner in which they would view the degree of change in competitive conditions. For this reason, they generally, in the course of their inquiries, determine in what area and between what persons there is competition in the purchase and sale of products meeting the same need. In contrast, Article 85 contains a general prohibition (paragraph 1) supplemented by an exception (paragaph 3). Thus the exemption of agreements falling within the general prohibition can be definitely evaluated only within the framework of paragraph 3, which makes it possible to take these various points into consideration. It is therefore only with respect to the last condition set forth by that provision (the enterprises concerned must not be able to eliminate competition for a substantial part of the products involved) that it might be necessary to determine the extent of the remaining competition. (2)

---

(5) *Ibid.*, at 7641 (CCH translation).

(1) *Id.* (CCH translation).

III. - The Doctrine Suggested by Advocate General Roemer

In his submissions to the Court of Justice, Advocate General Roemer approached Article 85(1) and the idea of restraint of trade in a manner undoubtedly inspired by the American Rule of Reason. He asked the Court of Justice to reverse the decision on several grounds and to remand the case to the Commission. He relied primarily on what he regarded as fallacy in the Commission's theory as to Article 85(1). (1) To him, Article 85(1) requires an investigation of the market effects produced by a restrictive agreement. One of the Commission's duties, he said, is to scrutinize the market conditions and to look, for instance, at the market share possessed by the firms. The *White Motor* case, (2) where restraints similar to those found in the *Grundig-Consten* case were present, was cited to illustrate the method which is applied in American law in assessing reasonableness, and more specifically the resort to economic investigation in order to ascertain the anticompetitive effect of a challenged practice. It would be artificial, he said, to apply Article 85(1) on the basis of purely theoretical considerations, and then to grant an exemption pursuant to Article 85(3), if a more detailed analysis would have revealed in the first place that the agreement under attack did not substantially restrain competition. According to the Advocate General, Article 85(1) requires the Commission to compare two market situations: the one existing after the restrictive agreement has been concluded and the one which would have developed in the absence of this agreement. Whether something has actually been changed by virtue of the agreement is the decisive test. The Advocate General argued that such an agreement might in fact be likely, in certain cases, to promote rather than to suppress competition, especially when it is the only practical means for a small company to break into a new competitive area. Thus he was clearly inspired by the *White Motor* case and by the considerations articulated by Justice Brennan in the concurring opinion. (3) In fact, the

---

(1) See the submissions of Advocate General Karl Roemer in the cases 56/64 and 58/64, *Consten-Grundig v. EEC Commission,* 2 CCH COMMON MARKET REPORTER, § 8046, especially at 7662-7674.

(2) White Motor Co. v. United States, 372 U.S. 253 (1963).

(3) *Id.*

language used by the Advocate General can be traced to the old *Chicago Board of Trade* case where Justice Brandeis had stated that the true test of legality was " whether the restraint imposed is such as merely regulates and perhaps thereby promotes competition or whether it is such as may suppress or even destroy competition. " (1) The Advocate General also adhered to the contention of the German Government that Article 85(1) requires the EEC Commission to consider interbrand as well as intrabrand competition.

IV. - The Ruling of the Court

The Court of Justice had to choose which of the conflicting views proposed by the EEC Commission and by Advocate General Roemer should prevail. Insofar as Article 85(1) was concerned, there was a complete conflict between the kind of rule of reason theory suggested by Roemer and the *per se* doctrine supported by the Commission. The Court took a middle road. The territorial confinement system of distribution set up by Grundig, and especially the insulation of the French market, were treated by the Court as amounting to a *per se* violation of Article 85(1); this will be explained later. (2) At the same time, the Court clearly implied that the exclusive franchise and the exclusive dealing term were not invalid under Article 85(1) by reason of their very nature. The Court held that the Commission had not adduced sufficient factual evidence to show that these agreements were anticompetitive in purpose or in effect.

It was stressed that even vertical arrangements can run foul of the basic purposes of the Treaty, especially when they are designed " to restore the national partitions in trade between Member States. " (3)

The distinctive feature of the distribution system set up by Grundig lay in the territorial confinement clauses imposed upon the dealers. Grundig dealers were granted an exclusive franchise

---

(1) Chicago Board of Trade v. United States, 246 U.S. 231, 238 (1918).

(2) See *infra*, p. 164-165.

(3) See Grundig-Consten v. EEC Commission, case no. 56/64 and 58/64, July 13, 1966, 2 CCH Common Market Reporter, § 8046 at 7651 (CCH translation).

for a specified area; for instance, Grundig had promised Consten not to sell goods to other outlets in France and not to sell directly to consumers within French territory. But Grundig had gone a step further. All dealers in Grundig products in the Common Market were forbidden to sell outside their exclusive territory. The German wholesalers were prevented from exporting Grundig products to France while, for instance, Consten, the French distributor, had in turn promised not to sell outside French territory. In that way, each distributor was in his territory completely protected against incursions by dealers located in other Common Market countries. The result was the absolute insulation of the French market and the elimination of any intrabrand competition in France. Moreover this system was supplemented by the registration in France in Consten's name of the trademark Gint. Thanks to this registration, the French distributor was in a position to sue any parallel importer for infringement of his trademark. The gist of the plan was thus to create territorial limitations along national boundary lines.

The Court construed the Commission decision to say that the violation of Article 85(1) of the Rome Treaty consisted in this closed territorial system of distribution. To this extent, the Court approved the Commission's decision. Clearly, the insulation of the French market resulted from the territorial restraints put upon dealers located in other Member States, and not from the agreement between Consten and Grundig itself, which was the only one to be challenged formally by the Commission. But the Court said that the committment of Grundig not to sell *indirectly* in France was implemented by the export prohibition imposed upon the German wholesalers. The Commission had taken into account the entire system of distribution established by Grundig. It was correct, the Court said, to place the particular agreement in its legal and economic context. (1)

> The situation (...) results in isolating the French market and makes it possible to apply to the products in question prices in which there is no effective competition. Furthermore, competition between producers generally loses its effectiveness as producers become more successful in their efforts to clearly differentiate their brands from other brands. Because distribution costs account for a substantial

(1) *Ibid.*, at 7653.

> part of the total cost price, it appears important that competition between dealers should also be promoted. Dealers are spurred to greater efforts by competition between distributors of goods of the same brand. Because the agreement is designed to isolate the French market for Grundig products and to artificially maintain separate national markets within the Community for products of a widely distributed brand, it distorts competition within the Common Market. (1)

The condemnation of the territorial confinement clauses reveals an adoption of a *per se* rule in that the Court denied the necessity of inquiring whether the territorial restraints, by regulating intrabrand competition, did not in fact improve interbrand competition. The Court explicitly met the argument of the petitioners, of the German Government and of Roemer that " the Commission, before declaring Article 85(1) applicable, should, in the interest of a reasonable application ('rule of reason'), have considered the economic effects of the contract in issue on competition between the various brands " (2). This rule of reason approach, inspired by the test which Justice Brennan suggested in his concurring opinion in *White Motor*, was rejected by the European Court.

> The principle of freedom of competition applies to all economic levels and all aspects of competition. Competition between producers is generally more apparent than competition between distributors of the same brand. This does not, however, mean that an agreement that restricts competition between distributors should escape the prohibition of article 85(1), because it might strengthen competition between producers. (3)

Although the Court elsewhere spoke only of the products of a " widely distributed brand ", it seems that territorial restraints of the kind imposed by Grundig will be held inherently anticompetitive, regardless of their effect upon interbrand competition, because they eliminate the possibility of intraband competition. This is clearly an adoption of the Commission's *theoretical* position as to the interpretation of Article 85(1) rather than merely a decision that the *facts* of the case did not warrant an application of the reasonableness test to validate the agreement.

---

(1) *Id.* (CCH translation).

(2) *Ibid.*, at 7652 (CCH translation).

(3) *Id.*

The Court emphasized that a violation of Article 85(1) does not in such a case depend upon any further economic considerations, for instance upon differences between prices in France and those in Germany. ([1]) Grundig's share of the French market was irrelevant. Thus, once a system of distribution similar to the one created by Grundig is found, the Commission will not have to present further factual evidence. To that extent, the Court formulated an abstract principle of law which amounts to a *per se* pronouncement. But this principle is limited. The Court did not say, for example, that every export prohibition, even if standing alone and unconnected with a whole system of distribution, is automatically in violation of Article 85(1).

Great importance was given in the *Grundig* case to the fact that territorial limitations coincided with national boundary lines. The restraints were for that reason regarded as incompatible with the basic policies of the Common Market to facilitate economic integration. One can wonder whether this factor was thought relevant in satisfying the jurisdictional requirement of Article 85(1) or had an independent substantive significance. Several questions are still unsolved. What about territorial division of markets between distributors of the same brand which cut across national borders (for instance, a distributor whose exclusive sales area would consist of part of Belgium, Germany and Holland)? What about a case where the French territory is allocated to five different Grundig dealers which are all forbidden to export to other Common Market countries and which are protected against exports from other Common Market countries by similar restraints? What would be the situation where the division of territories is within a single Member State and involves a product manufactured exclusively in this State? In my view, such vertical allocations of territories would fall within the automatic proscription adumbrated by the Court: the sole remaining issue would be to determine whether the effect upon interstate commerce is sufficient, and in that respect, the first two hypothetical cases mentioned above might well satisfy this test.

([1]) *Ibid.*, at 7653.

Nevertheless, even in the *Grundig* case, the *per se* rule formulated by the Court does not cover the entire agreement concluded between Consten and Grundig. The Court held that " the Commission did not furnish sufficient reasons why it considered it necessary to prohibit the agreement as a whole. It has not established that all the terms of the agreement violate article 85(1)." (1) The offence consisted rather of the territorial restrictions and of the terms of the agreement which were designed to prevent parallel imports. The Commission had not adduced sufficient *factual* evidence to show the anticompetitive effect or purpose of the exclusive franchise and of the exclusive dealing term. This implies that Article 85(1) *cannot* be applied mechanically to restraints of that type. Thus the Court condemned *per se* a territorial confinement system which amounted to a horizontal division of markets between Grundig dealers along national boundary lines, but it did not say that there was no room under Article 85(1) for a rule of reason to evaluate the other restraints of trade which were challenged by the Commission. A basis for justifying the different treatment of territorial restrictions and of exclusive franchises is that the latter do not exclude the possibility of intrabrand competition from dealers in other Common Market countries or from unauthorized dealers inside the exclusive territory who obtain supplies from dealers located in other Member States.

C. - Société Technique Minière v. Maschinenbau Ulm GmbH

I. - The Questions Posed by the Court of Appeal of Paris

As I have already stated, *Société Technique Minière v. Maschinenbau Ulm GmbH* gave the Court of Justice the opportunity to decide whether an exclusive franchise agreement or an exclusive dealing clause is *per se* prohibited under Article 85(1) and can only be exempted if it fulfills the requirements of Article 85(3) or whether it should rather be subject to a kind

(1) *Ibid.*, at 7654 (CCH translation).

of rule of reason under Article 85(1). [1] There is no doubt that this second alternative was adopted by the Court of Justice.

The Court of Appeal of Paris had raised its questions in a decision rendered on July 7, 1965, [2] *i.e.* before the EEC Commission had formulated its doctrine regarding exclusive franchises and exclusive dealing terms in the *Blondel, Hummel-Isbecque* and *Maison-Jallate* cases. [3] The contract which the French court had to evaluate was described by the French judges in general and abstract terms. The European Court of Justice was asked to formulate criteria for interpreting Article 85(1).

A French dealer had been granted an exclusive franchise by a German manufacturer covering the whole of France. The dealer was free to re-export the goods to other countries in the EEC. The manufacturer was not bound to prohibit his wholesalers in other countries from exporting to France. Thus this was not the case of an absolute territorial confinement system as in *Grundig-Consten* or *White Motor.* The dealers were only granted a simple exclusive franchise. But there was on their part nothing tantamount to a horizontal agreement between them. The dealers, and specifically the French distributor, were not insulated through territorial restraints against sales by neighboring dealers. Moreover, the agreement contained a requirement clause, inasmuch as the French distributor could not sell machinery that might compete with the equipment delivered under the franchise without prior authorization by the manufacturer.

As the Court of Appeal of Paris had no jurisdiction to apply Article 85(3) [4] its questions concerned only the scope of the prohibition of Article 85(1) and thus the concept or restraint of trade. Here too, there was a conflict between the views suggested by the EEC Commission and those of Advocate General Roemer.

---

(1) Société Technique Minière v. Meschineubau Ulm GmbH, case no. 56/65, June 30, 1966, 2 CCH Common Market Reporter, § 8047.

(2) See *supra*, this chapter, note 2, at 155.

(3) See *supra*, this chapter at 146-152.

(4) See Article 9(1) of Regulation no. 17, *Official Journal of the European Communities*, 204 (1962).

II. - The Thesis Defended by the EEC Commission

As in its prior decisions, *Blondel, Hummel-Isbecque* and *Maison Jallate,* the EEC Commission supported the point of view that " a restriction of competition ... is inherent both in the limitation of the freedom of action of the contracting parties and in the adverse effect on the position of third parties in the market. " (1) The Commission said that the position of the contracting parties or of third parties must be altered in a perceptible way by the restraint. (2) It thought that in the present case this test was satisfied. But, to support its opinion, the Commission again limited itself to a legal analysis merely of the terms of the contract.

> Because of the type of contract involved, competition is restricted at the distribution stage. Dealers and consumers cannot, in fact, be supplied by any but the licensee, who alone receives the goods from the licensor.. Furthermore, the licensee may not buy or sell competitive goods. A restriction of competition is especially perceptible when the products in question are individualized by their special characteristics. (3)

Thus in the view of the Commission, both types of restraints of trade—the exclusive franchise and the exclusive dealing term—should be considered as *per se* violations of article 85(1) without any need for a thorough market inquiry, and could only be exempted on the basis of Article 85(3).

III. - The Theory Proposed by Advocate General Roemer

Although he thought that the exclusive franchise and the exclusive dealing term *might* fall under Article 85(1) (4) Advocate General Roemer suggested a construction of Article 85(1) less strict than that of the Commission. To him, restraints of trade of the kind described by the Court of Appeal of Paris do not necessarily fall within Article 85(1). In other words, they are not prohibited by reason of their very nature. regardless of an investigation of their actual impact upon competition.

---

(1) Société Technique Minière v. Maschinenbau Ulm GmbH, case no. 56/65, June 30, 1966, 2 CCH COMMON MARKET REPORTER, § 8047, at 7689 (CCH translation).

(2) *Id.*

(3) *Id.* CCH translation).

(4) *Ibid.*, at 7701.

Roemer clearly advocated a rule of reason for Article 85(1), saying:—

> It would seem improper to subject every small impairment of competition, whether it is intended or only has that effect, to the strict prohibition of article 85(1) and to grant exemptions pursuant to Article 85(3) only. (1)

In support of his views, he quoted the German statute against restraints of competition which enables the cartel office to challenge the validity of exclusive franchises only if competition on the market for these or similar goods is substantially impaired. (2)

The Commission itself advocated that it was necessary to find at least a perceptible restraint of competition. But Roemer pointed out that the enforcement agency " considers suppositions or declarations by the parties in national proceedings to be sufficient for determining 'perceptible' impairments of competition without directing the national judge to evaluate the market situation in a specific case. " (3) His doctrine was that, in order to show a violation of Article 85(1), it is necessary to find a significant impairment of competitive conditions, whether this impairment actually exists or whether there is substantial evidence indicating that such a effect is going to occur. (4)

In regard to the exclusive dealing term, Roemer stated that when it is contained in the kind of agreement concluded between Société Technique Minière and Maschinenbau Ulm GmbH, it seldom endangers competition seriously, since " there are but few cases in which the access of certain products to the market can effectively be assured by a single specialized dealer. " (5) With respect to the exclusive franchise itself, it was Roemer's opinion that without such an agreement smaller enterprises will often not be able to penetrate a foreign market. It should be remembered, he said, that exclusive franchises do not prevent all intrabrand competition. The exclusive franchise in the present case was not accompanied by territorial limitations. Parallel imports were still possible. Finally, in his opinion, interbrand

(1) *Id.* (CCH translation).
(2) *Id.*
(3) *Id.* (CCH translation).
(4) *Ibid.*, at 7702.
(5) *Id.* (CCH translation).

competition should also be taken into account, not only in respect of mass-produced goods but also regarding highly technical instrument. (1)

> A realistic examination of the market may lead to the conclusion that in this area also there is keen competition between the products of various manufacturers—competition which makes the elimination of competition between the goods of one manufacturer seem unimportant. (2)

IV. - The Ruling of the Court

In *Grundig-Consten*, the Commission won the support of the Court for a *per se* condemnation of a territorial confinement system of distribution coinciding with national borders. The *per se* doctrine which was again propounded by the Commission in *Technique Minière* was here rejected by the Court, which ruled this time in favor of a reasonableness test. It was held that exclusive franchises as such, although they are restraints of trade within the technical meaning of this phrase, are not automatically banned by Article 85(1).

> A contract whereby a producer grants a single distributor the right to sell its products in a specified area does not automatically come under the prohibition of Article 85(1). Such a contract can, however, fulfill all of the conditions set forth in that provision, because of a particular factual situation... or because of the strictness of the clauses protecting the exclusive right... To decide whether a contract containing a clause " granting an exclusive selling right " must be considered as prohibited because of its object or because of its effect, it is necessary to take into account the following in particular: the nature of the products and whether or not their quantity was limited, the position and importance of the licensor and licensee on the market of the products concerned, whether the contract is isolated or is one of a group of contracts, and whether the clauses protecting the exclusiveness are rigid or possibilities are left open for other channels of trade in the same products through re-exports and parallel imports. (3)

The Court's pronouncement is undoubtedly an approval of a case-by-case method and implies an economic investigation into each factual situation. To that extent, it is reminiscent of the approach taken by the American Courts under the Rule of

---

(1) *Id.*
(2) *Id.* (CCH translation).
(3) *Ibid.*, at 7695-7696 (CCH translation).

Reason, and therefore reaches beyond the law on exclusive franchises. The Court seems to imply that to decide whether a specific agreement is meant to restrain competition or has that effect is a factual question. To ascertain the existence of a significant restraint of trade requires the collection of economic data to show the market structure has actually been changed, and that thereby the alternatives offered to consumers have been cut down. It is not sufficient to examine on their face agreements by which firms restrict their own market freedom, and then to declare them automatically in restraint of competition. This is, in my view, the essential doctrine of *Technique Minière.* The Commission had in fact interpreted the Treaty to say that every agreement by which a firm limits its ability to compete is in violation of article 85(1). It had replaced the broad language of the Treaty by a stricter version comparable to the provision of Section 1 of the Sherman Act which, before the Rule of Reason was announced, seemed to prohibit every contract in restraint of trade, regardless of how significant its actual effect on market competition might be. The Court reminds the Commission that Article 85(1) does not formulate such a mechanical standard and that the language of the Treaty cannot arbitrarily be cut down. Under Article 85(1), it is impossible to avoid assessing the significance of the interference with the free play of market forces.

It is not quite clear from the Court's opinion how this method will be applied to the vertical arrangement which was in issue. In my view, the Court failed to draw a clear distinction between three different kinds of restraints of trade: 1) the *exclusive franchise, i.e.* a promise by the manufacturer not to appoint another dealer or distributor in a given area; 2) the *territorial restriction, i.e.* a promise by several dealers or distributors not to sell outside an assigned area; 3) the *exclusive dealing* term, *i.e.* a promise by a distributor or dealer to handle the products of only one manufacturer or supplier to the exclusion of all others. The Court of Appeal of Paris had phrased its questions with great precision. A similar precision is unfortunately lacking in the answers of the European Court. The agreement between Société Technique Minière and Maschinenbau Ulm GmbH contained only restrictions of the first and of the third type.

Surprisingly the Court does not seem to concern itself with the exclusive dealing clause; its answers appear to apply only to the exclusive franchise. As to this latter restraint, the Court says that among other things its validity will depend on whether or not it is accompanied by territorial restrictions—which were not present in the contract described by the Court of Appeal of Paris.

However, the *Grundig* case made clear that territorial restrictions along national boundary lines are *per se* violations of Article 85(1), there being no need for a detailed economic analysis as to their actual effect on competition. Thus exclusive franchises coupled with territorial restrictions as found in the *Grundig* case will be able to escape the prohibition spelled out in Article 85(1) only if they meet the conditions of the exemption provided by Article 85(3). The severity toward territorial restrictions is in sharp contrast with the more liberal attitude toward simple exclusive franchises. The difference in treatment can be explained by the difference in effect on intrabrand competition. [1]. This is the sole justification for a *per se* rule in one case and for a rule of reason in the other.

Mere exclusive franchises stand a good chance of satisfying the reasonableness test formulated by the Court. The decisive test will be the share of the relevant market—which includes similar products of different brands. This means that an exclusive franchise granted by a dominant firm might well be in contravention of Article 85(1). The Court of Justice seems to agree with two American writers that, as the market share increases,

> The manufacturer's use of distribution restrictions becomes more difficult to justify. In the first place, a substantial share of the market indicates widespread consumer acceptance of his brand, and this advantage should make his franchise more attractive and so reduce the need for an exclusive on the part of his dealers and distributors. Moreover, as the market share of one manufacturer becomes larger, the importance to consumers of having some choice between competing sellers of the same brand increases (...). Furthermore, there is perhaps less interest in increasing a large manufacturer's ability to compete against its rivals (...) than in aiding a small manufacturer to do so. [2]

---

[1] See this chapter, *supra*, at 160 and 166.

[2] Note, Restricted Channels of Distribution under the Sherman Act, 75 HARV. L. REV. 795, 833-834 (1961-1962).

In the case which had to be decided by the Court of Appeal of Paris, Maschinenbau Ulm GmbH's share of the French market seemed to have been less than one per cent, so that this agreement should certainly escape the prohibition of Article 85(1). [1] Under the Rome Treaty, the law concerning exclusive franchises—as far as the concept of restraint of trade is concerned—will be stricter than in American law where the rule is one of virtual *per se* legality. [2] According to the test formulated by the European Court, certain exclusive franchises may be in restraint of competition and be prohibited by Article 85(1).

In regard to my thesis, the opinion of the Court in *Société Technique Minière* is of decisive importance, because it recognized that not every restraint of trade within the technical meaning of that phrase should be deemed to violate Article 85(1). There is no doubt that the Court finally ratified the doctrine supported by Roemer rather than that put forward by the Commission. The decisions of the EEC Commission in *Blondel, Hummel-Isbecque* and *Maison Jallate* are certainly not consonant with the guidelines issued by the Court in the present case, since the Commission did not undertake the market analysis which was later prescribed by the Court.

D. - Italy v. EEC Council and EEC Commission

I. - Prior Developments in the Policy of the European Authorities Toward Vertical Agreements

While it may be possible to reconcile *Technique Minière* with *Consten-Grundig* the opinion handed down by the European Court in the *Italian* case does not seem entirely consistent with the theory expounded in the two others. The *Italian* case concerned a suit brought by the Italian Government against the EEC Council and the EEC Commission to seek annulment of Regulation

(1) To my knowledge, the Court of Appeal of Paris has not yet reached a decision.

(2) See Handler, *Annual Antitrust Review*, 11 Record of the Ass'n of the Bar of the City of New York 367, 370 (1956). See also Packard Motor Car Co. v. Webster Motor Car Co., 243 F. 2d 418, 420 where Handler's view was adopted by the Court.

no. 19/65 by which the Commission was authorized to declare the prohibition of Article 85(1) inapplicable to certain groups of agreements, pursuant to Article 85(3) of the Rome Treaty. [1] This suit drew into question the whole policy of the European authorities on exclusive franchises and exclusive dealing terms. To understand the case, it is necessary to summarize briefly the successive developments of this policy. *Italy v. EEC Council and EEC Commission* is a good illustration of the proposition that in European antitrust law, procedural aspects have too often obscured the substantive law problems. There has been a tendency to interpret the substantive law provisions in the light of the procedural regulations, instead of adjusting the procedural rules to the substantive law concepts.

After the adoption of Regulation no. 17 by the EEC Council on March 13, 1962, the underlying doctrine professed by the EEC Commission has always been that contracts by which enterprises restrict their freedom of trade, regardless of their actual or probable impact on market conditions, should be registered in order to be able to claim the benefit of Article 85(3). Perhaps the Commission thought that this was the best way to secure control of the largest possible number of restrictions, and to ensure a uniform compliance with the Treaty. The emphasis was as a consequence put upon formal agreements rather than upon informal understandings. This theory was clearly at the back of a policy announcement on exclusive franchises and exclusive dealing terms which, because of their " restrictive " features, were considered automatically in restraint of competition under 85(1). [2] This announcement was later implemented by Regulation no. 153 which provided a simplified form for the registration of exclusive franchises not accompanied by territorial restrictions. [3] As a result, an enormous number

(1) Italy v. EEC Council and EEC Commission, case no. 32/65, July 13, 1966, 2 CCH Common Market Reporter, § 8048.

(2) See Official Notice on Contracts for Exclusive Representation concluded with Commercial Agents, *Official Journal of the European Communities*, 2921 (1962) and 1 CCH Common Market Reporter, § 2697.

(3) Regulation no. 153 Supplementing and Modifying Regulation no. 27 of May, 1962, issued by the EEC Commission December 21, 1962, *Official Journal of the European Communities*, 2918 (1962) and 1 CCH Common Market Reporter, § 2694.

of such agreements were filed with the Commission which faced the overwhelming task of examining each individual agreement to see whether it qualified for exemption under Article 85(3). This would have been an intolerable administrative burden. Although the Commission itself was partly responsible for this situation, it is quite understandable that it tried afterwards to find a way out. Action was taken along two lines. First, the Commission asked the EEC Council to be given the powers to grant a group exemption to certain classes of agreements responding to certain criteria. The result was Regulation no. 19/65. (1) Second, at the same time, through a number of similar decisions, the EEC Commission foreshadowed the conditions later to be incorporated in a regulation exempting certain groups of exclusive franchises and exclusive dealing terms from Article 85(1). Obviously, this was the purpose behind the *Blondel, Hummel-Isbecque* and *Maison-Jallate* cases all of which bore the imprint of the same pre-determined theory: a strict and mechanical approach toward the concept of restraint of trade set off by a fairly liberal application of Article 85(3). (2) The final aim was to prepare a regulation whereby exclusive franchises and exclusive dealing clauses meeting certain tests would be exempted from the prohibition of Article 85(1). To gain exemption, the agreements would have presumably to be purged of their most restrictive features; but, after this process, one might seriously doubt whether the agreements would ever have been caught by Article 85(1) in the first place. Was this whole regulatory scheme not simply meaningless?

In my view, this long procedure could have been avoided if the Commission had from the start refrained from generalization. Without asserting that exclusive dealing terms or exclusive franchises could under no circumstances come within the scope of the prohibition of Article 85(1), it was my thesis that those vertical types of arrangements might, but need not not necessarily, be so caught, and that this question could only

---

(1) Regulation no. 19/65, Application of Article 85(3) of the Treaty to Groups of Agreements and Concerted Practices issued by the Council, March 2, 1965, *Official Journal of the European Communities*, 533 (1965) and 1 CCH COMMON MARKET REPORTER, § 2725.

(2) See my discussion of these cases, *supra*, this chapter at 146-152.

be decided on a case-by-case analysis after a thorough market examination. It seems to me that all the procedural steps taken by the Commission and ratified by the Council were purely designed to avoid this case-by-case method. The underlying theory that every restraint of trade in the technical sense is prohibited by Article 85(1), was disapproved by the European Court of Justice in *Technique Minière* which spelled out a reasonable test for the application of Article 85(1) to exclusive franchises. In *Blondel, Hummel-Isbecque* and *Maison-Jallate,* the Commission should have granted a negative clearance saying that there was no violation of Article 85(1) instead of resorting to the exempting scheme of Article 85(3).

II. - Regulation No. 19/65 Sustained by the Court

The judgment of the Court of Justice regarding the action of the European authorities in the field of group exemptions could only be keenly anticipated. In challenging the Regulation no. 19/65, the Italian Government utilized an argument similar to my plea in favor of a Rule of Reason for Article 85(1). It was the opinion of the Italian Government that one could not implement Article 85(3), *i.e.* the exception to the rule, without deciding at the same time the applicability of the rule itself. According to the plaintiff, the European anthorities had, in fact, extended the scope of the prohibition laid down in Article 85(1). I cannot agree with all the grounds adduced by the Italian Government for the annulment of Regulation no. 19/65—for instance, the argument that vertical arrangements are necessarily outside the scope of Article 85(1). But I agree at any rate with the argument that a decision applying Article 85(3) is in effect a decision as so the extent of Article 85(1). I agree especially with the Italian Government that Regulation no. 19/65 violated Article 85(1) because, in enacting it, the Council had assumed that all agreements belonging to the exempted groups were to be considered as automatically prohibited under Article 85(1). In *Technique Minière,* the Court had recently held that one could not decide in the abstract whether an exclusive franchise is prohibited under Article 85(1). If the European Court had accepted the Italian Government's view as to the assumption behind Regulation no. 19/65, there is no doubt that its validity could not have been upheld since this assumption contradicted the Court pronouncement in *Technique Minière.* But to uphold Regulation no. 19/65, the European Court declined to agree that this was in fact the basis for the Regulation. The prudence shown by the Court is reminiscent of American constitutional law where:—

> When the validity of an act of the Congress is drawn in question, and even if a serious doubt is raised, it is a cardinal principle that this Court (the United States Supreme Court) will first ascertain whether a construction of the statute is fairly possible by which the question can be avoided. (1)

The Court rejected the suit brought by the Italian Government on the following grounds:—

> The first paragraph of article 85 sets forth a prohibition, its second paragraph describes its effects, and its third paragraph tempers these provisions by authorizing the granting of exemptions from the prohibition - exemptions that may be granted for entire groups... While a specific agreement can be exempted under Article 85(3) only if it is established that it falls under the prohibition of Article 85(1), in the case of group exemption authorized under paragraph 3, an agreement belonging to the group in question need not, because of this, necessarily fulfill the conditions of paragraph 1. In giving the Council the power to authorize group exemptions, Article 85(3) has created an obligation for the Council to exercise this power only with regard to groups of agreements likely to fulfill those conditions. [...] However, once a group has been defined, the definition is only a framework and does not mean that all agreements belonging to the exempted group but not fulfilling the various conditions of the definition necessarily come within the prohibition. Nor does a group exemption indirectly pass judgment on whether or not a specific individual agreement comes within the prohibition... Regulation no. 19/65 does not contravene those principles... Regulation no. 19/65 thus merely establishes the framework for the Commission's function, leaving it to the Commission to specify the conditions which an agreement must fulfill in order to qualify for a group exemption. The regulation was, as its title and its statement of reasons show, issued pursuant to paragraph 3 of Article 85, and not pursuant to paragraph 1, so that it does not create a legal presumption with respect to the interpretation of Article 85(1). It is designed to exempt from the prohibition groups of agreements and concerted practices and cannot therefore mean that

(1) Crowell v. Benson, 285 U.S. 22, 62 quoted in Mr. Justice Brandeis' concurring opinion in Ashwander v. TVA, 297 U.S. 288, 345-348.

the groups it intends to favor must first (even though by implication) be subject to the prohibition of Article 85(1) and particularly not give rise to the presumption that the conditions of that article are automatically fulfilled by any and all agreements. The regulation in issue could not therefore change the requirements that each individual agreement must satisfy to justify a finding that the conditions for the prohibition set forth in Article 85(1) are fulfilled... Regulation no. 19/65 simply authorizes the Commission to exempt as a group from the prohibition the agreements designated in it, and then only if they fall under Article 85(1). (1)

III. - Evaluation of the Court's Decision

It is quite understandable why the Court of Justice should try to find a way to preserve the constitutionality of Regulation no. 19/65. The purpose of the regulation was to free the Commission from the administrative burden which had been created in the field of vertical arrangements, so that the Commission could devote its efforts to the prosecution of more significant horizontal agreements. This was a matter of practical administration which has certainly not been overlooked by the Court. The annulment of Regulation no. 19/65 would have appeared as a bitter blow to the Council and to the Commission which would have been forced to implement its policy in another way. But the solution given by the Court is perhaps not completely satisfactory from a purely legal and logical point of view. It is really hard to perceive how a regulation granting an exemption does not imply that all agreements fall in principle within the prohibition. What otherwise would be the sense of granting a group exemption? The theory of the Court seems to be that, *in case* these agreements should be prohibited—which can only be decided on a case-by-case basis—they can be exempted by way of regulation. As a matter of fact, the Court has largely deprived the group exemption of its original meaning, since it says that the group exemption does not affect the evaluation of a restraint of trade under Article 85(1). The construction adopted by the Court to sustain the validity of the regulation is certainly contray to its spirit which was that the agreements

(1) Italy v. EEC Council and EEC Commission, case no. 32/65, July 13, 1966, 2 CCH COMMON MARKET REPORTER, § 8048, at 7718 (CCH translation).

described would come by reason of their very nature and regardless of an economic analysis, within the purview of Article 85(1). The solution provided by the Court is at best a compromise which, although upholding the constitutionality of Regulation no. 19/65, attempts at the same time to keep the door open to the rule of reason approach taken in *Technique Minière*. The main point of the Court's ruling is that although a specific agreement belonging to the group has not been filed with the Commission, it will not necessarily be void. The parties can still maintain the position that the agreement was never prohibited by Article 85(1), and under the *Technique Minière* doctrine, the question can only be answered after a factual analysis. If the *Italian* case is in fact difficult to reconcile with *Technique Minière*, it is because the latter case had formulated a rule under which most of the agreement described in Regulation no. 19/65 could escape the prohibition of Article 85(1), so that the need for the group exemption itself was no longer so great.

IV. - The Commission's Draft Regulation Exempting Exclusive Franchises and Exclusive Dealing Provisions

After the European Court had upheld the constitutionality of Regulation no. 19/65, the EEC Commission issued a draft exemption regulation which is to declare the prohibition of Article 85(1) inapplicable to certain groups of exclusive franchises and exclusive dealing terms, pursuant to Article 85(3) ([1]). This proposed regulation describes in general terms the agreements it concerns: it indicates the provisions which are to be contained in the contracts and the types of restrictions which those contracts may not contain if the parties want to avail themselves of the benefit of Article 85(3). The groups of agreements to which the Commission intends to grant an exemption by way of regulation are the so-called bilateral exclusive dealing agreements (" *accords bilatéraux d'exclusivité* "). These agreements are contracts by which a producer

(1) Proposed Regulation on the Application of Article 85(3) of the Treaty to Certain Groups of Bilateral Exclusive Dealing Agreement and Concerted Practices, issued by the Council, March 2, 1965, *Official Journal of the European Communities*, 2863 (1966) and 2 CCH COMMON MARKET REPORTER, § 9125.

located in one Member State grants to a dealer located in another Member State the *exclusive franchise* to distribute certain goods within a specified area. As a counterpart of this exclusive franchise, the dealer must in turn promise that he will only sell goods purchased from this producer (*exclusive dealing term*). The dealer must also commit himself to advertise only within his assigned territory, to sell the goods under the trade-mark of the producer, and to take certain measures designed to promote sales. (1) Provided that various other conditions are met, (2) these classes of contracts will be released from the prohibition of Article 85(1) pursuant to Article 85(3).

This draft regulation reveals once more the policy of the Commission and confirms my views as to the spirit which inspired the basic regulation issued by the Council and upheld by the Court. This policy consists of deciding by way of regulation that certain groups of agreements fall within Article 85(1), instead of justifying on a rule of reason analysis why a specific contract is caught by the prohibition. Again by way of regulation, these agreements are considered to qualify for the exemption. The EEC Commission is freed from its duty of ascertaining in the first place the anticompetitive significance of restrictive agreements. Regulations are replacing economic analysis. In its explanation of its draft regulation, the EEC Commission mentioned the opinion of the Court in the *Italian* case, saying that " every agreement belonging to the group need not fulfill the conditions of Article 85(1) " but the Commission was careful not to cite the opinion of the Court in *Technique Minière*. In effect, the Commission plans to grant a collective exemption to groups of vertical agreements which, according to the tests spelled out in *Technique Minière*, have neither as their purpose nor as their effect a discernible restraint of competition within the Common Market. Article 85(3) should not, I think, be applied to the agreements indicated in this draft regulation, because if all the conditions set up by the Commission are met, the agreements in question are not reached by Article 85(1) in the first place. Fulfillment of these conditions implies that

---

(1) See article 1 of the proposed regulation.

(2) See *infra*, p. 181-182.

competition is not substantially restrained as it has to be in order for Article 85(1) to apply.

The Commission states first that the group exemption should only apply if " the contract goods are subject to effective competition from similar goods in the contract territory. " [1] In other words there should be enough *interbrand* competition. In *Technique Minière,* this was precisely one of the tests announced by the Court to ascertain whether an exclusive franchise creates a significant restraint of trade under Article 85(1). A second condition for the group exemption would be that " it is not made difficult for the exclusive distributor to also supply customers outside the contract territory " [2]; this means that the exclusive franchise must not be accompanied by territorial restrictions like those condemned as *per se* violations of Article 85(1) in *Grundig.* This was another of the tests enunciated by the Court in *Technique Minière* to measure the anticompetitive significance of an exclusive franchise. The Commission plans to apply the group exemption only if the dealer is free to sell outside his assigned territory. Another requirement supplements this second condition: it must not be made " more difficult for middlemen or consumers to obtain the contract goods from another dealer in the Common Market. " [3] This condition demands that other dealers in the Common Market who are supplied by the same manufacturer are not prevented from exporting. Thus no group exemption will be granted if there is a territorial confinement system of distribution similar to the pattern set up by *Grundig.* Article 2 of the draft regulation also shows that the distribution agreement should not disguise a collusive division of market between competing manufacturers. [4] Article 2(4) which requires that " the exclusive distributor does not without valid objective reason exclude from supply certain groups of purchasers ", [5] is inspired by the German statute against restraints

---

(1) Article 2 (1) (CCH translation).

(2) Article 2 (6))CCH translation).

(3) Article 2 (5) (CCH translation).

(4) Article 2(3) provides that the group exemption shall only apply when " producers of competitive goods do not grant each other reciprocal distribution " (CCH translation). Compare with U.S. v. American Smelting and Refining Co., 182 F. Supp. 834 (SDNY 1960).

(5) CCH translation.

of trade which prohibits discriminatory refusals to deal. [1] Finally, Article 2(2) of the draft regulation is concerned with the exclusive dealing aspect of the agreement. The Commission also requires that " it is not more difficult for other producers to sell similar goods at the same trading level as that of the exclusive distributors " [2] but an agreement which satisfies this condition, does not substantially restrain competition, and so, on my interpretation of Article 85(1), is in no way subject to the prohibition of that section. All these conditions merely prove that the agreements exempted cannot have any discernible effect on competition, *i.e.*, that they do not fall within the prohibition of Article 85(1).

On the other hand, the reasons stated by the Commission to explain why these agreements should be exempted show that these types of agreements are often the sole way for small enterprises to penetrate a foreign market, and thus to increase competition. The Commission admits for instance:—

> In the present situation of trade, exclusive distributorship agreements in international trade generally result in an improvement of distribution because an enterprise can concentrate its selling activities, is not obliged to maintain a multiplicity of business ties with a large number of dealers, and, since it deals with only a single distributor, can more easily overcome the marketing difficulties resulting from linguistic, legal or other differences. The designation of a sole distributor facilitates the sales promotion of a product and makes possible an intensive exploitation of the market and a continuous supply while at the same time rationalizing distribution. Furthermore, the designation of an exclusive distributor, who assumes the sales promotion, the introduction of the product, customer service and the maintenance of stocks for the producer, *is often the only way small and medium-sized enterprises can enter the market as competitors.* [3]

V. - Conclusions

True, the European Court had sustained the validity of Regulation no. 19/65. But there the Court had instead limited itself to examining whether the Council had the constitutional

---

(1) See Section 26(2) of the German statute against restraints of competition.

(2) Article 2(2) (CCH translation).

(3) Explanation of the Commission (CHH translation), 2 CCH COMMON MARKET REPORTER, § 9125, at 8273. Emphasis supplied.

powers to authorize the EEC Commission to grant a group exemption, ruling merely that vertical arrangements are not necessarily outside the scope of Article 85(1). The main point at issue was not how Article 85(1) should be applied to exclusive franchise agreements—although there was undoubtedly a close connection between the two questions which has been overlooked by the Court, whether deliberately or not. In regard to the evaluation of the exclusive franchises under Article 85(1), *Technique Minière*, and not the *Italian* case, has laid down the decisive tests. The Commission in its draft regulation did not take the slightest account of those tests. The very same reasons which should have led the Commission not to apply the prohibition, led it, as I have shown, to apply the exemption. Another approach might have been to create a kind of collective negative clearance by way of regulation. Obviously Regulation no. 19/65 did not intend to give the Commission such a power. But even a collective clearance of this sort would have been unnecessary. Could not the Commission have backed out of the problem it had initially created for itself rather than have proceeded to extricate itself by way of regulation? The decision in *Technique Minière* provided an ideal opportunity for such a retreat. The Commission could have easily issued, in its capacity as an administrative agency, general guidelines by way of mere instructions which should have been a faithful implementation of the tests set up by the Court in *Technique Minière.*

Should these tests be applied, it appears that only a very small number of exclusive franchises and exclusive dealing terms will be covered by Article 85(1).

13. - Conclusions

A. - Necessity for a Case-by-Case Approach and Need for Economic Analysis

In a recent memorandum addressed to the Governments of the Member States, the EEC Commission declared:—

> According to the policy followed by the Commission, the prohibitions set forth in Articles 85 and 86 cannot be defined in the

abstract, but must be defined in the light of specific cases through the gradual development of a body of decisional law. (1)

This appears to be a good argument in favor of the case-by-case approach that I have consistently advocated in the present study. However, in fact, as the analysis of the cases decided by it has shown, the Commission has adhered to a very narrow definition of competition inspired by the German Act on horizontal agreements. In its application of Article 85(1), the Commission has precluded resort to any kind of rule of reason. Every agreement by which enterprises restrict their freedom and ability to compete has been considered as in restraint of competition for the purposes of Article 85(1). The test of market effect, " *Marktbeeinflussung* ", which is the second test under Section 1 of the German Act against restraints of competition, has also been taken over by the Commission when it decided that an agreement is prohibited under Article 85(1) only if it produces a "discernible" restraint of competition within the Common Market. (2) But similarly this test has been given a very narrow construction. Three decisions regarding exclusive franchises demonstrate that the Commission has relied on the mere terms of the agreement rather than on a thorough market inquiry. (3)

In the view which I have expounded, Article 85(1) demands on the contrary a real Rule of Reason in the sense which I have ascribed to the Rule in American law. Whether a particular agreement restrains competition can only be decided after a thorough factual analysis, on a case-by-case basis, in the light of economic investigation. Under EEC law, even a boycott would still have to be tested in terms of its effect on competition or of the purpose of the conspirators to affect competition in

---

(1) Concentration of Enterprises in the Common Market, memorandum of the Commission of the EEC to the Governments of the Member States, December 1, 1965. I am quoting the unofficial translation of the CCH Common Market Reports, no. 26, March 17, 1966, at 23.

(2) See the *Grosfillex case, supra,* this chapter at 140-141.

(3) See the *Blondel, Hummel-Isbecque, Maison-Jallate* cases discussed *supra,* this chapter, at 146-152.

some discernible way. ([1]) In 1955, the U.S. Attorney General's National Committee declared in its Report:—

> Practices which are not unreasonable *per se* are those from which a fixed set of effects does not follow. They are subject to more extensive market inquiry under the standards of the antitrust laws. This means that their actual or probable market consequences must be determined as part of their test of legality. ([2])

Only such an approach would give full effect to the policy embodied in Article 85(1) of the Rome Treaty.

B. - Rule of Reason Approach Partly Endorsed by the European Court of Justice

Partial support for this thesis can be found in the three recent decisions of the Court of Justice in *Grundig-Consten*, in *Technique Minière* and in the *Italian* case. Contrary to the theory that had been hitherto applied by the Commission, not every retriction which competitors impose upon themselves in regard to prices, terms of supply, quantities or descriptions of goods, process of manufacturing, cutomers or sales areas, will be deemed automatically in restraint of competition under Article 85(1) and subject only to the exempting provision of Article 85(3). The Court created the opportunity for some administrative or judicial discretion for ascertaining the existence of a restraint of competition under Article 85(1). Naturally the Court did not say that it was adopting unreservedly the American Rule of Reason. This could not be expected. The Rule of Reason is too closely connected with the developments of the Sherman Act, and it cannot be taken out of context and applied without more to the Rome Treaty. Also the scope of the rule announced by Chief Justice White is still uncertain even in America. The Court preferred thus to define certain criteria of application of Article 85(1), but in so doing, it in fact appears to have adopted the American dichotomy between the reasonableness test and the *per se* approach.

---

(1) *Cf.* for American law, Klor's Inc. v. Broadway-Hale Stores, Inc., 359 U.S. 207 (1959).

(2) At 315.

In *Grundig-Consten,* a vertical allocation of territories coinciding with national boundary lines was condemned for purposes of Article 85(1) because of its inherent anticompetitive character. There the Court rejected any query as to whether such an agreement had not in fact promoted competition between the various manufacturers. Economic evidence regarding the effects produced in the market was, the Court said, irrelevant for the application of Article 85(1). Restrictive agreements of this kind will always be in violation of Article 85(1), and it may be predicted that they will be extremely hard to justify under Article 85(3).

But *Technique Minière,* on the contrary, calls for an economic investigation of the restrictive effects brought about by exclusive franchises which are not accompanied by territorial restrictions. There the Court set up a reasonableness standard, meaning thereby that not every exclusive franchise will be deemed a *per se* offense of Article 85(1). Thus it is not sufficient in these cases that these agreements restrain or regulate the behavior of manufacturers. The European Court wants the Commission and the national courts to take a closer look at the actual effects on competitive conditions. It is no longer an abstract principle which can be applied mechanically, but an economic test which necessitates a case-by-case analysis.

Technique Minière was to that extent a disapproval of the dogmatic and rigid method followed by the Commission. Thanks to the European Court, Article 85(1) has been rendered more flexible. In that respect one can say that the exclusive franchises have played in European law a role comparable to that played by ancillary restraints in the early developments of the American Rule of Reason. They constitute the first, if hesitant, step toward a policy which would effectively protect market competition, and the first tentative reaction against a tedious administrative control of the business world. To make the rule more liberal, the European Court of Justice did not have to qualify the language of the Rome Treaty, for, as I attempted to show in this study, Article 85(1) had already incorporated the word " competition ", a word read into the Sherman Act after the reasonable construction prescribed by the United States Supreme Court.

C. - The Debate on the Application of a Rule of Reason to Article 85(1) Still Unresolved

Despite the three recent decisions of the Court of Justice, the debate over a rule of reason for Article 85(1) remains more than ever unresolved. First the law applicable to exclusive vertical arrangements should be more precisely restated by the Court. There is a conflict between the doctrine laid down in *Technique Minière* and the proposed group exemption regulation which has been issued by the Commission, pursuant to the powers granted by Regulation no. 19/65 and sustained by the Court in the *Italian* case. In my view, through Article 85(3) and the group exemption scheme, the Commission has taken jurisdiction over vertical types of arrangements which, according to *Technique Minière*, should almost always be considered beyond the scope of the prohibition of Article 85(1), because of their anticompetitive insignificance. It is highly desirable that the Court be given in the near future the opportunity to pass on the constitutionality of the Commission's regulation. Second, the Court has not yet decided any case concerning a horizontal agreement so that it is hardly possible to know whether the German definition of restraint of trade will be adopted in that field or whether the Court will here too leave some room for a case-by-case analysis. This issue should be solved very soon, for a case is now pending before the Court of Justice which involves a sizeable cartel by which Dutch, Belgian and German firms had engaged in market sharing, price-fixing and limitation of production. (1) What kind of economic evidence will be required by the Court to justify a finding of anticompetitive effect or purpose? What consideration will be given by the Court to the factor of market power? Hopefully the Court will be confronted with these problems in the case now pending.

---

(1) See the cases 8-66, 9-66, 10-66 and 11-66 concerning the *Noordwijks-Cement Accord* pending before the European Court of Justice, *Official Journal of the European Communities*, no. 52, March 23, 1966, at 738 and no. 63, April 2, 1966, at 913-915 and 2 CCH COMMON MARKET REPORTER, § 9085.

D. - *We Must Have a More Vigorous Antitrust Policy. The EEC Commission as a Prosecuting Body*

More than four years after the enactment of Regulation no. 17, it has become urgent to set the European antitrust policy at last upon a proper footing; this has not been the case so far. The recent opinions of the European Court have aroused certain hopes, because not only have they clarified the basic substantive provisions of the treaty but they have also revealed the Court's readiness to exercise fully its powers of judicial review in the important field of anticartel law. It is a regrettable irony that in an area where the Commission has the most extensive powers, it has acted so little. This shows, if demonstration is still necessary, that supranationality is not a magic formula: it only creates efficiency where the administration is competent and resolved to act.

Through its powers of judicial review in construing the substantive law of the Treaty, the European Court of Justice might be in a position to demonstrate that a few cases, carefully analysed, can gain more respect for community law than the strict administrative control of restrictive agreements which the Commission has tried to establish. The United States Supreme Court has played an extremely constructive role in the development of American antitrust law. Nothing in the Rome Treaty prevents the Court of Justice from following this example.

But the Commission which according to the Treaty is at one time a legislature, at another time a government or an enforcement agency, should be reminded that as far as antitrust policy is concerned, its more useful function is to be a prosecuting body comparable to the Antitrust Division of the American Department of Justice rather than to be limited to the passive and mechanical role of an agency in charge of handing out administrative permits.

E. - *More Flexibility Essential for Greater Effectiveness*

The same can be said of a rule of reason under Article 85(1) as was said by Professor Handler of the American Rule of Reason in 1941:—

> In our judgment, such a rule, properly understood and correctly applied, can be a source of strength rather than of weakness. Some

rule of reason was inevitable. A law which strait-jacketed business enterprise would fall of its own weight. (1)

So far the mechanical definition of " restraint of trade " adopted by the EEC Commission has led it to concern itself excessively with exclusive franchise agreements and to neglect horizontal agreements which undoubtedly exist in Europe and can be far more dangerous to the Common Market. This is not only bad law; it is bad policy. At a time when European countries are opening their old boundaries to each other and endeavoring to create larger economic spheres, Europe badly needs a vigorous antitrust policy in order to assure European consumers the benefits they expect from a Common Market. It is generally believed on the continent that antitrust law is only one of a number of tools by which economic control is exerted and policy implemented. But in a free society, it is nonetheless an essential tool. If the American approach to the concept of restraint of trade, *i.e.*, the rule of reason, had been adopted, the EEC Commission would not have been deluged with thousands of notifications. Most of the registered agreements appear to be simple exclusive franchise agreements, and thus must be of no substantial anticompetitive significance. Consequently, they hardly merited so much attention. The time thereby saved would have enabled the Commission to concentrate on horizontal agreements and to counteract more efficiently the more serious conspiracies. The thesis I have advocated may in certain instances prove more liberal than the conceptions adopted by the Commission. My main concern however is not with what is the more liberal rule, but with what is the more efficient one. If, at the same time, it is more liberal, let it be so. It is at all events clear that the narrowness of the approach taken by the Commission has not been conducive to efficiency but rather to bureaucratic paralysis.

Generally business groups in Europe, just as in America, complain about the lack of certainty in Antitrust law. At the same time, they are inclined to demand more flexibility. Such demands are irreconcilable. A rule of reason under Article

(1) HANDLER, A STUDY OF THE CONSTRUCTION AND ENFORGEMENT OF THE ANTI TRUS LAWS, TNEC Monograph, no. 38, 9 (1941).

85(1) would bring about more uncertainty for business men. But some uncertainty appears to be a fair price to pay for an effective antitrust policy. It is inherent in the nature of such policy not to rely on abstract legal criteria, but to discriminate between significant and insubstantial restraints of trade.

F. - Risk that the Adoption of a Rule of Reason will Lead to Divergent Decisions Within the Six

An important argument, which has been advanced in support of the strict definition of " restraint of trade " adopted by the EEC Commission deserves mention. Pursuant to Article 9(3) of Regulation no. 17, the national authorities, *e.g.*, the national courts have jurisdiction to apply Article 85(1). On the other hand, the EEC Commission is the only agency empowered to grant exemptions pursuant to Article 85(3) of the Rome Treaty. Thus while the Commission has exclusive jurisdiction over exemptions under Article 85(3), it has only concurrent jurisdiction to apply the prohibitions of Article 85(1), although once the Commission has initiated a procedure in a given case pursuant to Regulation no. 17, the authorities of the Member States lose their jurisdiction entirely as to that case. This partially concurrent jurisdiction creates a serious risk of lack of uniformity in the construction of the Treaty. The national courts may show more leniency in the application of the cartel prohibition than the European agency. To avoid, or at least to minimize, these risks, it has been suggested that the Commission should secure control of the greatest possible number of restrictive agreements by rejecting any rule of reason in the interpretation of Article 85(1), thus throwing the parties into the machinery of Article 85(3). Only this way, it is said, will uniformity in the construction of the Treaty be assured, despite concurrent jurisdiction, and Article 85(1) be efficiently enforced.

There is a simple answer to this argument. First, if the national courts were forced to apply a mechanical test, they would be abdicating their own role in the enforcement of Article 85(1). Since within the limits of Article 9 of Regulation no. 17 they retain competence, they thereby retain discretion, to determine when a restrictive agreement is actually producing or is intended to produce an adverse effect on competition. But on the above argument, this discretion would be indirectly limited. Second, the only way for the Commission to short-circuit the national courts in a case in which it fears a possible lack of uniformity is itself to initiate a procedure before the case is decided. Third, neither the Commission nor the national courts have the last word in regard to the interpretation of the Treaty. This belongs to the European Court of Justice either under Article 173 of the Treaty or pursuant to Article 177. (1) This policy argument should thus not be given decisive weight against a Rule of Reason under Article 85(1).

G. - *The Value of Comparative Anticartel Law*

My thesis seeks to exemplify a basic teaching. In the field of antitrust law, the comparative method has a more useful function to perform than merely to describe what is the applicable law in different countries without questioning why it is so. Antitrust law is an American tradition, as should always be remembered when comparisons are made and guidance is sought for the European law. Comparative law in this area is more than a fascinating intellectual game; it is a valuable tool; and indeed to the European lawyer an essential one.

---

(1) In his submissions to the European Court of Justice in *Technique Minière*, Advocate General Roemer squarely faced the argument concerning the risk of divergent developments of the law due to a rule of reason under Article 85(1). He stated: " The position of the Commisison and of Maschinenbau Ulm GmbH cannot be contested, as the Société Technique Minière attempts to do, on the basis that the application of such a 'rule of reason' (to designate it thus) would carry with it the danger that the law would develop differently in the various Member States or even within one State, because application of this rule would often be left to the national judge. As is illustrated by the instant case, Article 177 of the Treaty provides us with a valuable tool for meeting this danger through the gradual devlopment of criteria of interpretation by the European Court of Justice. " (CCH translation, 2 COMMON MARKET REPORTER, § 8047, at 7701). I completely agree with Roemer. I do not think however that the Commission advocated a true rule of reason. The Commission indeed admitted that the applicability of Article 85(1) depends on the existence of a discernible restraint of competition. But this was only a verbal concession, for, apart from *Grosfillex* and *Vitapro* (see *supra*, this chapter, at 140-143), this interpretation in no way led the Commission to adopt a more realistic attitude toward restrictive agreements.

This thesis represents an endeavor to dissipate some confusion—by calling into question certain oft-repeated theories such as that the American rule of reason allows social and economic justifications of substantial restraints of competition or that Section 1 of the German Act formulates a *per se* rule or that there is no room for a rule of reason under Article 85(1) of the Rome Treaty. I have tried, not to take for granted commonly-stated doctrines, but to question their accuracy, hoping that thereby I would perhaps take part in " the hunt for better understanding of the 'competition' we revere and of the free economic system which the Sherman Act symbolizes ". (1)

(1) J.A. Rahl, *Per Se Rules and Boycotts under the Sherman Act: Some Reflections on the Klor's Case,* 45 VA. L. REV. 1165, 1174 (1959).

SELECTIVE BIBLIOGRAPHY

Adams, *Rule of Reason: Workable Competition or Workable Monopoly*, 63 Yale L. J. 348 (1954).

Adelman, *Acquire the Whole or Part of the Stock or Assets of Another Corporation*, Aba Antitrust Section 111 (1953).

Adelman, *An Economist Looks at the Sherman Act*, 27 Aba Antitrust Section 32 (1965).

Adelman, *Effective Competition and the Antitrust Laws*, 61 Harv, L. Rev. 1289 (1948).

Baarman, Observations, Cahiers de Droit européen 669 (1966).

Barber, *Refusals to Deal under the Federal Antitrust Laws*, 103 U. Pa. L. Rev. 847 (1955).

Baumbach-Hefermehl, Wettbewerbs-und Warenzeichenrecht (1960).

Baumbach-Hefermehl, Wettbewerbs-und Warenzeichenrecht, Vol. 1 (1964).

Benisch, Annotation WuW 371 (1960).

Benisch, Annotation 433 (1963).

Biedenkopf-Callman-Deringer, Aktuelle Grundsatzfragen des Kartellrechtes (1957).

Blaise, Le Statut juridique des Ententes économiques (1964).

Blake and Jones, *The Goals of Antitrust: A Dialogue on Policy - In Defense of Antitrust*, 65 Colum. L. Rev. 377 (1965).

Blake and Jones, *The Goals of Antitrust: A Dialogue on Policy - Toward a Three-Dimensional Antitrust Policy*, 65 Colum. L. Rev. 422 (1965).

Bork, *The Rule of Reason and the Per Se Concept: Price-Fixing and Market Division*, 74 Yale L. J. 775 (1965) and 75 Yale L. J. 375 (1965).

Bork, *Ancillary Restraints and the Sherman Act*, 15 Aba Antitrust Section 211 (1959).

Bork, *The Goals of Antitrust: A Dialogue on Policy - Contrasts in Antitrust Theory*, 65 Colum. L. Rev. 401 (1965).

Börner, Die Marktbeherrschung im Kartellrecht der Montanunion und die Ruhrkohle (1960).

Bowman, *The Goals of Antitrust: A Dialogue on Policy - Contrasts in Antitrust Theory*, 65 Colum. L. Rev. 417 (1965).

Bowman and Bork, *The Goals of Antitrust: A Dialogue on Policy - The Crisis in Antitrust*, 65 Colum L. Rev. 363 (1965).

Buxbaum, *Patent Licensing: A Case Study on Antitrust Regulation within the European Economic Community*, 9 Antitrust Bull. 101 (1964).

Bye, *L'arrêt 13-60 du 13 mai 1963 sur les Comptoirs de la Ruhr*, Droit social 257 (1963).

CECA 1952-1962. - Rapport Wagenfuhr (1963).

Concentration of Enterprises in the Common Market, Memorandum of the Commission of the EEC to the Governments of the Member States, Dec. 1, 1965, CCH Common Market Reports, no. 26, March 17, 1966.

Chadwell, *Competition and Section 1 of the Sherman Act - Instant Antitrust or Long-Run Policy?*, 27 Aba Antitrust Section 60 (1965).

Dean, *Competition - Inside and Out*, 32 Harv. Bus. Rev. 63 (1954).

De Keyser, Exclusive Vertical Arrangements under United States and Common Market Antitrust Laws, Manuscript of a S.J.D. thesis, Northwestern University School of Law (1964).
De Keyser, *Territorial Restrictions and Export Prohibitions under the United States and the Common Market Antitrust Laws*, 2 Common Market Law Review 271 (1964-1965).
del Marmol, *Rapport introductif concernant les règles de concurrence applicables aux entreprises à l'intérieur du Marché Commun*, Ligue Européenne de Coopération Economique.
del Marmol, La Protection contre les Abus de Puissance économique en Droit Belge (1960).
Deringer, Das Wettbewerbsrecht der Ewg published by the German Periodical Wirtschaft und Wettbewerb, cited as *WuW/EWG - Wettbewerbsrecht.*
Deringer, *Exclusive Agency Arrangements with Territorial Protection under the EEC Antitrust Laws*, 10 Antitrust Bull. 601 (1965).
Deringer, *Alleinvertriebsverträge im Wettbewerbsrecht des Gemeinsamen Marktes*, NJW 1585 (1966).
Deringer, Annotation, 4 Common Market Law Review 220 (1966).
Deringer-Tessin, *Gruppenausnahmen in EWG-Kartellrecht für Alleinvertriebs- und Lizenzverträge*, AWD BB 54 (1965).
Deringer-Tessin, *EWG-Kartellrecht : keine Freistellung für Alleinvertriebsverträge mit absolutem Gebietsschutz*, AWD BB 329 (1964).
Dörinkel, Annotation, Grur 43 (1963).
Durry, *Ouragan Européen sur les contrats d'exclusivité*, Dalloz Chron. XXVIII (1963).

Ellis, *L'interprétation du Mot «Affecter» dans L'Article 85(1) Du Traité CEE par Rapport aux Mots «Empêcher», «Restreindre»,ou «Fausser» le Jeu de la Concurrence*, Dalloz 221-228 (1963).
Edwards, Maintaining Competition (1949).
Ententes et Monopoles dans le Droit moderne (1961).

Fikentscher, Annotation WuW 343 (1960).
Fikentscher, *Neuere Entwicklungen der Theorie zum Tatbestandsmerkmal der Wettbewerbsbeschränkung* § 1, WuW 788 (1961).
Fikentscher, *Sonstige Verträge im Gesetz gegen Wettbewerbsbeschränkungen*, in Festschrift für Alfred Hueck, 543 (1959).
Fikentscher, *Die Warenzeichenlizenz im Recht der Wettbewerbsbeschränkungen* in Die Warenzeichenlizenz, 412, 462 (1963).
Françon, *Les Ententes et les Monopoles selon le Traité de Rome, Premier Règlement d'Application des Art. 85 et 86*, 89 Journal du Droit international (Clunet) 400 (1962).
Frey, *Die Beeinflussung der Marktverhältnisse im Sinne des § 1 GWB*, WuW 17 1962).
Fulda, *The First Antitrust Decisions of the Commission of the EEC*, 65 Colum. L. Rev. 625 (1965).

Gabriel, *Aufeinander abgestimmte Verhaltensweisen unter wettbewerbspolitischem Aspekt*, WuW 802 (1961).
Gleiss, *Der Begriff der aufeinander abgestimmten Verhaltensweisen in Art. 85 EWG-Vertrag*, WuW 485 (1964).
Gleiss-Hirsch, *Das erste Negativtest der EWG Kommission*, NJW 1604 (1964).
Gleiss-Hirsch, *EWG-Kartellrecht*, Second Edition (1965).
Goldsmith, *En attendant l'arrêt Grundig-Consten : la notion d'abus d'exclusivité en vertu de l'Article 85 du Traité de Rome*, Dalloz, Chronique XL (1965).
Government Regulation of Business, Cases from the National Reporter System selected by Bowie, Rostow and Bork (1963).
Graupner, The Rules of Competition in the European Economic Community (1965).

GUIDE TO LEGISLATION ON RESTRICTIVE BUSINESS PRACTICES, Published by the Organization for Economic Cooperation and Development (Loose-leaf service).

HANDLER, CASES AND OTHER MATERIALS ON TRADE REGULATION (1937).
HANDLER, A STUDY OF THE CONSTRUCTION AND ENFORCEMENT OF THE ANTITRUST LAWS, TNEC Monograph no. 38 (1941).
HANDLER, ANTITRUST IN PERSPECTIVE (1957).
Handler, *The Polarities of Antitrust*, 60 NW. U. L. REV. 751 (1965-1966).
Handler, *Annual Antitrust Review*, 11 RECORD OF N.Y.C.B.A. 376 (1956).
Hefermehl, *Beurteilung von Fusionen und Konzernbildungen nach Art. 85 und 86 des EWG-Vertrages*, in FESTCHRIFT FÜR HANS CARL NIPPERDEY, Vol. 2, 771 (1965).
Hefermehl, Annotation, JZ 364 (1962).
Heinrich, *Die «conscious parallelism» Doktrin des U.S. Antitrustrechts und der Begriff «aufeinander abgestimmte Verhaltensweisen» in Art. 85 EWG Vertrag*, WuW (1965).
Heiseke, *Die warenrechtliche Problematik der Entscheidung der EWG-Kommission im Falle Grundig-Consten*, NJW 1409 (1965).
HONIG, BROWN, GLEISS, HIRSCH, CARTEL LAW OF THE EUROPEAN ECONOMIC COMMUNITY (1963).
HOUSSIAUX, CONCURRENCE ET MARCHÉ COMMUN (1960).

Jordan, *Exclusive and Restricted Sales Areas under the Antitrust Law*, 9 U.C.L.A.L. REV. 121 (1962).

KAUFMAN, RAUTMANN ET AL, KOMMENTAR ZUM GESETZ GEGEN WETTBEWERBSBESCHRÄNKUNGEN (Loose-leaf service).
KAYSEN and TURNER, ANTITRUST POLICY - AN ECONOMIC AND LEGAL ANALYSIS (1959).
Kirschstein, Annotation, WuW 560 (1964).
Kirschstein, Annotation, WuW 866 (1965).
Kirschstein, *Die EWG-Verordnung über Gruppenfreistellungen*, WuW 361 (1965).
Kirschstein, *Beurteilung von Alleinvertriebsverträge nach EWG-Kartellrecht*, WuW 77 (1966).
Klaue, *Zwei Jahre Rechtsprechung zum GWB*, WuW 391 (1960).
Knöpfle, *Zum Wettbewerb im Sinne des § 1 GWB*, WuW 159 (1962).
KRAWIELICKI, DAS MONOPOLVERBOT IM SCHUMAN-PLAN (1952).

LANGEN, KOMMENTAR ZUM KARTELLGESETZ (1957).
LA POLITIQUE DE LA HAUTE AUTORITÉ EN MATIÈRE D'ENTENTES ET DE CONCENTRATIONS (20 avril 1964) *Bulletin de la Communauté Européenne du Charbon et de l'Acier*, n° 47.
Le Tallec, *Die Wettbewerbsregeln in der Europäischen Wirtschaftsgemeinschaft nach der Rechtsprechung des Gerichtshofes*, AWD BB 437 (1966).
Letwin, *The English Common Law Concerning Monopolies*, 21 U. CHI. L. REV. 355 (1954).
Levi, *The Antitrust Laws and Monopoly*, 14 U. CHI. L. REV. 153 (1946-1947).
Levi, *A Two Level Anti-Monopoly Law*, 47 NW. U. L. REV. 567 (1952-1953).
Loevinger, *The Rule of Reason in Antitrust Law*, 50 VA. L. REV. 23 (1964).

Markert, *Alleinvertriebsverträge und Antitrustrecht*, WuW 299 (1964).
Markert, *Gemeinschaftsunternehmen und Antitrustrecht*, AWD BB 241 (1964).
MASON, *Market Power and Business Conduct: Some Comments on the Report of the Attorney General's Committee on Antitrust Policy*, in ECONOMIC CONCENTRATION AND THE MONOPOLY PROBLEM.
MATTHIES, DAS RECHT DER KARTELLE UND ZUSAMMENSCHLÜSSE IN DER MONTANUNION (1964).
Meyer-Cording, *Die Grundbegriffe des Wettbewerbsrechts*, WuW 461 (1962).
Montague, *Per Se Illegality and the Rule of Reason*, 12 ABA ANTITRUST SECTION 69 (1958).

Müller-Henneberg, *Zu den Begriffen «Kartell» und «Wettbewerbsbeschränkung»* WuW 877 (1963).
MÜLLER-HENNEBERG/SCHWARTZ, GESETZ GEGEN WETTBEWERBSBESCHRÄNKUNGEN, Kommentar, First Edition (1958).
MÜLLER-HENNEBERG/SCHWARTZ, GESETZ GEGEN WETTBEWERBSBESCHRÄNKUNGEN UND EUROPÄISCHE KARTELLRECHT, Gemeinschaftskommentar, Second Edition (1963).
MÜLLER-HENNEBERG/SCHWARTZ, NOVELLE 1965 ZUM GESETZ GEGEN WETTBEWERBSBESCHRÄNKUNGEN, Nachtrag zur 2. Auflage des Gemeinschaftskommentar (1966).

NEALE, THE ANTITRUST LAWS OF THE U.S.A. (1962).
Newes, *The European Commission's First Major Decision (Grundig-Consten)*, 20 BUS. LAW. 431 (1964-1965).
Niederleithinger, *EWG-Kartellrecht : Rechtsfolgen bei nicht angemeldetem Alleinvertriebsvertrag (Neukartell)*, Urteilsanmerkung, AWD BB 61 (1965).
Note, *Restricted Channels of Distribution under the Sherman Act*, 75 HARV. L. REV. 795 (1961-1962).
Note, *The Resurgence of the Exclusive Territorial Distributorship as an Antitrust Problem*, 40 MINN. L. REV. 853 (1956).

OBERDORFER, GLEISS and HIRSCH, COMMON MARKET CARTEL LAW (1963).
OPPENHEIM, FEDERAL ANTITRUST LAWS (1958) and 1964 Supplement.
Oppenheim, *Federal Antitrust Policy: Guideposts to a Revised National Antitrust Policy*, 50 MICH. L. REV. 1139 (1951-1952).
Oppenheim, *Selected Antitrust Developments in the Courts and Federal Trade Commission during Past Year*, 15 ABA ANTITRUST SECTION, 37-42 (1959).
Oppenheim, *Antitrust Booms and Boomerangs*, 9 ANTITRUST BULL. 641 (1964).

Pearson, *Tying Arrangements and Antitrust Policy*, 60 NW. U. L. REV. 626 (1965-1966).
Peppin, *Price-Fixing Agreements under the Sherman Antitrust Law*, 28 CALIF. L. REV. 297, 677 (1940).
PERSPECTIVES ON ANTITRUST POLICY, Edit. by A. PHILLIPS (1965).

Rahl, *Conspiracy and the Anti-Trust Laws*, 44 ILL. L. REV. 742 (1950).
Rahl, *Price Competition and the Price-fixing Rule*, 57 NW. U. L. REV. 137 (1962).
Rahl, *Antimerger Law in Search of a Policy*, Proceedings of the Fourth Annual Corporate Counsel Institute, 57 (1965), reprinted in XI ANTITRUST BULL. 325 (1966).
Rahl, *Antitrust Problems of Doing Business Abroad*, Remarks made at the Chicago Bar Association, March 11, 1965 (manuscript).
Rahl, *Per Se Rules and Boycotts under the Sherman Act: Some Reflections on the Klors' Case*, 45 VA. L. REV. 1165, 1174 (1959).
Rahl, *European Common Market Antitrust Developments concerning Horizontal Arrangements, Dominant Positions, and Mergers*, in INTERNATIONAL ASPECTS OF ANTITRUST, *Hearings Before the Subcommittee on Antitrust and Monopoly of the Committee on the Judiciary*, U.S. Senate, 89th Cong., Sec. Sess., Pt 1 at 377 (1966).
REPORT OF THE ATTORNEY GENERAL'S NATIONAL COMMITTEE TO STUDY THE ANTITRUST LAWS (1955).
RINCK, WIRTSCHAFTSRECHT (1963).
Rostow, *Report of the Attorney General's Committee in Perspective*, in CCH ANTITRUST LAW SYMPOSIUM, 64 (1956).
Rostow, *Monopoly Under the Sherman Act: Power or Purpose?*, 43 ILL. L. REV. 745 (1948-1949).
Ryziger, Annotation, CAHIERS DU DROIT EUROPÉN, 350 (1965).

Schapira, *La décision Grundig-Consten*, JOURNAL DU DROIT INTERNATIONAL, 67 (1965).
Schluep, *Die Rule of Reason des amerikanischen Antitrustrecht und das schweizerische Kartellgesetz*, Wirtschaft und Recht 36 (1966).

Shapiro, *The German Law Against Restraints of Competition - Comparative and International Aspects*, 62 COLUM. L. REV., 1, 201 (1962).
Schmidt, *Zum Begriff des Preiswettbewerbs nach § 17 GWB*, WuW 120 (1964).
Schwartz Ivo, *Antitrust Legislation and Policy in Germany - A Comparative Study*, 105 U. PA. L. REV. 617 (1957).
Schwartz Louis, *The Schwartz Dissent*, 1 ANTITRUST BULL. 37 (1955-1956).
Smith, Berge and Burns, *Proposals for Extended Application of the Rule of Reason*, U. of Mich. Law School Summer Institute, Federal Antitrust Laws, 231-162 (1953).
Sölter, *Die Ausnahmevorschrift des Artikel 85 Abs. 3 EWG-Vertrag*, WuW 665 (1961).
STEIN AND NICHOLSON, AMERICAN ENTERPRISE IN THE EUROPEAN COMMON MARKET: A LEGAL PROFILE (1960).
STEVENS AND YAMEY, THE RESTRICTIVE PRACTICES COURT (1965).
Stocking, *Rule of Reason, Workable Competition, and Monopoly*, 64 YALE L. J. 1107 (1955).
Stocking, *The Rule of Reason, Workable Competition and the Legality of Trade Association Activities*, 21 U. CHI. L. REV. 527 (1954).
STOCKING, WORKABLE COMPETITION AND ANTITRUST POLICY (1961).
Stone, *Closed territorial Distribution: An opening question in the Sherman Act*, 30 U. CHI. L. REV. 286 (1963).
Suetens, Annotations, CAHIERS DE DROIT EUROPÉEN, 243 (1965).

TAFT, THE ANTITRUST ACT AND THE SUPREME COURT (1914).
Teitgen, Annotation, DROIT SOCIAL, 483 (1965).
Tessin, *EWG-Kommission erteilt erstes Negativtest*, AWD BB 114 (1964).
Timberg, *Territorial Exclusives*, 56 TRADEMARK REP. 1 (1966).
THORELLI, THE FEDERAL ANTITRUST POLICY (1954).
Turner, *The Validity of Tying Arrangements under the Antitrust Laws*, 72 HARV. L. REV. 50 (1958-1959).
Turner, *The Definition of Agreement under the Sherman Act: Conscious Parallelism and Refusals to Deal*, 75 HARV. L. REV. 655 (1961-1962).
Turner, *Conglomerate Mergers and Section 7 of the Clayton Act*, 78 HARV. L. REV. 1313 (1965).
Turner, *Antitrust Policy and the Cellophane case*, 70 HARV. L. REV. 281 (1956-1957).
Turner, *Cooperation Among Competitors*, Address given at the Northwestern University Law School Corporate Council Institute, October 13, 1966 (manuscript to be published in NW. U. L. REV., January-February 1967 issue).

Ulmer, *Kartellvertrag und Gentleman's Agreement*, WuW 2 (1962).
Ulmer, *Wettbewerbsbeschränkende Absprachen im Rahmen von Unternehmenszusammenschlüssen*, WuW (1960).

Van Cise, *The Future of Per Se Illegality in Antitrust Law*, 50 VA. L. REV. 1165 (1964).
VON GAMM, DAS KARTELLRECHT IM EWG-BEREICH (1961).
Von der Groeben, *Die Wettbewerbspolitik als Teil der Wirtschaftspolitik im Gemeinsamen Market*, WuW 691 (1965).

Waelbroeck, *Trademark Problems in the European Common Market*, 54 TRADEMARK REP. 333 (1964).
Weiser, *Recent EEC Antitrust Activity Relating to Exclusive Distributorships and Trademarks*, 55 TRADEMARK REP. 863 (1965).
WILBERFORCE, CAMPBELL AND ELLES, THE LAW OF RESTRICTIVE TRADE PRACTICES AND MONOPOLIES (1966).
WILCOX, COMPETITION AND MONOPOLY IN AMERICAN INDUSTRY, TNEC Monograph 21 (1940).
WILCOX, PUBLIC POLICIES TOWARD BUSINESS (1955).
Wiley, *The Per Illegality of Price-fixing: Sans Power, Purpose or Effect*, 19 U. CHI. L. REV. 837 (1952).

WIRTSCHAFTSORDNUNG UUD RECHTSORDNUNG, FESTSCHRIFT FÜR FRANZ BÖHM (1965).
WOHLFARTH-EVERLING-GLAESNER-SPRUNG, DIE EUROPÄISCHE WIRTSCHAFTSGEMEINSCHAFT, Kommentar zum Vertrag (1960).
Wolf, *Zum Kartellrecht der EWG*, WuW 645 (1962).
ZEHN JAHRE RECHTSPRECHUNG DES GERICHTSHOFS DER EUROPÄISCHEN GEMEINSCHAFTEN (1965).

Asaociation Intercommunale
de MECANOGRAPHIE
88, rue Louvrex — LIEGE

GPSR Compliance

The European Union's (EU) General Product Safety Regulation (GPSR) is a set of rules that requires consumer products to be safe and our obligations to ensure this.

If you have any concerns about our products, you can contact us on ProductSafety@springernature.com

In case Publisher is established outside the EU, the EU authorized representative is:

Springer Nature Customer Service Center GmbH
Europaplatz 3
69115 Heidelberg, Germany

Batch number: 10830943

Printed by Printforce, the Netherlands